LONDON RECORD SOCIETY
PUBLICATIONS

VOLUME XXXV
FOR THE YEAR 1998

LONDON AND MIDDLESEX EXCHEQUER EQUITY PLEADINGS, 1685–6 AND 1784–5: A CALENDAR

EDITED BY

HENRY HORWITZ
Professor of History, University of Iowa
and
JESSICA COOKE, Ph.D.

LONDON RECORD SOCIETY
2000

ISBN 0 90095236 9

Typeset by
The Midlands Book Typesetting Company, Loughborough, Leicestershire
Printed and bound in Great Britain by
Quorn Selective Repro Ltd, Loughborough, Leicestershire

CONTENTS

LIST OF ABBREVIATIONS

For the annual legal terms: Mich, Easter, Hil, Trin.
For counties: Hants for Hampshire, Midd. for Middlesex, Norf. for Norfolk, etc.

(a), after defendant's name: indicates he/she answered (sometimes jointly with other defendants)

acct	account, accounts
ag	against
Bp	bishop
Cert	certificate
cl	common law
commn	commission
DR	Deputy Remembrancer
D, d, ds	defendant(s)
d1	first defendant, etc.
doc(s)	document(s)
E	the elder
EIC	East India Company
exam	examine, examination
gdn	guardian
inj	injunction
KB	Court of King's Bench
LMX	London and Middlesex (bill, suit)
n/f	next friend
nr	near
ord	order, ordered
ord *nisi*	order unless (other party responds)
P, p, p(s)	plaintiff(s)
p1	plaintiff 1, etc.
parlt	parliament
pet	petition
q	question (as in, land in question)
ref(s)	referee(s)
sbp	subpoena
sc	show cause
suff	sufficient, sufficiency (of answer)
w	with
w/i	within
w/o	without
Y	the younger

INTRODUCTION

Of the many only partially-listed 'series' of early modern documents in the Public Record Office [hereafter PRO], those of the central courts of equity (Chancery, Exchequer, and the shorter-lived Requests) have been notorious for their inaccessibility.[1] While it is difficult enough to identify and to trace suits brought by specific individuals using the extant listings and finding aids, subject-matter searches are even more problematic since listings providing such information are very much the exception.[2] At the same time, however, scholars have long been aware of the potential rewards to be found in these judicial archives – not only in the detailed bills of complaint (sometimes with attached schedules) by which suits were initiated, but also in the exhibits and other proofs submitted by the litigants, the depositions taken from their witnesses, the reports commissioned by the courts, and the decrees they handed down. Examples of successful searches carried out in recent years include Milhous's and Hume's collaborative work in opera and theatre history exploiting both Chancery and Exchequer records, Erickson's investigation of married women's property rights drawing upon an array of marriage settlements litigated in Chancery, and Stretton's study of women litigants in the Elizabethan Court of Requests.[3]

In the case of the Court of Exchequer's proceedings in equity, searchers proceeding along topical lines have had the benefit of one set of listings that does provide brief summaries of subject for certain suits – those for which witnesses' depositions were taken by commission in the provinces. These are the listings for E 134 (country depositions).[4] However, the suits so summarized constitute only a small fraction of the approximately 90,000 begun in Exchequer between the mid-seventeenth century, when the Court assumed a general jurisdiction in equity, and 1841, when this jurisdiction was merged

1. 'Series' supersedes the traditional category 'class' in the Public Record Office's archival lexicon in late 2000; i.e., E 134 will now be referred to as a series, not as a class.
2. Place name searches are, however, possible for a significant minority of document series for these courts.
3. Curtis Price, Judith Milhous, and Robert D. Hume, *Italian Opera in Late Eighteenth-Century London*, vol. I *The King's Theatre, Haymarket 1778–1791* (Oxford, 1995); Amy L. Erickson, *Women and Property in early modern England* (London, 1993); Tim Stretton, *Women Waging Law in Elizabethan England* (Cambridge, 1998).
4. These lists, published in the *Reports of the Deputy Keeper of Public Records* (vols. 38–42), cover the reigns Elizabeth I – George II and are continued for George III's reign in manuscript. They are available in the Map and Large Documents Room (hereafter Map Room) in the PRO at Kew, where most finding aids are shelved in series order and in numerical order within the specific series. In addition, a once distinct sub-series styled E 134 Miscellaneous is now listed in the 'Standard List' (hereafter SL) of PRO series under E 134.

into Chancery.[5] To begin with, relatively few Exchequer equity cases, certainly fewer than 10 per cent, ever reached the stage of having depositions taken (nor was it always necessary to depose witnesses in suits that did reach advanced stages). Moreover, these listings for E 134 do not cover the depositions taken by the four Barons of the Court (and their subordinates, the Examiners) chiefly in cases emanating from the metropolis (London and Middlesex) – that is, the depositions filed in E 133. This is no mean omission since, as will be discussed below, cases originating in the metropolis constituted a significant and growing proportion of all Exchequer suits filed, with a distinctive distribution of subject-matter. Rather, the only finding aid to the main portion of E 133 simply lists these cases by the surnames of the first plaintiff and first defendant (e.g. Smith v Jones) without providing the date either of the deposition in question or of the suit which occasioned it.[6] Thus, while researchers in the history of the city and the metropolis (e.g. the Survey of London, the Victoria County History) have, with a degree of success, been able to exploit Chancery records, little attempt has been made to make use of Exchequer equity materials, even though the two courts handled, with one major exception, much the same range of civil litigation and utilized very similar procedures.

It is the aim of this volume to illustrate the potential rewards of searches in Exchequer equity records for students of the history of London and the metropolis by way of calendaring a limited selection of the pleadings in equity (bills, answers, and related documents) consisting of every London and Middlesex suit filed for two years of the Court's operation as a general court of equity – the first year of James II's reign (6 Feb. 1685–5 Feb. 1686) and the twenty-fifth year of George III's (25 Oct. 1784–24 Oct. 1785).[7] All told, there are 151 suits for the former year, 194 for the latter.

Identification of London and Middlesex pleadings in the class E 112 is greatly facilitated by the practice of the Exchequer clerks of filing suits by county (a practice not paralleled in Chancery).[8] Together, these 345 sets of pleadings comprise all the surviving materials in E 112 filed as London and Middlesex bills and answers for these two years and so recorded in the Sworn Clerks' bill books (IND 1/16820–53). The bill books, in turn, list by suit name (*including first names*) the materials in E 112. Like the pleadings themselves, the bill book listings are subdivided by county. In turn, each set of pleadings

5. The standard work on the equitable jurisdiction of Exchequer is W. H. Bryson, *The Equity Side of the Exchequer* (Cambridge, 1975). The Court also had a jurisdiction in revenue matters and a common law jurisdiction (the Office of Pleas) but it devoted at least two complete days a week to equitable matters. The most complete guide to procedure is D. B. Fowler, *The Practice of the Court of Exchequer upon Proceedings in Equity* (2 vols, London, 1795).
6. The E 133 list is also to be found on the open shelves in the Map Room at Kew.
7. Revenue cases are excluded from consideration here, save as brought in a few instances by the Attorney General in the form of an 'English information' which, apart from the identity of the complainant and the use of the term 'English information', was virtually identical to a bill of complaint in equity. The selection of these particular years is explained below.
8. The normal rule was that a suit was entered 'under the head of that, where either the parties dwell, or the property to which the subject matter of the bill relates, appears to be situated': Fowler, *Practice of the Exchequer* I, p. 130.

is entered in the appropriate bill book under the legal term and regnal year in which it was filed in court, while the bill books themselves are divided by reign. For example, IND 1/6839 is vol. 2 of the set of bill books for George I's reign and within it a set of pleadings for a suit emanating from London/ Middlesex which was filed in Hilary term, 12 George I, is listed under that county designation and term designation.[9]

'Pleadings' constitute the initial stage of an equity or 'English bill' suit. They consist of the litigant's complaint and, in many but by no means all instances, the defendant's answer or other response (disclaimer, demurrer or plea), along with any subsequent pleadings (principally, the plaintiff's replication to the answer and the defendant's rejoinder to the replication).[10] In addition, the plaintiff might submit exceptions to an 'insufficient' answer (i.e. one not fully responding to the claims of the bill), contending that the defendant should submit a further, more responsive answer. Also included, as attachments to a plaintiff's bill of complaint (and, occasionally, to a defendant's answer), may be schedules itemizing goods or transactions in question (e.g. post-mortem inventories in an estate case or a cargo schedule in a marine insurance case). On occasion, one also encounters amended bills (usually to include or to delete defendants), supplementary bills, and bills of revivor (when an original party to a suit has died). The great majority of Exchequer equity suits (as in Chancery) never proceeded beyond the pleadings stage, being either abandoned or compromised, and for a substantial minority the only document that appears to have been filed is the bill of complaint. Subsequent stages of a contested suit usually, but not invariably, consisted of the taking of witnesses' depositions and the submission of documentary proofs (e.g. deeds),[11] the hearing of the case before the four Barons of the Exchequer,[12] the referral of factual question(s) either to the Court's own official, the Deputy to the King's Remembrancer (the equivalent of a Master in Chancery, hereafter referred to as the Deputy Remembrancer) or to a common law jury on an issue agreed upon by the parties, and the promulgation of the Court's decree in the light of the evidence, counsel's arguments, and (if any) the jury's verdict.

9. The entries by county are only in rough chronological order so that sets of pleadings for the same county and term may be entered pages apart. Dates were sometimes added to the bills by the clerks when filing, but only in relatively few instances in either 1685–6 or 1784–5. The bill books are not available on the open shelves and must be ordered under their IND numbers from the repository. The series list for E 112 in both the 'Standard List' and in the on-line catalogue provides a key to identifying the appropriate bill book volume.
10. For an account of 'English bill' procedure in Chancery, and other courts including Exchequer, see H. Horwitz, *Chancery Equity Records and Proceedings 1600–1800* (PRO Handbook No. 27, 2nd edn. 1998), chapter one.
11. One exception to the use of depositions is the collusive suit, such as the solicitation of a decree by representatives of a deceased seeking to preclude later challenges to their disbursement of assets.
12. From 1817 onwards, as a result of an attempted speed-up of Exchequer equity business, cases were normally heard by only a single baron, either the Chief Baron or his substitute: Bryson, *Equity Side*, p. 161.

On the whole, Exchequer equity records have been less intensively exploited than those of Chancery, in part because the archive is considerably smaller and has been less well known, and in part perhaps because of Exchequer's reputation as the pre-eminent forum for tithe disputes.[13] However, it should be noted that Exchequer's preoccupation with tithe cases was by no means constant: while over one-third of 'English bill' cases in 1685 concerned tithes, by 1785 that proportion had fallen to under one-sixth.[14] Moreover, in both years the number of tithe disputes arising in the metropolis was minimal. Rather, with respect to suits originating in the metropolis, Exchequer's equity business exhibits much the same array of subjects as those litigated in Chancery, with the principal categories of disputes concerning land, deceased's estates, debts and bonds, and commercial arrangements, initiated by a broadly similar profile of litigants.[15] Furthermore, a growing proportion of Exchequer cases emanated from the London metropolis – roughly one-fifth to one-quarter in the later seventeenth century, rising to a little over one-third by the later eighteenth and early nineteenth centuries.[16] Then, too, in both periods London and Middlesex generated disproportionately more suits than the prevailing metropolitan fraction of the total population of the kingdom.

Table I. Geographical origins of Exchequer equity cases

	Total bills	London and Middlesex	Rest of England and Wales
1685–86	630	20.2%	79.8%
1784–85	399	33.8%	66.2%
1818–19	448	35.3%	64.7%

Source: Bill books. Note the eighteenth-century fall-off in litigation (evident in the central royal courts, as well as in local jurisdictions) and the partial revival in the early nineteenth century to the end of George III's reign.

The pleadings calendared here have been gathered as part of a broader enquiry conducted in the course of the preparation of a PRO handbook on Exchequer equity records and proceedings, a project carried out by the editors of the present volume and funded by the Leverhulme Trust. For purposes of the handbook, the pleadings for 150 suits (selected from those filed for all of England and Wales) for each of four sample years (1685–86,

---

13. However, the potential value of these records has recently been underlined by J. Milhous and R. Hume, 'Eighteenth-century Equity Lawsuits in the Court of Exchequer as a Source of Historical Research', *Historical Research* 70 (1997), pp. 231–46. And see also T. Trowles, 'Eighteenth century Exchequer records as a genealogical source', *Genealogists' Magazine* 25–3 (Sept. 1995), pp. 93–98. It should be noted that there are distinct signs of a degeneration of record-keeping by the Exchequer equity staff over the course of the eighteenth century.
14. These data are derived from our samples of the two years' pleadings encompassing both metropolitan and provincial suits. See below for the samples.
15. For data on Chancery litigation, see Horwitz, *Chancery equity records,* chapter 2.
16. A similar trend is discernible in Chancery.

1734–35, 1784–85 and 1818–19) were read and analysed.[17] In addition, one-half of these 600 suits (those from the 1685–86 and the 1818–19 samples) were traced through the other relevant series of Exchequer equity records (especially the depositions and exhibits, Deputy Remembrancer's reports, and the Court's orders and decrees) as a way of gauging the behaviour of litigants and the modes of operation of the Court.[18] In turn, the suits calendared here include both those London and Middlesex cases which are part of the samples for 1685–86 and 1784–85 and all other surviving London and Middlesex pleadings for those two years.

Table II: London and Middlesex suits calendared in this volume

	1685–6	1784–5	Combined
From samples (see text)	34	51	85
From the rest of E 112	117	143	260
TOTAL	151	194	345

All told, the 345 sets of pleadings from London and Middlesex calendared here can be divided into six main subject-groupings: landholding and land transactions; tithes; estate (testamentary and intestacy) issues; debts and bonds; business transactions; and inter-vivos trusts. These are 'artificial' categories in the sense that Exchequer, as other courts of equity, knew no 'forms of action' (unlike the common law) and had no need to classify its business as we have chosen to.[19] Rather, the Court's focus was always on the conduct of the defendant, and from this perspective the gravamen of many bills of complaint was an allegation of fraud or of failure to honour an agreement.

In broad terms, suits categorized as related to landholding and other property questions include mortgage disputes, rental and leasehold claims, demands for specific performance of agreements to convey, as well as suits involving manorial rights, waste, and boundaries. Tithes have been reserved for a separate category given the prevalence of such disputes in Exchequer; complainants might be either parish incumbents or lay impropriators (or their agents or lessees). Suits classed as estate matters concern chiefly claims for

---

17. The years were chosen in large part to facilitate comparison with earlier work on Chancery litigation. See Henry Horwitz and Charles Moreton (eds.), *Samples of Chancery Pleadings and Suits: 1627, 1685, 1735 and 1785* (List & Index Society, vol. 257, 1995).

18. That is, for 1685–86 we have a total of 267 suits: 150 for the sample (including 34 from London and Middlesex) and 117 additional London and Middlesex cases. For 1784–85 we have a total of 293 suits: 150 for the sample (including 51 from London and Middlesex) along with 143 additional London and Middlesex cases. The 34 overlapping London and Middlesex cases for 1685–86 have been traced through the other Exchequer series but the 51 for 1784–85 have not. The sample sets will be calendared in a forthcoming volume (no. 278) published by the List and Index Society.

19. For illustration of our categorization of suits, 'business' = items **1, 5** and **7**; debt/bond = **6, 14** and **16**; estate = **2, 3**, and **4**; land = **21, 22** and **24**.

payment of legacies and for performance of other provisions of wills, including testamentary trusts. Under this rubric, too, have been placed suits by representatives of the deceased trying to bring in the deceased's property or to collect his/her debts. Suits classed as matters of debt include disputes concerning bonds and their enforcement and demands for sums owing (apart from mortgages and suits to recover the assets of a deceased). They also include the suits of creditors of deceased individuals against their representatives. However, when such credit relationships derive from a sale of goods or other business transaction, including an employment arrangement, they have been classified as matters of business. (From this perspective, then, the category of debts and bonds is a residual one.) Business transactions include, besides sales of goods and employment arrangements, matters of account between partners, as well as insurance and copyright cases. Finally, trusts refer exclusively to *inter vivos* trusts, principally the obligations of trustees under marriage settlements.

Using these six categories, and two supplementary ones – (1) cases involving royal revenue rights with the Attorney General as plaintiff (so-called 'English informations', to distinguish them from the usual Latin information) and (2) 'miscellaneous' matters – the 345 suits calendared in this volume have been grouped as indicated in Table III. The distinctive distribution of subject matter in the metropolitan cases in Exchequer is evident from a comparison of Table III with Table IV. Most striking is the very much higher proportion of tithe suits among non-metropolitan cases: tithe disputes constitute no more than 2 per cent of the London and metropolitan pleadings in the two years studied, but they generated 45 per cent and 23 per cent of the provincial cases respectively – a disparity reflecting the fact that by the terms of the act of 37 Henry VIII tithe disputes in the City were to be heard by the Lord Mayor's Court. Moreover, even leaving aside tithe suits, as in Table V, comparison of the profile of provincial litigation to that of the metropolitan suits in Table III underlines the fact that cases involving debts and bonds and business transactions were considerably less common among the former than among the latter.

Table III: Subject-matter of London and Middlesex suits in Exchequer equity cases

	1685–6 n*	%	1784–5 n	%
Land	28	18.5	19	9.7
Tithes	2	1.3	4	2.1
Estates (of deceased)	32	21.2	18	9.2
Debts and bonds	46.5	30.8	66	34.0
Business	31.5	20.9	84	43.3
Trusts	3	2.0	—	0.0
Royal revenue	2	1.3	—	0.0
Miscellaneous	6	4.0	3	1.5
TOTAL	151	100.0	194	99.8

* Five suits have been counted in more than one category, with each classification counting as 0.5

Table IV: Subject-matter of Exchequer equity suits emanating from the provinces

	1685–6		1784–5	
	n	%	n	%
Land	24	20.7	32	32.3
Tithes	53	45.7	23	23.2
Estates (of deceased)	12	10.3	17.5	17.7
Debts and bonds	14	12.1	16.5	16.7
Business	4	3.4	9	9.1
Trusts	2	1.7	—	0.0
Royal revenue	2	1.7	—	0.0
Miscellaneous	5	4.3	1	1.0
TOTAL	116	99.9	99	100.0

The provincial suits categorized here, and in following tables, are part of the samples taken for the Exchequer equity handbook, and will be calendared in the forthcoming List and Index Society volume. Two 1784–5 suits have been counted in two categories, each as 0.5.

Table V: Subject-matter of Exchequer equity suits from the provinces excluding tithe cases

	1685–6		1784–5	
	n	%	n	%
Land	24	38.1	32	42.1
Estates (of deceased)	12	19.0	17.5	23.0
Debts and bonds	14	22.2	16.5	21.7
Business	4	6.3	9	11.8
Trusts	2	3.2	—	
Royal revenue	2	3.2	—	
Miscellaneous	5	8.0	1	1.3
TOTAL	63	100.0	76	99.9

Just as London and Middlesex suits have a different subject profile than that of provincial suits, so the parties involved also differed in character, as evidenced in Tables VI and VII. One would indeed anticipate both from the distinctive socio-economic configuration of the capital and from the higher (and rising) proportion of credit and business cases among the London and Middlesex suits that the proportion of metropolitan plaintiffs in both years giving commercial or artisanal identifications would be substantially higher than those for the two provincial groups of plaintiffs. More surprising is the rise in the proportion of those styling themselves as gentlemen (or above) among metropolitan plaintiffs. While the commercial-artisanal group of London in 1685 was more than two-and-a-half times as large as that of the gentleman group, the situation is very different in 1785 when plaintiffs styling themselves gentlemen (or of higher ranks) constitute over one quarter (27.3 per cent) of the entire metropolitan group while plaintiffs styling themselves as gentlemen (or of higher ranks) constitute only 18.4 per cent of the provincial group of that year.[20] It is possible that this seeming anomaly reflects the freer adoption of the style 'gent.' by those of non-gentle birth among the better-off among the 'middling sort' by the later eighteenth century. And this speculation is reinforced by the simultaneous upward movement of debt and business suits in the metropolis (combined, from 52 per cent to 77 per cent: Table III) and the much smaller increase in commercial and artisanal first plaintiffs (from 43 per cent to 47 per cent: Table VI).

Table VI: Status and/or occupation of first-named plaintiffs in london and Middlesex suits

	1685–6: n = 151		1784–5: n = 194	
	n	%	n	%
Gentleman and above	25	16.6	53	27.3
Commercial and artisanal	64	42.4	91	46.9
Professional	17	11.3	24	12.4
Undesignated men	15	9.9	12	6.2
Women	17	11.3	13	6.7
Minors	3	2.0	—	
Miscellaneous men	1	0.7	1	0.5
Non-individual plaintiffs	9	6.0	—	
TOTAL		100.2		100.0

Table VII: Status and/or occupation of first-named plaintiffs in provincial suits (excluding tithes)

	1685–6: n= 63		1784–5 n=76	
	n	%	n	%
Gentlemen and above	20	31.7	14	18.4
Commercial and artisanal	13	20.6	22	28.9
Professional	7	11.1	6	7.9
Farmer	6	9.5	13	17.1
Undesignated Men	6	9.5	7	9.2
Women	8	12.7	14	18.4
Minors	1	1.6	—	0.0
Non-individual plaintiffs	2	3.2	—	0.0
TOTAL		99.9		99.9

20. Note that in Table VI and subsequent tables concerning the identity of first plaintiff, the category 'commercial and artisanal' embraces a wide range from merchants to craftsmen; 'farmer' includes all working farmers (though not agricultural labourers); 'professionals' includes all identifiable as clerics, lawyers (even if styling themselves 'gent' or 'esq'), medical men, and government officeholders. Well over two-thirds of the women were widows. Most of the 'undesignated men' did specify some role (e.g., executor) in relation to the suit.

To be sure, a minority of first-plaintiffs in London and Middlesex suits lived outside the metropolis while a smaller proportion of plaintiffs in provincial suits hailed from the metropolis.[21] But if the correlation between the first-named plaintiff's place of residence and the county of the origin of the suit was not one-to-one, most suits filed by the clerks as London and Middlesex featured first-named plaintiffs whose place of residence was London or the urban portions of Middlesex, and similarly most suits filed under the other English and Welsh counties featured first-named plaintiffs resident outside the metropolis.

As the subject of suits and, at least in 1685, the socio-economic profile of suitors in metropolitan cases diverged significantly from the suits and suitors from elsewhere in England and Wales, so the course of metropolitan suits and of those from the provinces also differed. Above all, metropolitan suitors were often seeking injunctions from the Exchequer to inhibit proceedings against them in other courts, primarily the common law courts and, in particular, King's Bench. As Table VIII indicates, close to three-tenths of the metropolitan bills from 1685 sought injunctions to inhibit proceedings in other courts and this proportion doubled in 1785. By contrast, provincial suitors were much less often in search of injunctions, even if we exclude tithe cases in which relief of this type was rarely requested.

Table VIII: Injunctions sought in Exchequer equity to halt proceedings in other courts

	1685–6	1784–5
London & Middlesex suits	43 of 149	116 of 190
Other suits	10 of 63	24 of 76

In their pursuit of injunctions, metropolitan suitors in Exchequer also can be distinguished from suitors in Chancery, whether from the provinces or the metropolis. Only 10 per cent of Chancery complainants in 1685 sought injunctions, and only 8 per cent in 1785. This, then, is to confirm the observation of the barrister James Wigram, testifying before the House of Lords inquiry of 1840 on the future of the Exchequer equity jurisdiction: 'when I used to draw more bills in the Court of Exchequer, a large proportion ... were bills for the mere purpose of obtaining injunctions to restrain proceedings at law. If a party wished to use a Court of Equity as the means of defeating a Plaintiff at Law, he generally had recourse to the Court of Exchequer'.[22]

---

21. Those categorized as 'provincials' include a few individuals from rural Middlesex. Among the London and Middlesex suits (excluding tithe suits), 21 of 122 individual first plaintiffs in 1685 (who stated their place of residence) and 24 of 187 in 1785 came from outside the metropolis. Conversely, among provincial cases, 6 plaintiffs of 54 in 1685 and 1 of 75 in 1785 came from the metropolis.

22. As quoted in H. Horwitz, 'Chancery's "Younger Sister": the Court of Exchequer and its Equity Jurisdiction, 1649–1841', *Historical Research* 72 (1999), p. 175. See also Fowler, *Practice of the Exchequer*, 1 pp. 249–51, 259–60. Both discuss the greater scope and efficacy of Exchquer injunctions.

As metropolitan plaintiffs, by comparison both with their provincial counterparts in the Exchequer and with Chancery complainants generally, were considerably more likely to be responding to legal actions elsewhere, so metropolitan defendants in Exchequer (often plaintiffs in other proceedings) were rather more likely to submit an answer (or other response) to the bill of complaint than were their provincial counterparts. As Table IX indicates, less than a quarter of metropolitan complaints in 1685 and less than three-tenths in 1785 went unanswered, whereas almost double the proportion of provincial suits never went further than the filing of the bill of complaint (over two-fifths in 1685 and over five-eighths in 1785).

Table IX: Exchequer equity suits in which there are bills only (no responses)

	1685–6	1784–5
London & Middlesex suits	36 of 151	56 of 194
Other suits	49 of 116	64 of 99

(Comparable figures for Chancery 'bill only' pleadings are 34 of 146 suits in 1685 and 33 of 140 in 1785)

The greater readiness of defendants in Exchequer suits emanating from the metropolis to respond, in turn, means that metropolitan suits tend to contain more information about the issue in question than do suits coming from the provinces. To be sure, complainant and defendant tend to tell very different stories, but at the least the researcher is reminded that a bill of complaint may be a very partial presentation of the facts in question. Indeed, since the bill was not supported by oath whereas the defendant was bound to answer under oath, the balance of credibility may well incline to the latter's side.

One further type of document, not infrequently found in these pleading files, may also contribute to the researcher's information and understanding – the schedules attached by some parties to their pleadings, spelling out in detail the state of matters in litigation. Among the more interesting schedules found among the 1685 sets of pleading are a list of debts allegedly owed by Middlesex water customers (**23**); a schedule of clay sold by a Dorset merchant to a London tobacco-pipe maker (**37**); both sides' lists of goods and effects left by a sea captain who died on a voyage from Guinea to Barbados (**44**); a schedule of logwood and other items in transactions involving one of the farmers of the Customs (**61**); accounts between a Cambridgeshire gentleman and a merchant tailor of Hatton Garden (**90**) with respect to dealings in malt; accounts of Anthony Row, purveyor to Charles II's stables (**103–04**); financial dealings of a onetime Master of the Mint with the moniers of the Mint (**113**); and an inventory of goods seized from a brewhouse by commissioners of the excise (**141**). Similarly, among the 1785 pleadings, we encounter a set of accounts of a friendly society of London porters (**169**); accounts of a vessel shipping rice from South Carolina to London which was lost at sea (**221**); the captain's narrative of a cargo ship, the *Success*, which sank in the Delaware on a voyage from Dublin to Philadelphia (**230**); a list of buildings erected by the architects James and Samuel Wyatt using a newly-invented method of slating roofs (**296**); lists of musical compositions, including works by Bach (probably Johann Christian) in two copyright disputes (**288, 299**). All told, roughly one in four of the 345 sets of pleadings calendared in this volume incorporate such schedules or listings, but such schedules are more commonly associated with metropolitan suits than provincial ones, as illustrated by Table X.

Table X: Schedules by origin of suit

	1685–6	1784–5
Metropolitan	34 of 151 = 22.5%	49 of 194 = 25.3%
Provincial	9 of 116 = 7.8%	11 of 99 = 11.1%

What of the subsequent course of the suits whose pleadings are calendared here? One way to answer is to describe the documentation that such litigation, if continued through later stages, would generate. Three main types of documents were usually, though not invariably produced, in the course of subsequent litigation. One type would be motions and resultant orders as minuted in E 161, with the orders written out and filed in E 131 and then entered in E 127.[23] A second type would be the questions (interrogatories) put to witnesses and their sworn depositions (in E 133 and occasionally in E 134).[24] Finally, there are the reports of inquiries or accounts in references prepared by the Deputy Remembrancer (E 194, E 195), and the summaries of hearings (including counsel's arguments as well as relevant portions of the evidence) and the Court's decrees in cases that reached a conclusion (accounts of hearings and statements of decrees survive in E 162 , and also in E 126 and E 130).

Of these various records, perhaps the richest for the majority of searchers will be the depositions. Additional ancillary material can be found in E 193 (strayed replications and rejoinders); in E 103, E 207, and E 218 (affidavits, usually relating to matters of process); E 140 and E 219 and related series (documentary exhibits submitted by the parties and not removed from Court).

As depositions will constitute the most interesting source beyond the pleadings for most inquirers, it is worth saying something about the frequency with which witnesses were called on by one or both parties. To begin with, we may consider the course of the thirty-four London and Middlesex suits that are part of our 1685–6 sample and, as such, have been traced through the records. Of this total, only three were carried on beyond the pleadings stage, and two of these have extant depositions. A somewhat similar result is produced by analysis of the traced 1818–19 sample. This contains 53 London and Middlesex suits of which twelve went beyond the

---

23. Abortive motions are only minuted in E 161, while certain routine processes (referred to from the courtroom location where they occurred as 'side-bar' motions) tended to be entered only in E 127.
24. Similarly, occasional witnesses in suits originating in the provinces found it convenient to make their depositions in London.

pleadings stage, with depositions taken in only three.[25] These data suggest that the taking of depositions was quite uncommon, at least in metropolitan suits. However, too much stress should not be put on these small samples, especially in light of the course of proceedings in some 258 suits which reached the hearing stage between 1695 and 1697. Of these 258 suits, 57 emanated from London and Middlesex, and for these depositions survive in 42 instances mainly in E 133, but also in four instances in E 134 as well).[26] On the one hand, then, the researcher in Exchequer equity materials can hardly expect to find depositions as a matter of course; yet it would appear that subject to the limitations of the existing finding aid for E 133, depositions would prove a useful supplement to investigation of the pleadings in E 112.

It remains to describe the form of an Exchequer bill and also of an answer.[27] For our purposes, there are five leading characteristics of a bill of complaint in Exchequer equity. First, it is in English. Second, it spells out in detail and in layman's language the nature of the litigant's grievance or complaint (though this may entail technical descriptions of the matter in question – e.g. practice in transferring bills of exchange). Third, the plaintiff asks the Court's assistance (via subpoena) to compel the defendant to answer, and might also ask for relief by way of injunction from defendant's proceedings in the matter at hand that either were under way in other courts or being conducted to the plaintiff's irreparable harm (e.g. the cutting of timber on a contested parcel of land or a breach of copyright).[28] Fourth, plaintiffs were required to state their place of residence, and usually also provided some indication of occupation and/or status.[29] Fifth, the bill was to bear the signature of the complainant's counsel to indicate that he vouched for the seriousness of the complaint.

Similarly, answers were also in English (as, indeed, were most Exchequer equity documents); they differ from the bills chiefly in the requirement that defendants swear to the truth of their assertions, with the date of their oath recorded on the document. In this fashion, then, defendants in equity may be regarded, for some purposes at least, as testifying under oath, a privilege not given to defendants at common law.

Both bills and answers, as found in E 112, are on parchments of varying sizes, with lengthy bills sometimes sewn together to make single sheets as long as eight feet. Bills, answers, and other pleadings were supposed to be kept together (and the clerks normally tied them together, thus sometimes making them difficult to handle) but with the passage of time (and the

---

25. This finding also reflects the limited proportion of metropolitan suits pursued beyond the pleadings. Of the 1685 sample of 150, 27 of the 30 suits that were litigated beyond the pleadings emanated from the provinces. However, in the 1819 sample, only sixteen of 98 provincial suits went beyond the pleadings as compared to twelve of 52 London and Middlesex cases. Even so, depositions survive for eight of the sixteen provincial cases and for only three of the twelve metropolitan ones.
26. These suits are analysed in Horwitz, 'Chancery's "Younger Sister"', pp. 166 ff.
27. A full description of Exchequer pleadings can be found in Bryson, *Equity Side*, pp. 93–128.
28. As in Chancery, and despite the prohibition of 4 Anne cap. 16, sec. 22, subpoenas were often issued before the complainant's bill was actually filed.
29. As evidenced by Tables VI and VII, this requirement was complied with more fully and consistently in 1785 than in earlier sample years.

lengthening of the pleading process) some replications and rejoinders were never filed in E 112; some of these strays survive in E 193.

Note on editorial method

In calendaring the pleadings from E 112 for London and Middlesex for these two years, our particular concerns have been threefold: (1) to indicate the archival locations of all pleadings relating to the suit in question; (2) to summarize the substance of the dispute, relying chiefly on the complainant's allegations; and (3) to list all the parties to the suit (along with their places of residence and status or occupation), as well as other individuals of significance.

In turn, the calendar includes all London and Middlesex pleading recorded in the bill books for the two years in question, save in those few instances in which the pleadings themselves are not to be found in E 112 and for a small number of stray replications and rejoinders that have ended up in E 193.

Proper names are spelled as in the documents. In some instances this has meant spelling a given surname differently in one pleading than in another. Such inconsistencies are reconciled in the indexes. There are individual indexes for persons and subjects for each of the two years calendared.

New style dating has been employed throughout. Documents relating to individual pleadings are listed in chronological order by year and by legal term. If two documents are extant for a given term, one of which is dated to day and month and the other only by term, the latter will be listed first (e.g. a document dated simply Michaelmas 1685 will precede one dated 18 November 1685).

Cross-references to related suits have been inserted in the calendar where the suits in question appear to be directly related.

Acknowledgements

This calendar was made possible by the generosity of the Leverhulme Trust in supporting the work of Dr. Jessica Cooke in connection with the preparation of Professor Henry Horwitz's *Exchequer Equity Records and Proceedings 1649–1841*, forthcoming as a Public Record Office Handbook. The editors would like to express their gratitude to Dr. Trevor Chalmers, formerly of the Public Record Office, who provided invaluable and patient technical support for this project. We would also like to thank for assistance and support Mr. Guy Holborn, Librarian, Lincolns Inn, and Mr. Aidan Lawes, Dr. Elizabeth Hallam-Smith, and Dr. David Thomas, all of the Public Record Office, and Miss Margaret Condon, formerly of the Public Record Office. Finally, we are most grateful for the scrupulous care with which Dr. Vanessa Harding has proceeded in readying our text for the press.

BIBLIOGRAPHY

R. M. Ball, 'Tobias Eden, Change and Conflict in the Exchequer Office, 1672–1698', *Journal of Legal History* 11 (1990), pp. 70–89

idem, 'The King's Remembrancer's Office in the 18th century', *Journal of Legal History* 11 (1990), pp. 90–113

Charles Barton, *An Historical Treatise of a Suit in Equity* (London, 1796)

William Hamilton Bryson, *The Equity Side of the Exchequer: Its Jurisdiction, Administration, Procedures and Records* (Cambridge, 1975)

Idem, 'Equity Reports and Records in Early-Modern England', in Alain Wijffel (ed.), *Case Law in the Making The Techniques and Methods of Judicial Records and Law Reports* (Comparative Studies in Continental and Anglo-American Legal History, 17 (2 vols., 1995)), I, pp. 69–82, and II, pp. 53–84

C. Churches, '"The most unconvincing testimony": the genesis and historical usefulness of the country deposition in Chancery', *Seventeenth Century* XI (1996), pp. 209–227

David Burton Fowler, *The Practice of the court of Exchequer upon Proceedings in Equity* (London, 2 vols., 1795)

Henry Horwitz, *Chancery Equity Records and Proceedings 1600–1800* (PRO Handbook no.27, 2nd edn. 1998)

H. Horwitz, 'Chancery's "Younger Sister": The Court of Exchequer and its Equity Jurisdiction, 1649–1841', *Historical Research* 72 (1999), pp.160–82

M. Macnair, 'Common law and statutory imitations of equitable relief under the later Stuarts', in C.W. Brooks and Michael Lobban (eds.), *Communities and Courts in Britain 1150–1900* (London, 1997), pp. 115–31

J. Milhous and R. D. Hume, 'Eighteenth-century Equity Lawsuits in the Court of Exchequer as a Source for Historical Research', *Historical Research* 70 (1997), pp. 231–46

T. Trowles, 'Eighteenth century Exchequer records as a genealogical source', *Genealogists' Magazine* 25–3 (Sept. 1995), pp. 93–98

CALENDAR OF EXCHEQUER EQUITY PLEADINGS 1685–6

1. Albyn v Farmer

P: (1) Benjamin Albyn, merchant, London. D: (1) Henry Farmer, packer, London; (2) Richard Yarbury, dry salter, London, allegedly invested with d1's power of attorney; (3) Richard Perkins, allegedly d1's creditor; (4) William Love esq., merchant, London, p & d1's arbitrator, p's deponent, aged 65 years; (5) Richard Onslow, merchant, London, p & d1's arbitrator, p's deponent, aged 51 years; (6) John Harvey esq., merchant, London, p & d1's arbitrator, p's deponent, aged 65 years. C: (1) Edward Hildegard, counsel for p's bill; (2) William Killingworth, counsel for p's exceptions; (3) P. Crawford, counsel for d1; (4) Anthony Upton, counsel for d2. P seeks relief from any suit of ds for payment of bonds totalling £582 which p was allegedly compelled in 1682 to issue d1 by ds4-6, arbitrators of p & d1's dispute concerning cloth sold & sums owed to each other. P claims d1 had agreed in 1681 to sell him cloth & ship it to Turkey (where p was living) but substituted inferior cloth. D1 had p arrested & p sued him in Chancery. P asserts d1 & d3 (allegedly d1's creditor) assigned the bonds to d2, who claims to have d1's power of attorney.

1685, Easter	E 112/589	Bill. LMX 52; dated 1 June.
1685, June 19	E 112/589	Answer. Swearing date of d2's answer.
1685, June 20	E 112/589	Answer. Swearing date of d1's answer & plea.
1685, Nov 23	E 112/589	Further answer. Swearing date of d1's further answer.
1685, Mich	E 112/589	Exception. P's exceptions concern his business dealings with d1.
1686, Feb 19	E 112/589	Further answer. Swearing date of d1's further answer.
1686, Easter	E 112/589	Replication. P asserts ds' answers are insufficient.

2. Aldridge v Cocke

P: (1) Mary Aldridge, J. Aldridge's widow & administratrix. D: (1) Mary Cocke, Bishopsgate St., London; (2) Benjamin Hart, pawnbroker, London. C: (1) L. Owen, counsel for p; (2) D. Roy, counsel for d2. Add: (1) John Aldridge, looking-glass maker, London, deceased, p's husband; (2) Martha Drew, pawnbroker, London, deceased. P, J. Aldridge's widow & administratrix, seeks recovery of household goods which she claims ds1-2 acquired by some

1

means unknown to her. D1 reportedly asserts J. Aldridge asked her to pawn the goods to d2. D2 claims when he was apprentice to M. Drew (deceased), p pawned goods which she could not redeem and were therefore sold.

| 1685, Mich | E 112/598 | Bill. LMX 584; dated 12 October? (cf. E 112/594 LMX 305 Aldridge v Milburne). |
| 1685, Nov 24 | E 112/598 | Answer. Swearing date of d2's answer. |

3. Aldridge v Dyke

P: (1) Mary Aldridge, J. Aldridge's widow & administratrix. D: (1) Jonathan Dyke, d2's husband; (2) Elizabeth Dyke, d1's wife, J. Clarke's widow. C: (1) L. Owen, counsel for p. Add: (1) John Aldridge, looking-glass maker, London, deceased, p's husband; (2) John Clarke, looking-glass maker, deceased, d2's former husband. P, administratrix of her husband, J. Aldridge, deceased, seeks payment of debts which she claims ds owed her husband for looking-glasses. Ds deny they owed p's husband, but d2 claims after her first husband John Clarke, looking-glass maker, died, she gave his tools to J. Aldridge in return for work.

| 1685, Mich | E 112/594 | Bill. LMX 308. |
| 1686, Jan 21 | E 112/594 | Answer (with attachments). Swearing date of ds' answer; accounts between J. Aldridge & d2 attached. |

4. Aldridge v Milburne

P: (1) Mary Aldridge, St. Buttolphs out Bishopsgate, London, J. Aldridge's widow & administratrix. D: (1) Mary Milburne, pawnbroker, Howndsditch, St. Buttolphs, London. C: (1) L. Owen, counsel for p. Add: (1) John Aldridge, looking-glass maker, London, deceased, p's husband; (2) Mary Cocke. P, J. Aldridge's widow and administratrix, seeks recovery of her husband's household goods which she alleges M. Cocke delivered to d as security for some debt of J. Aldridge's. D reportedly refuses to return the goods.

| 1685, Mich | E 112/594 | Bill. LMX 305 (cf. E 112/598 LMX 584 Aldridge v Cocke). |

5. Arthur v Beane

P: (1) Owen Arthur gent., parish of St. Botolph, Aldgate, London, married to H. Beane's daughter, lessee of hearth duties for Devon & Cornwall. D: (1) Katherine Beane, H. Beane's widow & executrix; (2) Mathew Clements, Wapping, London, H. Beane's executor; (3) Humphrey Arthur, H. Beane's legatee; (4) Beane Arthur, H. Beane's legatee; (5) Samuel Clarke, H. Beane's legatee. C: (1) Edward Ward, counsel for p; (2) William Rowney, counsel for d5; (3) Thomas Smith, counsel for ds1-2. Add: (1) Humphrey Beane esq., deceased, p's father in law, d1's husband, farmer of the hearth duties for Devon & Cornwall; (2) Sir Richard Piggott, knight, farmer of the hearth duties for Devon & Cornwall; (3) Perient Trott, farmer of the hearth duties for Devon & Cornwall; (4) Edward Rutter gent., London, lessee of hearth duties for Devon & Cornwall; (5) Thomas Collier, St. Olave's, Southwark, Surrey, lessee of hearth duties for Devon & Cornwall; (6) John Parsons, brewer, parish of St. Katherine's, Midd, lessee of hearth duties for Devon & Cornwall; (7) Thomas Birkhead, lessee of hearth duties for Devon & Cornwall. P seeks payment of his debts by ds. P became lessee of 1/8 part of the hearth duties for Devon &

Cornwall with E. Rutter, T. Collier, J. Parsons & T. Birkhead, from the farmers of the duties R. Piggott, P. Trott & p's father in law H. Beane. When p became indebted to the farmers & others he assigned his brewhouse and a £2000 judgement to H. Beane to pay his debts & a £100 annuity to p. P claims H. Beane did not pay his creditors & died in 1679, leaving the judgement to ds3-5, with his wife d1 & d2 as executors. Ds1-2 claim the judgement was for debts p owed H. Beane. D5 has allegedly sued ds1-2 in Chancery for the judgement.

1685, Hil	E 112/589	Bill. LMX 65; dated 29 January (37 Charles II), but entered as 1 James II.
1685, June 17	E 112/589	Answer. Swearing date of answer of ds1-2.
1685, July 6	E 112/589	Answer. Swearing date of d5's answer.

6. Auberry v Gwyn

P: (1) Samuel Auberry, coachmaker, St. Martin in the Fields, Midd, E. Auberry's son & administrator. D: (1) Edward Gwyn esq., Heref, d2's husband; (2) Dame Frances Gwyn, d1's wife, previously Throckmorton; (3) Sir Thomas Geary, St. Giles in the Fields, Midd, knight; (4) Henry Phillipps, d3's trustee; (5) Richard Aillsbury, d3's tenant. C: (1) William Ettricke, counsel for p; (2) Ra. Darnall, counsel for ds1-2; (3) Ri. Bayly, counsel for d3. Add: (1) Edmond Auberry, coachmaker, St. Martin in the Fields, Midd, deceased intestate, p's father. P, as administrator & son of E. Auberry (deceased intestate), seeks possession of a Warwickshire farm in payment of £180 damages for which he obtained a judgement in KB in 1682 ag ds1-2. D3 claims d2 had mortgaged the farm to his trustee d4 for £200 in 1676, which d2 did not repay so d3 possessed & transferred it to another party. Ds1-2 claim they had agreed with p (& are willing) to pay him £108 in instalments.

1685, Mich	E 112/592	Bill. LMX 228; dated 7 November; amended 4 May 1687 to include ds4-5.
1686, May 10	E 112/592	Plea. Swearing date of plea of ds1-2.
1687, April 14	E 112/592	Answer. Swearing date of d3's answer.

7. Axton v Renew

P: (1) Thomas Axton, merchant, London, owned 1/4 of a ship, the *St. Mary*. D: (1) Peter Renew, merchant, London, or resident in France; (2) Peter Hasler, Fareham, Hants, P. Richards' administrator. C: (1) A. Newnam, counsel for p; (2) Robert Gillmore, counsel for d1. Add: (1) Paul Richards, merchant, deceased intestate, owned 1/2 of a ship, the *St. Mary*; (2) George Perin, merchant, Kensington, London. P seeks relief ag ds' suits for payment of a £97 2s 2d bill of exchange which p drew upon G. Perin in 1675 allegedly as a loan for P. Richards, who endorsed it to d1. Perin refused to accept the bill. P claims Richards also owed him for sums spent building a ship, the *St. Mary*, & for payment of a £400 bond to the Crown, etc. Richards died intestate & d2 became his administrator. Ds claim the bond was for debts p owed Richards, & that p allowed Richards to endorse it to d1.

1685, Mich	E 112/590	Bill. LMX 106.
1685, Nov 12	E 112/590	Answer. Swearing date of d1's answer.
1685, Mich	E 112/590	Copy bill.
1685, Nov 28	E 112/590	Commission. For d2's answer.
1686, Jan 27	E 112/590	Answer. Swearing date of d2's answer.

8. Barrington v Smith

P: (1) Abraham Barrington gent., London. D: (1) Richard Smith, apothecary, Thames St., London, first d listed in the schedule. C: (1) Charles Porter, counsel for p. Add: (1) Joseph Ayloffe esq., barrister, Gray's Inn, Midd, deceased, owner of London Bridge waterhouse. P (lessee of London Bridge waterhouse for past 13 years from J. Ayloffe) seeks payment of arrears of rent from d and others listed in the schedule, for pipes laid and water transported to the ds' houses. The ds reportedly assert they received no water when the pipes were frozen, but p claims this was for a short time for which he is not responsible.

1685, Easter   E 112/588   Bill (with attachments). LMX 12; dated 8 May; schedule attached of arrears of rent owed by d and others.

9. Bennett v Bennett

P: (1) Thomas Bennett the younger, cheesemonger, St. James Market, Midd, John Bennett's son, d1's nephew, M. Bennett's brother, T. Bennett the E's grandson. D: (1) James Bennett, uncle of p & M. Bennett, John Bennett's executor, T. Bennett the E's executor; (2) Elizabeth Bennett, T. Bennet the E's widow & executrix. C: (1) Robert Rawlins, counsel for p. Add: (1) John Bennett, tanner, Westminster, Midd, deceased, father of p & M. Bennett, T. Bennett the E's son; (2) Thomas Bennett the elder, tanner, deceased, grandfather of p & M. Bennett, d2's husband, John Bennett's father & executor; (3) Mary Bennett, deceased, p's sister, John Bennett's daughter, T. Bennett the E's granddaughter. P seeks possession of estates willed to him & his sister M. Bennett (deceased) by his father John Bennett (deceased in 1667) & grandfather T. Bennett the E (deceased in 1679). John appointed his father T. Bennett the E & d1 as his executors. T. Bennett the E appointed his widow d2 & d1 as his executors. 9 months ago p reached 21 years, but ds reportedly deny the estates were willed to him, or claim they are of little value.

1685, Mich   E 112/594   Bill. LMX 339.

10. Bennett v Ironsides

P: (1) Richard Bennett, infant under 21, Dame B. First's grandson. D: (1) Ralph Ironsides, doctor in physic, M. Ironsides' husband; (2) Thomas Gallopp the elder esq., Netherberry, Dors, p's trustee, T. Gallopp the Y's father; (3) Thomas Gallopp the younger gent., Netherberry, Dors, p's trustee, T. Gallopp the E's son; (4) Robert Freke the elder gent., Upway, Dors, p's trustee, R. Freke the Y's father; (5) Robert Freke the younger, Upway, Dors, p's trustee, R. Freke the E's son. N/f: (1) George Bennett, p's father & next friend. C: (1) Thomas Jenner, counsel for p. Add: (1) Dame Bridget First, deceased, p's grandmother, M. Ironsides' mother; (2) Margaret Ironsides, d1's wife, Dame B. First's daughter; (3) Dr William Denton, p's previous trustee; (4) Dr Henry Jones, p's previous trustee. P, under 21, with his father & next friend G. Bennett, seeks payment of interest from £421 7s willed to him by his grandmother Dame B. First, or possession of a leasehold manor, Stottingway, Dorset, which d1 mortgaged to ds2-5 for the £421 7s. In 1678 p transferred the money by a suit in this Court from trustees W. Denton & H. Jones to ds2-5, who lent it to d1. D1 has not paid the interest. Ds claim if p dies before 21 the

4

money goes to d1's wife M. Ironsides (Dame B. First's daughter), who should be a defendant to this suit.

1685, Mich	E 112/589	Bill. LMX 83.
1685, Mich	E 112/589	Copy bill. (truncated).
1686, Feb 12	E 112/589	Commission. For ds' answer.
1686, April 29	E 112/589	Answer. Answer of ds2-5, sworn by ds2-3 on this date, sworn by ds4-5 on 1 May.
1686, May 30	E 112/589	Answer. Swearing date of d1's answer.

11. Bertie v Dickins

P: (1) Peregrine Bertie esq., London, N. Bertie's son & heir. D: (1) William Dickins esq., barrister, Gray's Inn, Midd; (2) John Dickins gent., St. Dunstan's in the West, London. C: (1) P. Crawford, counsel for p; (2) Thomas Skipwith, also counsel for p; (3) W. Vaughan, counsel for d1. Add: (1) Nicholas Bertie esq., Westminster, London, deceased, p's father; (2) Paul Elliott gent., London, deceased; (3) Henry Owen gent., Fulham, Midd, deceased. P seeks relief from d1's suit for payment of a £400 counter bond issued by p's father N. Bertie as part of an agreement N. Bertie made with ds & H. Owen (deceased) to imbank his marshes in Ely & Lincs in 1664. P claims his father, ds & Owen became bound to P. Elliott (deceased) for £100 to pay d1's expenses, & that N. Bertie issued a £300 counter bond to d2 & the £400 counter bond to d1. D1 claims N. Bertie agreed to settle 1/6 of the marshes on him.

| 1685, Trin | E 112/589 | Bill. LMX 55; dated 8 July. |
| 1685, Nov 9 | E 112/589 | Answer. Swearing date of d1's answer. |

12. Bickerton v Taylor

P: (1) George Bickerton, merchant, Midd. D: (1) Samuel Taylor, button seller, parish of St. Andrews, Holborn, Midd; (2) Peter Squoles, d3's husband; (3) Anne Squoles, d2's wife, E. Williams's widow & administratrix. C: (1) Henry Hatsell, counsel for p; (2) William Brooke, counsel for d1. Add: (1) Edward Williams, tailor, St. Martin in the Fields, Midd, deceased intestate, d3's former husband. P seeks payment of a judgement for £500 he had obtained at KB in 1676 ag E. Williams, who, before paying, died intestate in 1678, leaving his widow & administratrix, d3. P agreed with d3 that he & d1 (another creditor of E. Williams) would collect the debts. P now claims d1 conspires with d3 & her new husband d2 to receive the debts & defraud p of his £500, and that d1 also owes p £19 for goods. D1 claims d3 received debts without accounting for them with p or d1.

| 1685, Mich | E 112/598 | Bill (with attachments). LMX 578; dated 26 October; account attached of goods for which d1 allegedly owes p. (cf. E 112/598 LMX 577 Taylor v Bickerton). |
| 1685, Nov 11 | E 112/598 | Answer. Swearing date of d1's answer. |

13. Birt v Searne

P: (1) Richard Birt, mariner, parish of St. Pauls, Shadwell, Midd. D: (1) Mary Searne, R. Searne's widow; (2) Nicholas Mann gent., solicitor, employed by d1; (3) William Nash, served on the *Robert* of London. C: (1) Mich. Drew,

5

counsel for p; (2) Francis Browne, counsel for ds1-2. Add: (1) Richard Searne, boatswain, St. Pauls, Shadwell, Midd, deceased, d1's husband, served on the *Robert* of London. P seeks inj ag the suit at cl of d1, executrix of her deceased husband R. Searne, for full payment of her husband's wages while boatswain on a ship, the *Robert* of London, bound for Jamaica. P offered to pay her the wages minus board and lodging, medical and funeral bills, but ds claim the receipts are false.

1685, Mich	E 112/598	Bill. LMX 595; dated ?6 November.
1685, Nov 20	E 112/598	Answer. Swearing date of answer of ds1-2.
1686, Trin	E 112/598	Replication. P asserts the answer of ds1-2 is insufficient.

14. Blaney v Howard

P: (1) Isaac Blaney, mariner, Stepney, Midd. D: (1) Edward Howard, mariner, Stepney, Midd, d2's husband; (2) Mary Howard, Stepney, Midd, d1's wife. C: (1) J Hordesnell, counsel for p; (2) Godfrey Thacker, counsel for d2. P seeks inj ag ds' suit for payment of a £32 bond he was allegedly compelled to issue after ds had him arrested in the Court of White Chapel for board & lodging debts. P lodged in d2's house while d1 was at sea & claims d2 borrowed £13 from him, for which she compelled him to issue a release after his arrest. D2 denies borrowing the sum or receiving a release.

| 1685, Easter | E 112/589 | Bill. LMX 72. |
| 1685, May 26 | E 112/589 | Answer. Swearing date of d2's answer. |

15. Booth v Hayter

P: (1) Richard Booth, merchant, London; (2) Samuel Story, merchant, London. D: (1) Charnell Hayter. C: (1) Philip Neve, counsel for ps; (2) John Heames, counsel for d. Ps seeks relief ag a judgement for £80 damages which d obtained ag p1. P1 claims he sold d 5 hogsheads of tobacco at £52 13s 5d, which d did not then pay. P1 had the hogsheads removed from d's shop by a Replevin which proved irregular. D obtained the £80 judgement ag p1 in an action of Trover and Conversion at KB. D claims this cause, concerning damages, is not a matter for equity.

| 1685, Mich | E 112/593 | Bill. LMX 273, dated 17 November. (cf. E 112/590 LMX 101 Booth v Wybourne). |
| 1685, Nov 23 | E 112/593 | Demurrer. Swearing date of d's plea & demurrer. |

16. Booth v Wybourne

P: (1) Richard Booth, merchant, London; (2) Samuel Storey, merchant, London. D: (1) Isaac Wybourne, d2's husband; (2) Elizabeth Wybourne, d1's wife, R. Wymondesold's widow & executrix. C: (1) Francis Fuller, counsel for ps; (2) Sam. Dodd, counsel for ds. Add: (1) Richard Wymondesold, tobacconist, London, deceased, d2's husband. Ps seek discovery of the personal estate of R. Wymondesold (deceased), & payment of a £530 18s 5d debt Wymondesold owed them for goods. Ps claim Wymondesold's widow & executrix d2 paid them £150 towards the debt, but after her marriage to d1, refused to pay the rest. Ps sued ds in the Court of Common Pleas, where ds pleaded that Wymondesold owed bonds exceeding his estate.

| 1685, Mich | E 112/590 | Bill. LMX 101. |
| 1686, April 24 | E 112/590 | Answer (with attachments). Swearing date of ds' answer; inventory attached of R. Wymondesold's personal estate. |

17. Bowd v Allen

P: (1) Isaac Bowd, draper, Hertford, Herts, p2's son, p3's brother; (2) Adlord Bowd the elder, draper, Hertford, Herts, father of p1 & p3; (3) Adlord Bowd the younger, draper, Hertford, Herts, p2's son, p1's brother. D: (1) Samuel Allen, merchant, London. C: (1) Edward Ward, counsel for ps; (2) Jason Kingsman, counsel for d. Ps seek inj ag d's suit at KB for payment of a £500 penal bond. In 1682 p1 became partners with d as merchants in New Hampshire, America. D advanced £750 to the business as his 3/4 share, & lent p £250 for his 1/4 share, in return for the £500 penal bond of p1 & his father p2. P1 claims he sent d the profits, & bought a ship on account of the business, but that d compelled him to sign erroneous accounts & had him imprisoned. D claims ps1-2 did not repay the bond on time.

1685, Easter	E 112/589	Bill (with attachments). LMX 37; dated ?15 May; account book attached.
1685, May 26	E 112/589	Answer. Swearing date.
1685, Trin	E 112/589	Exception. Ps' exceptions, dated 19 June, concern the bond, accounts & terms of p1 & d's partnership.

18. Brandon v Peirce alias Ash

P: (1) John Brandon, framework knitter, London, R. Peirce's nephew, heir at law & administrator. D: (1) Richard Peirce alias Ash gent., London; (2) John Bland, merchant tailor, College Hill, London. C: (1) R. Lechmere, counsel for p. Add: (1) Richard Peirce, cook, London, deceased intestate. P, nephew, heir at law & administrator of R. Peirce (deceased intestate in 1681 leaving realty & a personal estate worth £20,000), seeks recovery of Peirce's estate from ds. D1 reportedly claimed he paid Peirce's debts & obtained an order in this Court to possess his estate. D2 reportedly refuses to pay p a £100 debt he owed Peirce & has also possessed some of the estate, asserting Peirce owed him for clothes made.

| 1685, Mich | E 112/590 | Bill. LMX 129; 23 November. |

19. Brereton v Tanner

P: (1) Ralph Brereton gent., Beech, Staffs. D: (1) John Tanner, merchant, London. C: (1) Francis Browne, counsel for p; (2) William Brooke, counsel for d. Add: (1) Richard Brereton, p's son, d's former apprentice. P seeks inj ag d's suit for payment of a £50 bond, half the fee p agreed to pay for his son to become d's apprentice. Having initially paid £50, p claims he became suspicious of d, delayed paying the bond, then d went insolvent and absconded. D denies going insolvent, claims he went abroad on business, whereupon p's son left his service.

| 1685, Hil | E 112/589 | Bill. LMX 41. |
| 1685, Oct 22 | E 112/589 | Answer. Swearing date. |

20. Brooker v Adams
P: (1) Joseph Brooker, pewterer, Minories, London. D: (1) John Adams, haberdasher, London. C: (1) Edm. Jones, counsel for p; (2) ? Hely, counsel for d. P seeks repayment of £50 he paid d as a deposit on a £300 lease for a messuage with pewter and tools in Leadenhall St. P claims d received a higher bid, and prevented p from raising the rest of the £300 by encouraging p's creditors to sue and have him imprisoned. D claims p delayed the execution of the lease, and that the £50 was for goods he sold p.

| 1685, Mich | E 112/590 | Bill. LMX 103. |
| 1685, Nov 6 | E 112/590 | Answer. Swearing date. |

21. Broome v Browne
P: (1) John Broome gent., London. D: (1) Elizabeth Browne, T. Browne's widow & administratrix; (2) William Millett gent., scrivener, London, renounced executorship of T. Browne's will; (3) Sir William Gostlin, sheriff of London; (4) Sir Peter Vandeputt, sheriff of London. C: (1) William Ettricke, counsel for p; (2) William Cherry, counsel for ds1-2. Add: (1) Thomas Browne, deceased, d1's husband; (2) John Forth, brewer, London; (3) Collett, (no forename given). P seeks repayment of £100 he was compelled to pay ds3-4 after d1 (T. Browne's widow & administratrix) revived her husband's suit ag p in KB for arrears of rent on a cellar. P claims in 1681 he leased the cellar as J. Forth's trustee at £14 per annum for 7 years from T. Browne (deceased). P repaired the cellar, but Forth then refused to lease it, so p leased it to a Mr Collett, who quit the premises. T. Browne sued p for remaining rent on the lease, but died leaving d2 who renounced executorship.

1685, Mich	E 112/595	Bill. LMX 368; dated 19 November.
1689, May 8	E 112/595	Answer. Swearing date of d2's answer & disclaimer.
1689, May 9	E 112/595	Answer. Swearing date of d1's answer.

22. Bryant v Wordell
P: (1) Elizabeth Bryant, Totnam, Midd. D: (1) John Wordell gent., Totnam, Midd; (2) Thomas Chipps, chirurgeon, Totnam, Midd. C: (1) Jo. Danyell, counsel for p; (2) Edward Ward, counsel for d2. P, a widow, seeks recovery of a brewhouse d1 allegedly mortgaged to her in 1684 as security for a £600 debt. P claims d1 was later imprisoned in KB, and d2 persuaded her to become security for d1's bond, and to assign the mortgaged brewhouse to d2 in case the marshall of KB should seize it. D2 claims p & d1 absconded after issuing the bond to KB, and sold d2 the brewhouse absolutely for £250.

| 1685, Mich | E 112/591 | Bill. LMX 135; cf. E 112/591 LMX 136 Wordell v Chipp. |
| 1686, Jan 25 | E 112/591 | Answer. Swearing date of d2's answer. |

23. Bucknall v Barton
P: (1) Ralph Bucknall esq., St. Giles in the Fields, Midd; (2) John Bucknall esq., Oxhey Place, Herts; (3) William Thompson esq., solicitor, Middle Temple, London; (4) William Gulston esq., solicitor, Middle Temple, London; (5) William Hall gent., London; (6) John Tomkins gent., Abington, Berks; (7) William Green gent.. D: (1) William Barton; (2) Thomas Priggs; (3) Henry

8

Doble; (4) George Shuttleworth; (5) Sir Richard Dutton, Pall Mall, Midd, knight, & other ds. C: (1) Edward Smyth, counsel for ds3-4; (2) William Ettricke, counsel for d5. Ps, licensed to raise Thames water in York House Garden, Midd., seek payment of rent from ds, residents of Middlesex, for water piped to their premises. D3 claims he leased a watercourse from ps, who failed to supply water. D3 also maintains the bill is vexatious as his lease includes penalties for ps' failure to supply water. Ds4-5 deny any knowledge of the water rent, claiming they only lease their premises.

1685, Mich	E 112/590	Bill (with attachments). LMX 111; bill is damaged, counsel's name illegible. Schedules attached of debts owed by ds for water.
1685, Nov 28	E 112/590	Answer. Swearing date of d4's answer.
1685, Nov 28	E 112/590	Answer. Swearing date of d3's answer & demurrer.
1686, Nov 26	E 112/590	Answer. Swearing date of d5's answer.
1687, Trin	E 112/590	Replication. P denies the sufficiency of d5's answer.

24. Chace v Sterling

P: (1) Robert Chace. D: (1) James Sterling, J. Rouse's executor, d2's husband; (2) Mary Sterling, d1's wife, J. Rouse's executor. C: (1) James Dodd, counsel for p. Add: (1) Jarvis Rouse, deceased; (2) John Lindsay, goldsmith, p's former partner; (3) Peirce Reeve, goldsmith, p's former partner. P seeks revival of suit he filed ag J. Rouse seeking enforcement of an alleged agreement that Rouse would accept £400 in lieu of farm rents for which p and his former partners had offered to cancel their three bonds to Rouse. Rouse was suing p at KB for full payment of the bonds, denying any such agreement. Rouse then died, leaving ds as executors.

| 1685, Easter | E 112/588 | Bill of revivor. LMX 7; dated 30 May. |

25. Chancellor v Castle

P: (1) Marke Chancellor, joiner, London, J. Chancellor's son, R. Chancellor's brother, N. Knapp the E's grandson. D: (1) Richard Castle, yeoman, Chilton, Berks, M. Castle's husband. C: (1) Richard Knapp, counsel for p. Add: (1) Nicholas Knapp the elder, Chilton, Berks, deceased, grandfather of p, N. Knapp infant & R. Chancellor, father of N. Knapp Y & J. Chancellor; (2) Nicholas Knapp the younger, deceased, N. Knapp the E's son, M. Castle's prior husband, N. Knapp the infant's father; (3) Nicholas Knapp, deceased, infant, son of M. Castle & N. Knapp the Y, N. Knapp the E's grandson; (4) Jane Chancellor, deceased, insane, mother of p & R. Chancellor, N. Knapp the E's daughter; (5) Rebecca Chancellor, p's sister, J. Chancellor's daughter, N. Knapp the E's granddaughter; (6) Mary Castle, deceased, d's wife, N. Knapp the Y's widow, N. Knapp the infant's mother. P seeks possession of a messuage & lands which his grandfather N. Knapp the E left to his son N. Knapp the Y, who died leaving his son N. Knapp the infant, who died, so the premises reverted to p's mother J. Chancellor (N. Knapp the E's daughter), who went insane & died in 1678. D claims the premises had belonged to his wife Mary (N. Knapp the Y's widow, deceased) for her life, and that p's mother conveyed the premises to her daughter R. Chancellor, who sold it to d for £264.

1685, Mich	E 112/590	Bill. LMX 117.
1685, Mich	E 112/590	Copy bill.
1685, Nov 28	E 112/590	Commission. For d's answer.
1686, Jan 21	E 112/590	Answer. Swearing date.

26. Cherry v Cooper

P: (1) Richard Cherry, vintner, London. D: (1) Thomas Cooper, fishmonger, Thames St., London; (2) John Haughton, attorney at law; (3) Joseph Saunders, Indian gown man, Royal Exchange, London. C: (1) John Yalden, counsel for p. P seeks payment of £20 d1 allegedly borrowed but did not repay, so p sued him in one of the Compter's Courts, London. D1 engaged d2, an attorney at KB, who issued a bond to d3 in trust for p as security for d1's debt. The ds now reportedly conspire to defraud p, with d1 claiming he repaid p, or d2 denying he issued the bond, or claiming it was irregular and void.

| 1686, Hil | E 112/594 | Bill. LMX 324; entered as I James II. |

27. Clarke v Morgan

P: (1) Richard Clarke, wire drawer, Little Britain, London, p2's husband; (2) Mary Clarke, Little Britain, London, p1's wife, daughter of C. Morgan & d. D: (1) Elizabeth Morgan, C. Morgan's widow & administratrix, p2's mother. C: (1) William Ettricke, counsel for ps. Add: (1) Charles Morgan, wire drawer, Little Britain, London, deceased intestate, p2's father, d's husband. Ps seek possession of a distributive share of the estate of p2's father C. Morgan (deceased intestate). D (C. Morgan's widow & p2's mother) became administratrix, & ps claim she has issued shares to p2's 3 sisters but not to p2. D reportedly claims C. Morgan's estate is worth very little, & that his debtors are insolvent.

| 1685, Hil | E 112/589 | Bill. LMX 42. |

28. Coape v Gwynn

P: (1) Henry Coape, mercer, St. Paul's, Covent Garden, Midd, partner with ps2-4; (2) William Nicholas, mercer, St. Paul's, Covent Garden, Midd, partner with p1 & ps3-4; (3) Samuell Coape, mercer, St. Paul's, Covent Garden, Midd, partner with ps1-2 & p4; (4) Richard Alchorne, mercer, St. Paul's, Covent Garden, Midd, partner with ps1-3. D: (1) Ellen Gwynn, St. Martins in the Fields, Midd, named Ellinor in the bill. C: (1) John Powell, counsel for ps; (2) W. Barnsley, counsel for d. Add: (1) John Leonard Millins, lieutenant, Ireland, deceased; (2) Abraham Yarner, Ireland, Dublin. Ps, mercers & partners, seek payment for silks & goods they sold d. In 1683 d agreed to pay ps a £100 bond towards debts which J. L. Millins in Ireland owed her, if p2 could collect on it. D issued the bond & a letter of attorney to A. Yarner, ps' colleague in Ireland, who sued J. L. Millins, who was killed in a duel leaving no assets. Ps assert d refused to receive back the bond & pay her debts, but d claims ps refused to return the bond to her.

1685, Mich	E 112/590	Bill. LMX 107.
1686, April 21	E 112/590	Plea. Swearing date of d's plea & answer.
1686, May 19	E 112/590	Answer (with attachments). Swearing date; schedule attached of d's accounts with ps.

29. Dallow v Lyford
P: (1) Edward Dallow, glassware maker, Whitechapel, Midd, partners with ps2-3; (2) John Dallow, glassware maker, Whitechapel, Midd, partners with p1 & p3; (3) Phillip Dallow, glassware maker, Whitechapel, Midd, partners with ps1-2. D: (1) Robert Lyford, imprisoned in KB. C: (1) Edward Ward, counsel for ps. Ps, partners as glassware makers & owners of glasshouses in Well Close, Whitechapel, seek relief ag d's suit for payment of £411 10s which d reportedly claims ps owe him for carriage of coal, ash, metal, timber, etc., to their glasshouses before 1683. Ps claim d owes them for glass bottles totalling £464, for which ps obtained a judgement in KB.
1685, Mich   E 112/598   Bill. LMX 598.

30. Daniell v Griffin
P: (1) Anne Daniell, Dukes Place, London, P. Griffin's sister. D: (1) Joane Griffin, P. Griffin's widow. C: (1) Samuel Blackerby, counsel for p; (2) Francis Brown, counsel for d. Add: (1) Peircy Griffin, mariner, Stepney, Midd, deceased, gunner's mate of the ship *Constantinople Marchant*, p's brother, d's husband. P, a widow, seeks payment of half the personal estate of her brother P. Griffen, who she claims died intestate. D, Peircy's widow and administratrix, claims her husband fell ill and died on a voyage from the East Indies and made his will by word of mouth, leaving everything to his wife.
1685, Mich   E 112/590   Bill. LMX 122; dated 17 November.
1685, Dec 1   E 112/590   Answer (with attachments). Swearing date; inventory of P. Griffin's personal estate attached.

31. Davis v Goldsmith
P: (1) Benjamin Davis the younger, chirurgeon, London, B. Davis the E's son. D: (1) Alice Goldsmith, St. Albans, Herts; (2) Joane Goldsmith; (3) Francis Goldsmith; (4) William Kilboe. C: (1) Paul Pulling, counsel for p; (2) Ja. Wittewronge, counsel for ds1-2. Add: (1) Richard Davis, deceased, p's great-uncle; (2) Benjamin Davis the elder, deceased, p's father. P seeks possession of premises in Bedford left by his grandfather for his sons. P's great-uncle, R. Davis, possessed the estate as guardian of the eldest son, a lunatic. The second son, p's father, B. Davis the E, sued R. Davis in Chancery for the estate. B. Davis the E & R. Davis died. Now d1 allegedly conspires with ds2-3 & d4 (tenant of the premises) in claiming she bought the premises from R. Davis.
1685, Easter   E 112/589   Bill. LMX 73; dated 1 June.
1685, June 23   E 112/589   Answer. Swearing date of answer of ds1-2.

32. Dawes v Royal African Co.
P: (1) Nicholas Dawes, merchant, London; (2) Thomas Ducke, merchant, London; (3) Ransford Waterhouse, merchant, London; (4) Samuel Pett, merchant, London; (5) John Lowe, merchant, London; (6) Isaäc Heath, merchant, London; (7) Christopher Dodsworth, merchant, London; (8) Benjamin Thompson, merchant, London, master of a ship, the *Eaglet*, in 1683. D: (1) Royal African Co., England; (2) Henry Greenhill esq., agent general for the Royal African Co. of England; (3) Sir Robert Sawyer, Attorney General, knight, also

counsel for d1. C: (1) Edward Ward, counsel for ps; (2) John Hollis, counsel for d2; (3) Francis Browne, counsel for d1. Ps seek a writ of distringas ag d1, & recovery of £810 in gold dust which p8, master of a ship, the *Eaglet*, was transporting in 1683 when the ship was captured by pirates. P8 hid the gold in a canoe but his servants ran away with it. D2, agent general for the Royal African Co. of England, recovered it for p8 but later refused to return it to ps. Ds claim a 1672 charter of Charles II entitles only d1 to trade in that part of Africa, & to seize unlawful traders' goods & transfer 1/2 to the Crown.

1685, Mich	E 112/590	Bill. LMX 115.
[1685, undated]	E 112/590	Answer. D3's answer, undated.
1686, March 30	E 112/590	Answer. Swearing date of d2's answer.
1687, Easter	E 112/590	Answer. D1's answer & plea; seal missing.

33. Deeble v Wade

P: (1) Samuel Deeble, merchant, Totnes, Devon, p2's husband; (2) Grace Deeble, Totnes, Devon, p1's wife, S. Putt's administratrix. D: (1) Peter Wade, goldsmith, London. C: (1) Jo. Hely, counsel for ps. Add: (1) Samuel Putt, merchant, London, deceased. Ps seeks payment to p2 (administratrix of S. Putt, deceased in 1682) of money Putt allegedly entrusted to d, for which Putt received no receipts. D reportedly denies Putt left money outstanding, & has allegedly altered his accounts.

1685, Easter	E 112/589	Bill. LMX 66; dated 21 May.

34. Dodsworth v Edwards

P: (1) Christopher Dodsworth, mercer, London, trustee for the children of R. Pooke & E. Andrews, E. Dodsworth's husband. D: (1) Benjamin Edwards gent., London, G. Pooke the E's nephew, d2's husband; (2) Sarah Edwards, d1's wife, daughter of R. Pooke & E. Andrews, sister of d3 & E. Dodsworth; (3) Susanna Charlton, daughter of R. Pooke & E. Andrews, sister of d2 & E. Dodsworth. C: (1) Ambrose Phillipps, counsel for p; (2) Edward Ward, counsel for ds. Add: (1) Richard Pooke, grocer, London, deceased intestate, father of ds2-3 & E. Dodsworth, E. Andrews' previous husband; (2) Elizabeth Andrews, deceased, R. Pooke's widow & administratrix, mother of ds2-3 & E. Dodsworth, Daniel Andrews' wife; (3) George Pooke the elder, deceased, uncle of ds2-3 & E. Dodsworth; (4) Stephen Charlton esq., barrister, Temple, London, deceased, d3's husband; (5) Daniel Andrews, merchant, London, E. Andrews' husband; (6) Elizabeth Dodsworth, p's wife, daughter of R. Pooke & E. Andrews, sister of ds2-3. P, trustee of London premises for ps2-3 & other children of R. Pooke (deceased intestate in 1647) appointed by R. Pooke's widow & executrix E. Andrews & her husband D. Andrews, seeks relief from ds' suit in this Court for payment of rents from the entrusted premises. P claims the fire of 1666 burnt houses on the premises including those left to ds2-3 by their uncle G. Pooke the E, & p was compelled to build new houses for which ds allegedly promised to reimburse him £560, but did not.

1685, Trin	E 112/589	Bill. LMX 67; cf. E 112/588 LMX 13 Edwards v Dodsworth.
1685, Nov 7	E 112/589	Answer. Swearing date of ds' answer.
1686, Hil	E 112/589	Exception. P's exceptions concern the deeds & rents of the premises.

12

35. Draper v Ottiwell

P: (1) Richard Draper, milliner, London, M. Ottiwell's administrator. D: (1) Joseph Ottiwell, clerk, Elesmere, Salop, M. Ottiwell's father, d2's husband; (2) Elizabeth Ottiwell, Elesmere, Salop, M. Ottiwell's mother, d1's wife; (3) Nathaniel Williams, clerk, Malpas, Ches, d4's husband; (4) Frances Williams, Malpas, Ches, d3's wife; (5) Francis Nichols, Wrexham, Denb. C: (1) Giles Duncombe, counsel for p. Add: (1) Mary Ottiwell, milliner, seamstress, Wrexham, Denb, deceased intestate, daughter of ds1-2. P seeks discovery of the personal estate of M. Ottiwell (deceased intestate) and payment of a £35 debt from it. P claims ds possessed the estate, so p took out letters of administration entitling him to receive payment from it. Ds1-2, M. Ottiwell's parents, claim the estate is insufficient to pay the debts, and ds3-4 deny any involvement whatsoever.

1685, Mich	E 112/590	Bill. LMX 95; dated 14 November.
1685, Mich	E 112/590	Copy bill.
1685, Nov 28	E 112/590	Commission. For ds' answer.
1686, Feb 1	E 112/590	Answer (with attachments). Swearing date of ds' answer; inventory attached of M. Ottiwell's personal estate.

36. Edwards v Dodsworth

P: (1) Benjamin Edwards gent., London, p2's husband; (2) Sarah Edwards, London, p1's wife, daughter of R. & E. Pooke, sister of p3, E. Dodsworth, G. Pooke & S. Pooke; (3) Susanna Charleton, daughter of R. & E. Pooke, sister of p2, E. Dodsworth G. Pooke & S. Pooke. D: (1) Christopher Dodsworth, London, E. Dodsworth's husband. C: (1) Edward Ward, counsel for ps; (2) Ambrose Phillipps, counsel for d's answer; (3) W. Williams, counsel for d's further answer. Add: (1) Richard Pooke, grocer, London, deceased intestate, E. Pooke's husband, father of ps2-3, G. Pooke, S. Pooke & E. Dodsworth; (2) Elizabeth Andrewes, D. Andrewes's wife, R. Pooke's widow & administratrix, mother of ps2-3; (3) Daniel Andrewes, merchant, London, E. Andrewes's husband; (4) Elizabeth Dodsworth, London, d's wife, R. Pooke's daughter, sister of ps2-3, G. Pooke & S. Pooke, G. Pooke's administratrix; (5) George Pooke, deceased, R. Pooke's son, brother of ps2-3, E. Dodsworth & S. Pooke; (6) Stephen Pooke, R. Pooke's son, brother of ps2-3, E. Dodsworth & G. Pooke. Ps seek payment to ps2-3 of 1/4 share each of profits from London premises left by R. Pooke (deceased intestate in 1657, father of ps2-3, E. Dodsworth, G. Pooke & S. Pooke), which Elizabeth, his widow & administratrix, entrusted for his children before she married D. Andrewes. The premises were burnt in the great fire of 1666, & d (as his wife's husband & next friend of R. Pooke's other children) recovered the premises from the trustees, bought S. Pooke's share & sold some of the premises. G. Pooke died & E. Dodsworth became his administratrix.

1685, Easter	E 112/588	Bill. LMX 13; dated 16 May; cf. E 112/589 LMX 67 Dodsworth v Edwards.
1685, July 24	E 112/588	Answer (with attachments). Swearing date; 4 schedules attached of accounts for the premises.
1685, Mich	E 112/588	Exception. Ps' exceptions concern rents d received for the premises.

1686, Jan 8   E 112/588   Further answer (with attachments). Swearing date of d's further answer; 2 schedules attached of accounts for premises.

37. Evans v Smith

P: (1) Edward Evans, tobacco pipemaker, London. D: (1) Dennis Smith, merchant, Poole, Dors; (2) George Morton, factor, employed by d1; (3) John Hunt, tobacco pipemaker, Salisbury Court. C: (1) W. Williams, counsel for p; (2) Whitlock Deane, counsel for ds. P seeks relief ag d1's suit for payment of debts totalling £320 for tobacco pipe clay which d1 agreed to supply only to p & d3 in 1685 for one year. P claims d1, his factor d2, & d3 have sold large quantities of clay to other parties. Ds claim p refused to account with d1 for clay sold, so d1 had p arrested & caused p's customers to pay d1 directly.

1686, Hil	E 112/590	Bill. LMX 94; dated 29 January.
[1686, undated]	E 112/590	Demurrer (with attachments). D1's demurrer, undated, claims p's case is a matter for law, not equity; schedule attached of clay sold by d1.
1686, Feb 8	E 112/590	Answer. Swearing date of d2's answer.
1686, Feb 8	E 112/590	Answer. Swearing date of d3's answer.

38. Fisher v Baltin

P: (1) John Fisher gent., solicitor, Middle Temple, London, P. Palmer's executor. D: (1) Thomas Baltin, sadler, St. Martins in the Fields, Midd, P. Palmer's executor. C: (1) Edward Ward, counsel for p; (2) Ro. Warren, counsel for d. Add: (1) Penelope Palmer, St. Martins in the Fields, Midd, deceased; (2) Viscountess Baltinglasse, P. Palmer's debtor. P seeks payment of £48 17s 6d which P. Palmer owed him upon 5 bonds, & £30 Palmer willed him after her death in d's house in 1684, leaving p & d as executors. Palmer's estate included securities owed by Viscountess Baltinglasse & others. P claims d conspires with Palmer's debtors to defraud him of the bonds & legacy. D claims Palmer's estate is insufficient to pay all debts, as she had issued d a £479 6s 8d judgement in the Court of Common Pleas for board & lodging bills.

1685, Mich	E 112/590	Bill. LMX 112; dated 4 November.
1685, Nov 14	E 112/590	Answer (with attachments). Swearing date; inventory attached of P. Palmer's personal estate.

39. Gardner v Gardner

P: (1) Robert Gardner, haberdasher, London, N. Gardner's son and executor. D: (1) Frances Gardner, p's stepmother, N. Gardner's widow. C: (1) Nicholas Courtney, counsel for p; (2) Richard Catlyn, counsel for d. Add: (1) Nathaniel Gardner, deceased, p's father, d's husband; (2) Benjamin Bonwicke gent., Reigate, Surrey. P, N. Gardner's son & executor, seeks discovery of personal estate and rents which d (p's stepmother and N. Gardner's widow) allegedly retained after N. Gardner's death. D claims N. Gardner was bound for £1000 to her brother B. Bonwicke to leave d £100, which p has not done. D also claims N. Gardner had given her items from his personal estate.

1685, Easter	E 112/588	Bill. LMX 18.

1685, May 28	E 112/588	Answer. Swearing date.
1685, Trin	E 112/588	Exception. P's exceptions concern the items and money in d's possession from N. Gardner's personal estate.
1685, Oct 30	E 112/588	Further answer. D lists items which N. Gardner gave her.

40. Gibbs v Bebington

P: (1) Marmaduke Gibbs esq., barrister, Gray's Inn, Midd. D: (1) Michael Bebington esq., St. Martin in the Fields, Midd; (2) Isaac Dorisla, merchant, London; (3) William Jobson, St. Martin in the Fields, Midd. C: (1) Thomas Lyng, counsel for p. Add: (1) John Vaughan esq., late receiver of the 18-month tax for South Wales & Monmouthshire, 1672-3; (2) Richard Gwynn esq., Swansea, Glam; (3) David Thomas gent., Lisworney, Glam. P seeks inj ag any suit of d at KB for payment of an £800 judgement p issued d in 1682 as security for a £150 loan d made D. Thomas. In 1678 d had become bound to Queen Katherine for £640 to perform his duties as receiver & bailiff for Northants & Bucks, with p as security. In 1679 R. Gwynn had paid the Crown £1372 3s 4d, as security for J. Vaughan, receiver of the 18-month tax in 1672-3 for South Wales and Monmouthshire. The Crown entrusted the arrears of taxes to d3 for p, d1 & d2. P claims d agreed to discharge the £800 judgement in return for p's share of the arrears of taxes. When p sought to remove himself as security for d's bond to the Queen, ds conspired to deny the trust was ever set up.

| 1685, Trin | E 112/588 | Bill. LMX 16. |

41. Gittings v Dickinson

P: (1) William Gittings, parish of St. Brides, London, p2's next friend; son & administrator of Edward Gittings; (2) Edmund Gittings, p1's brother under 21 years. D: (1) William Dickinson esq., previous administrator of Edward Gittings. C: (1) William Bannaster, counsel for ps; (2) Ed. Ward, counsel for d. Add: (1) Edward Gittings, marchant tailor, London, deceased intestate, ps' father. Ps seek payment of p2's share of the estate of Edward Gittings (deceased intestate in 1679) from d, previous administrator. 4 of Edward's 5 children are now over 21 years, and p1 has assumed the administration. P2 (15 years old) seeks his share to become an apprentice attorney, which d is only willing to transfer if this Court indemnifies him.

| 1685, Trin | E 112/594 | Bill. LMX 323. |
| 1685, June 29 | E 112/594 | Answer. Swearing date. |

42. Gomes v Humphryes

P: (1) Antonio Gomes, yeoman, St. Martin in the Fields, Midd, previously of Lisbon, Portugal. D: (1) Edward Humphryes, broker, St. Martin in the Fields, Midd. C: (1) Thomas Montgomery, counsel for p; (2) Edward Ward, counsel for d. P, previously d's lodger, seeks discovery of accounts for the sale of Navarre wines and other goods p asked d to sell for him, and an inj ag d's suit for payment of arrears of rent from p. D claims his wife sold the wine, which was inferior, and the small proceeds have already been paid to p.

| 1685, Easter | E 112/588 | Bill. LMX 10; dated 12 May. |
| 1685, May 19 | E 112/588 | Answer. Swearing date. |

43. Goodall v Lattimer

P: (1) John Goodall, butcher, London. D: (1) John Lattimer, cook, London; (2) William Morgan, tapster, London. C: (1) Paul Pullein, counsel for p. P seeks payment of a £20 debt allegedly owed to him by d1, with whom he did business. D1 reportedly promised to pay p when he received payment of a debt from d2, but now d1 allegedly denies owing p, and d2 denies owing d1.

1685, Trin   E 112/589   Bill. LMX 70; 29 June.

44. Gowen v Cope

P: (1) William Gowen, chirurgion, London. D: (1) Mary Cope, W. Cope's widow & executrix; (2) Daniell Hill, linen draper, London. C: (1) Robert Gillmore, counsel for p; (2) Sam. Dodd, counsel for d1. Add: (1) William Cope, ship's captain, deceased, d1's husband, master of a ship, the *George and Betty*; (2) Thomas Beard, chief mate, deceased. P seeks inj ag ds' suit at KB for payment of £400 in goods & £1000 in gold allegedly left by W. Cope, captain of a ship, the *George and Betty*, on a voyage in 1682 from Guinea to Barbados. P was chirurgion on the voyage, authorised to take command when W. Cope and T. Beard, the 1st mate, died. W. Cope had instructed p to sell his goods & transfer the proceeds & his effects to d1, his wife, who would recompense p. P claims he paid d1 £600 & £200 for clothes, which d1 denies receiving & claims p retains the goods & money.

1685, Mich	E 112/590	Bill (with attachments). LMX 116; dated 4 November; p's schedule attached of W. Cope's goods & effects.
1685, Nov 12	E 112/590	Answer (with attachments). Swearing date of d1's answer; d1's schedule attached of W. Cope's goods & effects.

45. Grant v Parsons

P: (1) John Grant gent., Kingston upon Thames, Surrey. D: (1) Richard Parsons; (2) Henry Craycroft, formerly p's agent at the brewhouse; (3) Daniel Forth, J. Forth's administrator; (4) Henry Forth, J. Forth's son and heir. C: (1) Henry Trinder, counsel for p; (2) Fr. Fuller, counsel for d1. Add: (1) John Forth esq., London, deceased. P seeks relief from d1's suit in this Court claiming p had no authority to receive payment of a mortgage on d1's messuage owed to a brewhouse which p bought from J. Forth (deceased). P's agent d2 allegedly told d1 that p was so unauthorised, also alleged by ds3–4 (J. Forth's administrator and son). D1 claims p's deeds to the brewhouse recording the mortgage now compromise d1's title to the messuage.

1685, Trin	E 112/589	Bill (with attachments). LMX 38; dated 22 June; schedule of debts owed to the brewhouse attached (cf. E 112/590 LMX 25 Parsons v Grant).
1685, July 10	E 112/589	Answer. Swearing date of d1's answer.

46. Gratinger v Salisbury

P: (1) Jacob Gratinger, shoemaker, St. Martin le Grand, London, allegedly sells abroad shoes unfit for sale in England. D: (1) Gilbert Salisbury, shoemaker, St. Martin le Grand, London; (2) John Coopestake, d1's nephew & servant; (3)

Edward Lambert, scrivener, St. Martin le Grand, London. C: (1) Thomas Jones, counsel for p; (2) Edward Baldwyn, counsel for d1 & d3. P seeks inj ag d1's suit in the Court of Common Pleas for payment for shoes p bought from d's nephew & servant d2. P claims he bought shoes from d2, who embezzled the money. Ds1-2 then conspired with d3 to imprison p & his wife for receiving stolen goods & had p's goods seized. D1 claims p did not pay d2 for the shoes, & denies seizing p's goods but suggests the parish churchwardens may have seized them as indemnity ag the charge of p's wife & children.

1685, Mich	E 112/589	Bill. LMX 82; dated 23 October.
1685, Oct 30	E 112/589	Answer. Swearing date of d3's answer & disclaimer.
1685, Oct 30	E 112/589	Answer. Swearing date of d1's answer.
1685, Mich	E 112/589	Exception (with attachments). P's exceptions concern his imprisonment, whether he paid for the shoes, & the sum for which d sues him. (Replication from E 112/589 LMX 84 mistakenly attached.).

47. Hall v Winter

P: (1) Edward Hall gent., London. D: (1) Daniel Winter, Farnham, Surrey; (2) Thomas Sutton. C: (1) John Dorrington, counsel for p; (2) William Killingworth, counsel for d1. P seeks repayment of a £20 deposit which d2 paid on p's behalf to d1 for £220 worth of wheat in 1684. P claims d1 agreed to house the wheat until January 1685 in return for rent, but ds then sold it. D1 denies agreeing to house it, & claims after p's deposit was paid, the price of wheat dropped, d2 claimed p had small pox & could not collect it, & never paid the balance.

| 1685, Mich | E 112/592 | Bill. LMX 209. |

48. Hankinson v Manning

P: (1) John Hankinson, p2's husband, p3's guardian; (2) Sarah Hankinson, p1's wife, p3's sister; (3) Elizabeth Bullock, p2's sister, under 21 years. D: (1) Thomas Manning, S. Newby's son and trustee; (2) William Bradford, Blackfriars, London, S. Newby's trustee. C: (1) Francis Winnington, counsel for ps; (2) Henry Hatsell, counsel for ds. Add: (1) Sarah Newby, London, deceased, grandmother of ds2-3, named Mary in bill; (2) Joseph Bullock, S. Newby's son, father of ps2-3; (3) Launcelot Monroe, fishmonger, London. Ps seek profits supposedly left to J. Bullock and his daughters ps2-3 by S. Newby from a messuage (with ds as trustees), and silver, a diamond ring, bedding and furniture Newby left to p2. Ds claim Newby changed her mind and sold the messuage to d2 and L. Monroe, gave the bedding and furniture to d1's wife, and sold and pawned the silver and ring.

1685, Easter	E 112/588	Bill. LMX 4.
1685, June 25	E 112/588	Answer. Swearing date of ds' answer.
1685, Trin	E 112/588	Replication. Ps assert ds' answer is insufficient.

49. Hardwick v Fortune

P: (1) Ralph Hardwick, merchant, London. D: (1) Edward Fortune, ship's master, part owner of a ship, the *Sidmouth*. C: (1) Edward Ward, counsel for p;

(2) Ambrose Phillips, counsel for d. Add: (1) Abraham Lee, p's agent. P seeks relief ag d's suit for payment of £1000 after p hired d (master of a ship, the *Sidmouth*) to transport wheat from Chichester to Teneriffe & the Canary Islands, and a cargo of wines back. P claims d delayed his arrival at Chichester & the price of wheat had risen, that the ship was leaky & p's agent refused to load it with the wines. D asserts he had the ship surveyed, pumped out & pronounced seaworthy.

| 1685, Trin | E 112/589 | Bill. LMX 54; dated 20 June. |
| 1685, Oct 1 | E 112/589 | Answer. Swearing date. |

50. Harris v Daniel

P: (1) John Harris, E. Harris's son, brother of ps2-3 & p5, A. Ely's administrator; (2) Spicer Harris, E. Harris's son, brother of p1, p3 & p5, A. Ely's administrator; (3) Benjamin Harris, E. Harris's son, brother of ps1-2 & p5, A. Ely's administrator; (4) Ralph Studd, p5's husband, A. Ely's administrator; (5) Rebecca Studd, p4's wife, E. Harris's daughter, sister of ps1-3, A. Ely's administratrix. D: (1) Sir Peter Daniel, knight, W. Osbalston's executor; (2) Robert Townson, W. Osbalston's executor; (3) Robert Osbalston the younger, W. Osbalston's son & sole executor upon his majority in 1681. C: (1) F. Crawford?, counsel for ps (name damaged); (2) Henry Hatsell, counsel for ds. Add: (1) Elizabeth Harris, deceased, mother of ps1-3 & p5, D. Spicer's neice; (2) David Spicer gent., parish of St. Olave's, Southwark, Surrey, deceased, E. Harris's uncle, A. Ely's brother; (3) Anne Ely, deceased, W. Ely's wife, D. Spicer's sister; (4) William Ely, silk throster, St. Olave's, Southwark, Surrey, deceased, A. Ely's husband; (5) Robert Osbalston the elder, haberdasher, London, deceased, d3's grandfather, D. Spicer's executor; (6) Elizabeth Spicer, deceased, D. Spicer's widow & executrix; (7) William Osbalston, mercer, St. Olave, London, deceased, R. Osbalston the E's son, d3's father. Ps seeks payment of duties from lighthouses in Kent which D. Spicer (deceased in 1650) willed to his sister A. Ely (deceased) & his neice E. Harris (mother of ps1-3 & p5), leaving as executors his widow E. Spicer (deceased in 1658) & R. Osbalston the E (deceased in 1669 leaving his son W. Osbalston). W. Osbalston died in 1678 leaving ds1-2 as executors & his son d3, who possess the lighthouses & receive the duties. Ps became A. Ely's administrators. Ds claim d3's father & grandfather bought the interests of p1 & W. Ely (A. Ely's husband) in the lighthouses.

| 1685, Easter | E 112/589 | Bill. LMX 47; dated 21 April. |
| 1685, Oct 23 | E 112/589 | Answer. Swearing date of ds' answer. |

51. Harris v Jeffryes

P: (1) Richard Harris the elder, chandler, St. Giles without Cripplegate, London, p2's father; (2) Richard Harris the younger, glazier, St. Giles without Cripplegate, London, p1's son. D: (1) Robert Jeffryes, bricklayer, London. C: (1) Godfrey Thacker, counsel for ps; (2) Thomas Dickins, counsel for d. Ps seek inj ag d's suit at KB for £80 bond p2 issued with p1 as security for performance by p2 of £43 worth of glazier's work. Ps claim in 1684 d sold p2 a leasehold messuage in Rotherithe, Surrey, for £83: £40 in cash & £43 worth of glazier's work. P2 asserts d prevented him from performing the work, then had him arrested. D claims p2 only performed £11 worth of work, which was

18

inferior & 6 weeks late, so d had to hire another glazier.
1685, Easter   E 112/590   Bill. LMX 123; dated 14 May.
1685, May 23   E 112/590   Answer. Swearing date.

52. Harrison v Wolstenholme

P: (1) Richard Harrison esq., Balls, Herts, Sir J. Harrison's son, heir & executor. D: (1) Sir Thomas Wolstenholme, bart., Sir J. Wolstenholme's son, heir & executor, d2's father; (2) Thomas Wolstenholme esq., d1's son, Dr L. Wright's administrator. C: (1) Richard Holford, counsel for p's bill; (2) Francis Brown, counsel for p's replication; (3) Henry Trinder, counsel for ds. Add: (1) Sir John Harrison, deceased, knight, p's father, member of the House of Commons, farmer of the customs; (2) Sir John Wolstenholme, deceased, d1's father, member of the House of Commons, farmer of the customs; (3) Sir Paul Pindar, member of the House of Commons, farmer of the customs; (4) Dr Lawrence Wright, doctor of physic, deceased, Lady Vere's trustee; (5) Lady Vere. P seeks relief ag ds' suit for payment of a £4000 bond d1's father Sir J. Wolstenholme issued in 1640 with p's father Sir J. Harrison & Sir P. Pindar (members of the House of Commons & farmers of the customs under Charles I) to Dr L. Wright as Lady Vere's trustee for a £2000 loan. D1 claims his father was compelled to repay more than his share of a £150,000 fine to the Crown & a £50,000 loan owed by the farmers, including Lady Vere's bond. P claims this bond was repaid, that Sir J. Wolstenholme was not just surety but equally liable for the debts, & that Sir J. Harrison paid his share.
1685, Trin   E 112/589   Bill. LMX 58; dated 8 July; cf. E 112/588 LMX
                              23 Wolstenholme v Turner.
1685, Nov 3   E 112/589   Answer. Swearing date of ds' answer.
1686, Trin   E 112/589   Replication. P asserts ds' answer is
                              insufficient.

53. Hartus v Kettlewell

P: (1) Henry Hartus, stationer, St. Dunstan in the West, London. D: (1) Robert Kettlewell, bookseller, St. Dunstan in the West, London, d2's husband; (2) Bridget Kettlewell, St. Dunstan in the West, London, d1's wife, W. Moore's widow, d3's daughter, named Elizabeth in bill; (3) Valentine Howard, d2's father. C: (1) Whitlock Deane, counsel for p; (2) John Barnesley, counsel for ds. Add: (1) Joseph Martin, merchant, London, absconded; (2) William Moore, silkman, London, deceased; (3) John Arnold, goldsmith, London, absconded. P seeks payment of £110 bond from J. Martin, with W. Moore and J. Arnold as security. Martin and Arnold have absconded, and Moore died leaving d2 his executrix who possessed his estate and married d1. P asserts ds should pay the bond from Moore's estate, but ds claim Moore died owing debts and the estate is insufficient to pay the bond.
1685, Easter   E 112/588   Bill. LMX 14; dated 27 May.
1685, June 19   E 112/588   Answer. Swearing date of ds' answer.

54. Harvey v Bull

P: (1) Hon. Dame Elizabeth Harvey, Swallow St., Midd. D: (1) Richard Bull gent., St. Martin in the Fields, Midd. C: (1) Samuel Keck, counsel for p; (2) Edward Ward, counsel for d. P, a widow, seeks abatement of a 21 year lease from d allowing her access through a passageway between her house and d's coachyard. P claims she later discovered that the passage was a common way but d demands full payment of the lease. D asserts he built the passage on a common footpath, but that he is entitled to charge rent for coaches and horses.

| 1685, Mich | E 112/590 | Bill. LMX 120. |
| 1686, Jan 18 | E 112/590 | Answer. Swearing date. |

55. Harvey v Munday

P: (1) Gideon Harvey, doctor in physic. D: (1) Josiah Munday, yeoman, Hillingdon, Midd. C: (1) Sa. Johnson, counsel for p; (2) E. Reeve, counsel for d. Add: (1) Dudley Pennard, mercer, Amersham, Bucks, J. Pennard's son; (2) Jane Pennard, D. Pennard's mother. P seeks possession of a messuage in the manor of Cowley Hall at Hillingdon whose tenancy he allegedly bought from D. & J. Pennard a year ago. D claims he leased it from the Pennards two years ago, but was persuaded to rent rooms in it to p, who locked d and his family out when they were away from home.

| 1685, Easter | E 112/590 | Bill. LMX 108. |
| 1685, July 21 | E 112/590 | Answer. Swearing date. |

56. Hathersich v Shute

P: (1) Job Hathersich, mercer, Litchfield, Staffs. D: (1) Margaret Shute, Z. Shute's widow & executrix; (2) Thomas Rowney; (3) Cawen Mason, previously p's servant/agent. C: (1) John Yalden, counsel for p; (2) Richard Holford, counsel for d1. Add: (1) Zachary Shute, linen draper, London, deceased, d1's husband. P seeks possession of his remaining real & personal estate which he assigned in 1679 to his creditors, in particular to pay Z. Shute debts of £2300 & £823. P claims in 1675 he became receiver for the revenues of Excise & Hearth Money in Litchfield on Z. Shute's behalf, but that in 1679 Z. Shute confined & forced him to issue a £3000 bond to the Crown as security for the revenues. Z. Shute died leaving his widow & executrix d1. D3 (previously p's agent) & d2 have allegedly received sums from p's debtors & threaten to pay them to d1. D1 is suing p for the £3000 bond to the Crown, claiming she has only received £105 16s from p's estate.

1685, Hil	E 112/589	Bill. LMX 43.
1685, Nov 26	E 112/589	Answer (with attachments). Swearing date of d1's answer; schedule attached of accounts for p's estate.
1686, Hil	E 112/589	Replication. P asserts d1's answer is insufficient.

57. Hensley v Fuller

P: (1) Joseph Hensley, cooper, London. D: (1) Richard Fuller, vintner, London; (2) Anthony Beverley, J. Beverley's father. C: (1) Lewis Owen, counsel for p; (2) F. Fuller, counsel for d1; (3) John Viney, counsel for d2. Add: (1) John Beverley, vintner, d2's son. P seeks payment of £152 2s 8d which ds allegedly owe him for wine. P claims in 1683 d1, d2 & his son J. Beverley bought a pipe of canary wine, a hogshead of port wine, & subsequent wines, for which they still owe £152 2s 8d. P claims d2 issued d1 a £200 warrant of attorney in KB for d1 to pay p fully, d1 had d2's goods seized, but did not pay p. D1 denies he was party to d2's purchases from p after the pipe & hogshead, but claims the warrant was for a £100 debt d2 owed him.

1685, Easter	E 112/589	Bill. LMX 46; dated 12 April.
1685, May 25	E 112/589	Answer (with attachments). Swearing date of d1's answer; schedule attached of d2's goods which d1 had seized.
1685, June 29	E 112/589	Answer. Swearing date of d2's answer.
1685, Trin	E 112/589	Exception. P's exceptions to d1's answer, dated 4 July, concern d2's debt to d1 & d2's goods seized by d1.
1685, Nov 20	E 112/589	Further answer. Swearing date of d1's further answer.

58. Hilliard v Cooke

P: (1) Thomas Hilliard, merchant. D: (1) Thomas Cooke, goldsmith, London; (2) Nicholas Cary, goldsmith, London; (3) Thomas Kilburne, goldsmith, London; (4) Edward Caple, goldsmith, London. C: (1) Henry Hatsell, counsel for p. Add: (1) Thomas Yoatly, merchant, London; (2) Arthur Cooke, currier, parish of St. Paul, Shadwell, Midd. P seeks discovery of the sum outstanding on a mortgage he made to ds3-4 of his premises in Ivelchester, Somerset, in 1676 with T. Yoatly & A. Cooke as trustees. P did not repay on time, so ds3-4 took possession & assigned the premises to ds1-2 as their trustees, reportedly as security for an £800 debt ds3-4 owe ds1-2.

1685, Hil	E 112/589	Bill. LMX 31.

59. How v Hicks

P: (1) Dame Sarah How, Sir R. How's widow & administratrix. D: (1) Sir Michael Hicks, knight, d2's husband, Sir W. Hicks's son; (2) Dame Susannah Hicks, Sir R. How's daughter, d1's wife; (3) James Reading esq., St. Mary Newington, Surrey, trustee for ds1-2, d4 & Sir W. Hicks; (4) Thomas Lowfield, mercer, London. C: (1) Edward Ward, counsel for p; (2) William Cherry, counsel for ds. Add: (1) Sir Richard How, London, deceased intestate, knight, alderman of the City of London, p's husband; (2) Sir William Hicks, Ruckholts, Essex, bart., deceased, d1's father; (3) Thomas Browne gent., scrivener, Cornhill, London, deceased, trustee for ds1-2, d4 & Sir W. Hicks. P, Sir R. How's widow & administratrix, seeks relief from any suit of ds for payment of a £5000 penal bond that Sir R. How issued to repay £2575 (with security of a mortgage on his leasehold premises) to d3 & T. Browne (deceased), entrusted by ds1-2, d4 & d1's father Sir W. Hicks to purchase property. Sir R. How died intestate in 1683, & p claims ds refuse to accept payment of the £2575 & threaten to possess the mortgaged premises. Ds claim to be willing to accept the £2575 in return for indemnity.

1685, Easter	E 112/588	Bill. LMX 20.
1685, June 12	E 112/588	Answer. Ds' answer, sworn by ds1-2 on this date, sworn by ds3-4 on 17 June.

60. Hughes v Webb

P: (1) John Hughes, draper, London; (2) Christopher Markham, bailiff for St. Clements Danes; (3) William Hayes, bailiff for St. Clements Danes. D: (1)

Thomas Webb, salesman, tailor, parish of St. Clements Danes, Midd, absconded; (2) Mary Webb, d1's mother; (3) Peter Courtney gent., attorney. C: (1) Jo. Methwen, counsel for ps. Ps seek payment of d1's debts to p1, & relief ag ds' suit in the Court of Common Pleas for £14. P1 claims in 1682 he supplied d1 with cloth worth £28 9s 5d, & lent him £3 10s. D1 absconded without paying. In 1683 p1 caused 4 attachments to be taken out of the Duchy Court of Lancaster for the Liberty of St. Clements Danes (of which ps2-3 are bailiffs), & p1 received £5 from a sale of d1's goods. D1's mother d2 hired d3 who obtained a judgement in KB for £14 damages for the goods.

| 1685, Hil | E 112/597 | Bill (with attachments). LMX 521; schedule attached of cloth goods p1 supplied d1. |

61. Isaacson v Shaw

P: (1) Radolph Isaacson gent., Five Fields, Essex, Officer of the Customs under Charles II. D: (1) Sir John Shaw the younger, bart., Sir J. Shaw the E's son & executor; (2) Joseph Dawson gent., London. C: (1) Edward Ward, counsel for p; (2) William Ettricke, counsel for ds. Add: (1) Sir John Shaw the elder, Eltham, Kent, bart., deceased, d1's father, Farmer of the Customs under Charles II. P seeks payment of £6551 8s 3d which Sir J. Shaw the E (Farmer of the Customs, deceased in 1670) allegedly owed p for profits from receiving logwood and board & lodging. P claims d1 (Shaw the E's son & executor) or d2 have paid sums towards the debt, but have now caused a judgement to be recovered ag d1 affecting Shaw the E's estate, & have committed waste on the estate. D1 claims p issued him a release of all demands in 1681. D2 denies any interest in the estate.

1685, Mich	E 112/591	Bill (with attachments). LMX 133; schedule attached of Sir J. Shaw the E's alleged debts to p.
1686, Feb 12	E 112/591	Answer. Swearing date of d1's plea & answer.
1686, Feb 16	E 112/591	Answer. Swearing date of d2's answer.

62. Jenings v Anderson

P: (1) William Jenings, Whitechapel, London, p2's husband; (2) Sarah Jenings, Whitechapel, London, p1's wife, J. Howard's widow & executrix or administratrix with the will annexed. D: (1) Thomas Anderson, innkeeper, London, the Crown Inn without Aldgate. C: (1) Samp. Warde, counsel for ps' bill; (2) Robert Rawlins, counsel for d; (3) Edward Ward, counsel for ps' exceptions. Add: (1) John Howard, smith, farrier, Whitechapel, London, deceased, p2's previous husband. Ps seek payment of bills totalling £81 4s for work which d, innkeeper, hired p2's previous husband J. Howard, smith & farrier (deceased), to perform. Howard appointed p2 as his executrix. D denies owing Howard for work, & claims Howard owed him for bonds & a horse.

1685, Mich	E 112/590	Bill. LMX 92; dated 28 November.
1686, Jan 27	E 112/590	Answer. Swearing date, amended 15 April, sworn again on 4 June.
1686, Easter	E 112/590	Exception. Ps' exceptions concern J. Howard's work & accounts with d.
1686, Mich	E 112/590	Replication. Ps assert d's answer is insufficient.

63. Keeling v Boone
P: (1) Thomas Keeling, barber surgeon, London. D: (1) Mary Boone, R. Boone's widow & administratrix; (2) Mary Erwin, London; (3) William Boone, R. Boone's brother. C: (1) James Selby, counsel for p; (2) John Pratte, counsel for ds1-2. Add: (1) Richard Boone, vintner, Wapping, Midd, deceased intestate, d1's husband. P seeks payment of £28 he lent R. Boone in 1684 in return for a £55 penal bond as security. R. Boone died intestate, leaving d1 his widow & administratrix. In 1679 R. Boone had mortgaged 2 messuages to d2 for £200, which he had not repaid. P claims ds conspire to defraud him of the £28. D1 claims the estate is insufficient to pay debts.

1685, Easter	E 112/588	Bill. LMX 19.
1685, May 27	E 112/588	Answer (with attachments). Swearing date of answer of ds1-2, also sworn 12 June; schedule attached of R. Boone's personal estate.

64. King v Hoyle
P: (1) Sarah King, widow of T. King deceased; sole daughter and heir of W. and G. Fox. D: (1) Samuel Hoyle, scrivener, London, G. Fox's brother, p's uncle; (2) Chamberlen Donne, parker (park-keeper), London, spelled Chamberlaine Dunn in bill. C: (1) Nat. Axtell, counsel for p; (2) Thomas Goodinge, counsel for d2. Add: (1) William Fox, pewterer, London, deceased, p's father, G. Fox's husband; (2) Grace Fox, London, deceased, p's mother, W. Fox's wife. P seeks recovery of deeds to lands in Wales and a leasehold messuage in Aldersgate which p claims ds fraudulently obtained from her father W. Fox after her mother died. P asserts ds committed her father to Bedlam (where he died before p was 21), and assumed the administration of his estate. D2 claims he bought the land from d1 who bought it fairly from Fox, whom d2 denies committing.

1686, Hil	E 112/589	Bill. LMX 85; dated 5 February; entered as 1 James II.
1686, April 27	E 112/589	Answer. Swearing date of d2's answer.

65. Langrish v Burton
P: (1) Barrell Langrish, milliner, St. Martin in the Fields, Midd. D: (1) Deborah Burton, p's mother in law; (2) John Hales esq., barrister, Inner Temple, London; (3) Edward Carlton, St. Martin in the Fields, Midd; (4) William Hell; (5) John Johnston; (6) Jacob Whidden; (7) John Wilkinson; (8) James Chizard, attorney at law. C: (1) John Yalden, counsel for p; (2) John Powell, counsel for ds2-3. P seeks relief ag suits of ds1-3 for payment of debts. In 1682 p issued d1 (p's wife's mother) a £500 judgement for a £200 debt, d2 an £816 judgement for a £408 debt, & d3 a £440 judgement for a £220 debt, in return for ds1-3 securing p's goods ag his other creditors. P claims ds1-3 had his goods seized, undervalued & sold for £350 (deposited with d8) to repay his creditors. P also asserts his wife gave d1 his copies of the judgements. P claims ds1-3 & d8 conspire with d3's partners ds4-7 to retain his goods. Ds2-3 deny p's goods were under-valued, & claim p's debts are still largely due.

1685, Mich	E 112/590	Bill. LMX 87.
1686, May 13	E 112/590	Answer. Swearing date of answer of ds2-3.

66. Lewin v Rackett
P: (1) Margaret Lewin, E. Lewin's widow & executrix. D: (1) Michael Rackett gent., merchant, the Minories, London; (2) Daniel Lewin, E. Lewin's son. C: (1) Edward Warde, counsel for p; (2) Humphrey Dolman, counsel for d1; (3) John Yalden, counsel for d2. Add: (1) Edmund Lewin esq., deceased, p's husband, d2's father; (2) Joseph Buckmaster, E. Lewin's tenant; (3) Underhill Brees. P, E. Lewin's widow & executrix, seeks payment of £135 17s 9 1/2d arrears of rent that J. Buckmaster owed for E. Lewin's premises. E. Lewin ejected Buckmaster, who sued in this Court, but E. Lewin died leaving the premises to his son d2. Buckmaster revived the suit ag p & d2 & got a verdict to pay arrears & costs in return for a new lease. Buckmaster deposited the money with d1, & d2 granted the lease to U. Brees. D2 claims he is entitled to the arrears of rent, while d1 is willing to deliver it to whom this Court decides.

1685, Easter	E 112/588	Bill. LMX 5; dated 6 May.
1685, May 21	E 112/588	Answer. Swearing date of d1's answer.
1685, June 21	E 112/588	Answer. Swearing date of d2's answer.

67. Lilburne v Thursby
P: (1) George Lilburne, druggist, London. D: (1) John Thursby, goldsmith, Lombard St., London; (2) John Coleman, merchant, London, R. Phillipps' assignee; (3) John Thorpe, merchant, London, R. Phillipps' assignee. C: (1) John Hely, counsel for p; (2) William Killingworth, counsel for d1; (3) Gi. Duncombe, counsel for ds2-3. Add: (1) Richard Phillipps, merchant, bankrupt. P seeks relief ag d1's suit in KB and any suit of ds2-3 (assignees of R. Phillipps, bankrupt) for payment of a £73 4s note p issued Phillipps in 1685. Before the note was due, Phillipps went bankrupt & absconded, so ds2-3 were appointed his assignees, & seek payment for the note. D1 likewise seeks payment, claiming Phillipps endorsed the note to him. Ds2-3 assert Phillipps went bankrupt before endorsing the note to d1.

1685, Mich	E 112/589	Bill. LMX 79.
1685, Nov 3	E 112/589	Answer. Swearing date of d1's answer.
1685, Nov 30	E 112/589	Answer. Swearing date of answer of ds2-3.

68. Lister v Awnsham
P: (1) Frances Lister, M. Lister's widow, daughter of H. & J. Mildmay; (2) Timothy Whitfield esq., barrister, Gray's Inn, Midd, p3's husband; (3) Mary Whitfield, p2's wife, p1's sister, daughter of H. & J. Mildmay. D: (1) Margaret Awnsham, G. Awnsham's widow & executrix. C: (1) Giles Duncombe, counsel for ps; (2) Thomas Jenner, counsel for d. Add: (1) Mathew Lister, deceased, p1's husband; (2) Gideon Awnsham, deceased, d in original bill, d's husband; (3) Margaret Awnsham, deceased, d in original bill, G. Awnsham's previous wife, sister of J. Mildmay & R. Awnsham; (4) Henry Mildmay esq., Heston, Midd, deceased, father of p1 & p3, J. Mildmay's husband; (5) Jane Mildmay, Heston, Midd, deceased, mother of p1 & p3, H. Mildmay's wife, sister of R. Awnsham & M. Awnsham the 1st; (6) Robert Awnsham, deceased, brother of J. Awnsham & M. Awnsham the 1st. Ps seek revival ag d (G. Awnsham's widow) of the 1682 suit in this Court of p1 & her husband M. Lister (deceased) ag G. Awnsham (deceased) & his previous wife M. Awnsham the 1st (deceased) for payment of rents from premises. R. Awnsham (deceased)

had left the premises to J. Mildmay, her husband Henry (parents of p1 & p3), M. Awnsham the 1st & G. Awnsham. Ps claim some of the premises were sold, £1500 paid to G. & M. Awnsham the 1st, £1000 entrusted for p1 & p3 each (then minors), & rents from the residual premises were to go to p1 & p3. D claims ps have mistaken her for G. Awnsham's previous wife, & that the residual premises were never intended for p1 & p3.

1685, Hil   E 112/589   Bill of revivor. LMX 44; dated 9 February.
1685, May 13   E 112/589   Answer. Swearing date.

69. Litton v Kinsey

P: (1) Rowland Litton esq., Ansty, Herts. D: (1) Thomas Kinsey, vintner, Crown Tavern, Bloomsbury, Midd; (2) Thomas Goodall gent., solicitor, d1's attorney; (3) Lionell Copley esq., Wadworth, Yorks; (4) Orlebar Wilson gent., solicitor, d3's attorney. C: (1) John Yalden, counsel for p; (2) G. Duncombe, counsel for ds1-2. P seeks relief from any suit of ds for payment of a £600 bond d3 issued d1 with p as security, conditioned for the payment of £330 for debts d3 owed d1, who had caused d3 to be arrested. P claims ds1-2 now conspire with ds3-4 to compel him to pay the bond, but ds1-2 claim p was aware of the liability when he became d3's security.

1685, Easter   E 112/588   Bill. LMX 3.
1685, July 21   E 112/588   Answer. Swearing date of d1's plea & answer & d2's answer.

70. Love v Thornehill

P: (1) Barnaby Love, clerk, Wouston, Hants. D: (1) Robert Thornehill, London; (2) Anne Stevens, St. Martin in the Fields, Midd; (3) Thomas Tayler, d2's lessee; (4) Edward Love gent., p's son & alleged trustee. C: (1) Thomas Prichard, counsel for p; (2) John Powell, counsel for d4; (3) Edward Warde, counsel for d1. Add: (1) Hon. George, Earl of Berkeley. P seeks inj ag the suit of ds2-3 for a £100 penal bond which p issued d2 in 1670 with a warrant of attorney for entering a judgement on the bond as security for a £50 loan. P claims in 1672 he repaid d2, who deposited the judgment with the Earl of Berkeley, who assigned it to p's son & trustee d4, who assigned it to d1 for an alleged £17 10s loan. D1 claims p only repaid £15 to d2, who sold the judgement to the earl for £35, who paid it as wages to his servant d4, who sold it to d1 for £27.

1685, Easter   E 112/588   Bill. LMX 9; dated 14 May.
[1685, undated]   E 112/588   Plea. Plea of ds1-2, claiming p is outlawed after a suit for debt in the Court of Common Pleas.
1685, May 18   E 112/588   Answer. Swearing date of d4's answer.
1685, Oct 23   E 112/588   Answer. Swearing date of d1's answer.

71. Ludlow v Vermuyden

P: (1) Nathaniell Ludlow gent., London, Dame E. Ludlow's son & executor. D: (1) Cornelius Vermuyden esq., Westminster, Midd. C: (1) Edward Ward, counsel for p; (2) John Rowes, counsel for d. Add: (1) Dame Elizabeth Ludlow, deceased, p's mother; (2) John Beck, merchant, London, deceased insolvent; (3) Edmund Ludlow esq., Westminster, Midd, convicted of high treason. P, son & executor of Dame E. Ludlow (deceased), seeks payment of £100 bond that d issued in 1657 with J. Beck (since deceased insolvent) for repayment of £50 to Edmund Ludlow allegedly in trust for Dame E. Ludlow. Edmund was convicted in high treason in 1660 & his goods were forfeit to the Crown. D requests relief ag p's suit as the bond is 30 years old, or claims that J. Beck's executors should also be sued.

| 1685, Easter | E 112/589 | Bill. LMX 50; dated 20 June. |
| 1686, May 14 | E 112/589 | Answer. Swearing date. |

72. Major v Manning
P: (1) Thomas Major, mercer, London, d4's assignee. D: (1) Edward Manning esq., St Mary Cray, Kent, A. Bonham's brother & administrator, T. Bonham's residual administrator; (2) Henry Adderley, M. Bonham's executor, omitted in amended bill; (3) Thomas Peachell, M. Bonham's executor, omitted in amended bill; (4) William Shorte, cheesemonger, London, bankrupt, A. Shorte's husband. C: (1) Nat. Axtell, counsel for p; (2) Edwin Wyatt, counsel for d1; (3) Edward Ward, counsel for ds2-3. Add: (1) Alice Shorte, d4's wife; (2) Thomas Bonham, deceased, A. Bonham's husband, M. Bonham's father; (3) Ann Bonham, deceased intestate, T. Bonham's widow & executrix; (4) Margaret Bonham, deceased, T. Bonham's daughter. P, assignee of d4 (bankrupt), seeks payment of legacies & money which T. Bonham (deceased), his widow & executrix A. Bonham (deceased intestate) & daughter M. Bonham (deceased) allegedly left to A. Shorte, d4's wife. A. Bonham's brother d1 became her administrator, & ds2-3 are M. Bonham's executors. P claims ds retain the legacies, d1 holds £300 & ds2-3 hold £200 due to d4 & his wife. D1 claims d4 & his wife dispute T. Bonham's will, & denies receiving M. Bonham's legacy to A. Shorte. Ds2-3 claim M. Bonham only left A. Shorte £50 for when she reaches 21 years.

1685, Mich	E 112/589	Bill. LMX 80; dated 12 November; cf. E 112/598 LMX 556 Manning v Higgins.
1685, Nov 27	E 112/589	Answer. Swearing date of d1's answer.
1688, Jan 23	E 112/589	Amended bill. Date of amended bill, which omits ds2-3 & asserts d1 possesses all the legacies & money due to d4.
1688, June 14	E 112/589	Answer. Swearing date of answer of ds2-3.

73. Manning v Higgins
P: (1) Edward Manning esq., St. Mary Cray, Kent, T. Bonham's residual administrator, A. Bonham's brother & administrator. D: (1) Baldwin Higgins; (2) Graveley Norton, scrivener, Chancery Lane, London. C: (1) Edwin Wyatt, counsel for p; (2) William Peisley, counsel for d2. Add: (1) Thomas Bonham esq., Valens in Daggenham, Essex, deceased unadministered, A. Bonham's husband; (2) Anne Bonham, Valens in Daggenham, Essex, deceased intestate, p's sister, T. Bonham's widow & executrix. P, residual administrator of T. Bonham & administrator of T. Bonham's widow Anne (p's sister), seeks discovery & payment of sums T. Bonham had entrusted to d2. T. Bonham died in 1676, leaving his widow & executrix Anne, who died intestate in 1678 leaving her husband's estate unadministered. P claims d2 also colludes in concealing a £100 bond d1 owed T. Bonham. D2 claims he has accounted for all the sums, including d1's bond.

1685, Mich	E 112/598	Bill. LMX 556 (cf. E 112/589 LMX 80 Major v Manning).
1685, Nov 17	E 112/598	Answer. Swearing date of d2's answer.
1686, Hil	E 112/598	Exception. P's exceptions to d2's answer concern T. Bonham's personal estate still in d2's hands.
1686, May 14	E 112/598	Further answer. Swearing date of d2's further answer.

74. Mathew v Neave
P: (1) Nathaniell Mathew the elder gent., London, E. Mathew's father & administrator, J. Mathew's father; (2) Nathaniell Mathew the younger, J. Mathew's son; (3) Abraham Kewids, dyer, Wansworth, London, p4's husband; (4) Mary Kewids, p3's wife, J. Mathew's daughter; (5) Thomas Mathew, J. Mathew's son; (6) Elizabeth Harwell. D: (1) John Neave the younger, J. Neave the E's son & surviving executor; (2) Henry Church, J. Neave the E's grandson; (3) William Weaver, d4's husband; (4) Martha Weaver, d3's wife, J. Darbyshire's mother, M. Darbyshire's mother & administrator; (5) Edward Harwell, J. Harwell's uncle & trustee, uncle of ds6-7; (6) Elizabeth Harwell, sister of J. Harwell & d7; (7) Mary Harwell, sister of J. Harwell & d6; (8) ? Church, d2's sister (no forename recorded); (9) ? Church, d2's sister (no forename recorded). C: (1) Francis Browne, counsel for ps; (2) Edward Ward, counsel for ds3-4; (3) Sam. Dodd, counsel for d5. Add: (1) John Neave the elder, clothier, Ipswich, Suff, deceased, d1's father, grandfather of d2, J. Harwell, J. Darbyshire & J. Mathew; (2) John Mathew, deceased, father of p2 & ps4-5, p1's son, J. Neave the E's grandson; (3) John Harwell, deceased, J. Neave the E's grandson, brother of ds6-7; (4) John Darbyshire, deceased, d4's son, J. Neave the E's grandson; (5) Elizabeth Mathew, deceased intestate, p1's daughter, J. Mathew's sister; (6) Martha Darbyshire, deceased, d4's daughter, J. Darbyshire's sister. Ps seeks payment to p1 (father of J. Mathew, deceased, & father & administrator of E. Mathew, deceased), p2 & ps4-5 (J. Mathew's children), & p6, of a share of legacies left by J. Neave the E to his grandchildren d2, J. Mathew, J. Harwell (deceased) & J. Darbyshire (deceased), payable within 2 years, with d1 as surviving executor. Should the legatees die within 2 years of J. Neave the E's death, the legacies would descend to their siblings. Ps claim entitlement to J. Mathew's legacy, & part of those of J. Harwell & J. Darbyshire who allegedly died within 2 years. D5 denies J. Harwell died within 2 years.

1685, Mich	E 112/590	Bill. LMX 86.
1686, Feb 3	E 112/590	Plea. Swearing date of d5's plea.
1686, April 27	E 112/590	Answer. Swearing date of answer of ds3-4.

75. Maynard v Maynard
P: (1) Gabriel Maynard, Hanwell, Midd, d1's brother, T. Maynard's son. D: (1) John Maynard, p's brother, T. Maynard's son; (2) William Greenhill, customary tenant of the manor of Harrow; (3) Richard Snapp, customary tenant of the manor of Harrow. C: (1) John Hawles, counsel for p; (2) Henry Appleton, counsel for d1. Add: (1) Thomas Maynard, yeoman, Roxheth,

Midd, deceased, father of p & dl. P, dl's brother & son of T. Maynard (deceased), seeks possession of a close copyhold of the manor of Harrow, Midd., which his father allegedly surrendered to ds2-3 for p's use for life. P claims dl conspired with ds2-3 to seize the premises & receive the rents. Dl claims their father never surrendered the close, so it descends to dl.

1685, Trin   E 112/597   Bill. LMX 528.
1685, June 30   E 112/597   Answer. Swearing date of dl's answer.

76. Miller v Birkhead

P: (1) Andrew Miller gent., solicitor, Gray's Inn, Midd. D: (1) Edward Birkhead, timber merchant. C: (1) R. Cooke, counsel for p; (2) R. Freeman, counsel for d. Add: (1) John Stone, attorney in KB. P seeks inj ag d's suit in KB for completion of payment for timber p bought from d in 1681 to build houses in Longlane, Southwark. P claims he paid d fully for the timber, which was rotten, so d promised to reimburse him, but instead hired J. Stone, attorney in KB, to sue him. D denies the timber was rotten & claims p paid only £24 10s 6d of the full price £27 12s 2d, & still owes £3 1s 8d.

1685, Easter   E 112/589   Bill. LMX 48; dated 23 April.
1685, June 1   E 112/589   Answer. Swearing date of d's plea & answer.

77. Milner v Geoard

P: (1) Jonathan Milner, cutler, London. D: (1) John Geoard, merchant, London, otherwise spelled Geoart, R. Geoard's husband. C: (1) ? Bennett, counsel for p. Add: (1) Rebecca Geoard, Avemary Lane, London, d's wife, J. Parke's sister; (2) Jane Parke, R. Geoard's sister. P seeks payment of 100 guinea bond allegedly owed by d. P claims he agreed to introduce d to sisters Jane and Rebecca Parke in return for 100 guineas if d married one of them. P also claims he lent d 5 guineas and sold him goods for which d did not pay. D married Rebecca, but now reportedly denies issuing the bond, receiving the loan or buying the goods.

1685, Mich   E 112/590   Bill. LMX 104.

78. Mole v Rugeley

P: (1) John Mole gent., London. D: (1) Henry Rugeley, milliner, Exeter Exchange in the Strand, Midd; (2) Charles Wilson, attorney, in the Court of Common Pleas. C: (1) J. Winchcombe, counsel for p. P seeks inj ag ds' suit in the Court of Common Pleas for payment of £20 for milliner's wares. P claims in 1684 he bought millinery from dl on the basis that dl would receive back & deduct the cost of unused goods. P returned some parcels, but dl allegedly charged him for more wares than he had originally ordered. Dl hired d2 to sue p.

1685, Trin   E 112/593   Bill. LMX 269; dated 25 June.
1686, Hil   E 112/593   Replication. P asserts dl's (missing) answer is insufficient.

79. Moniers v Slingsby

P: (1) Provost & Corporation of Moniers, his Majesty's Mint, Tower of London. D: (1) Henry Slingsby esq., master & worker of his Majesty's gold & silver monies. C: (1) Thomas Prichard, counsel for ps; (2) Edward Warde, counsel for d. Ps, Provost & Corporation of Moniers of his Majesty's Mint in the Tower of London, seek payment of £16108 19s 1d for the years 1676-80 following an agreement d, master & worker of his Majesty's gold & silver monies, made with ps to pay them 3 shillings for coining each pound of gold, & 8 pence for each pound of silver. Ps claim d paid some of the debt but not all. D pleads that ps are not entitled to style themselves a corporation.

1685, Easter	E 112/588	Bill. LMX 6; dated 6 May; cf. E 112/588 LMX 8 Sawyer v Slingsby & E 112/590 LMX 128 Slingsby v Anderson.
1685, June 11	E 112/588	Plea. Swearing date of d's plea.

80. Neale v Lyford

P: (1) Thomas Neale, St. Andrews, Holborn, Midd, infant of 17 years, son of F. Neale & A. Lyford. D: (1) Thomas Lyford gent., Berks, A. Lyford's husband. N/f: (1) James Smith gent., St. Andrews, Holborn, Midd, p's next friend & guardian. C: (1) William Rowney, counsel for p; (2) Sa. Dodd, counsel for d. Add: (1) Francis Neale gent., Staines, Midd, deceased, p's father, A. Lyford's previous husband; (2) Anne Lyford, deceased, p's mother, d's wife, F. Neale's widow & executrix. P, infant of 17 years, with his next friend J. Smith, seeks inj to prevent d from committing waste upon premises p's father F. Neale (deceased in 1677) left to his widow & executrix Anne for her life, then to p & other sons. Anne re-married d & died in 1680. P asserts d wrongly claims to be p's guardian, retains the premises, receives rents & fells timber. D claims he promised Anne to be p's guardian, & only felled 3 small elm trees.

1685, Mich	E 112/593	Bill. LMX 271.
1685, Dec 24	E 112/593	Answer (with attachments). Swearing date; accounts attached of rents d received from premises.
1686, Mich	E 112/593	Replication. P asserts d's answer is insufficient.

81. Nelson v Williamson

P: (1) Thomas Nelson, distiller, Ratcliffe, Midd. D: (1) Searne Williamson, Norway, R. Menlove's administrator; (2) Champion Ashby, merchant, London, part owner of a ship, the *William and Betty*, d1's attorney. C: (1) Richard Knapp, counsel for p. Add: (1) Rowland Menlove, mariner, Ratcliffe, Midd, deceased; (2) John Clarke, merchant, London. P seeks payment of a £60 penal bond R. Menlove issued him in 1682 for a £31 loan. Menlove later issued a £250 bond with d2 (part owner of a ship, the *William and Betty*) to J. Clarke for the repayment of £127 10s to repair the ship, for which d2 indemnified Menlove & appointed him ship's master. In 1683 Menlove sailed the ship to Guinea & drowned. D1 (Menlove's administrator) issued d2 his power of attorney to receive debts owed to Menlove, & ds now refuse to repay p's bond.

1685, Easter	E 112/589	Bill (with attachments). LMX 68; cf. E 112/589 LMX 60 Strong v Ashby; inventory attached of R. Menlove's goods on board the ship.

82. Newby v Manning

P: (1) George Newby gent., Leicester, Leics, H. Newby the E's brother & administrator, H. Newby the Y's uncle & administrator. D: (1) Thomas

29

Manning, S. Newby's son & executor, d2's husband; (2) Mary Manning, d1's wife; (3) William Bradford, tailor, S. Newby's trustee; (4) Samuell Berry, carpenter, S. Newby's trustee; (5) Jonathan Shaw, scrivener, S. Newby's trustee; (6) Lady Lumley; (7) Sir John Chickley; (8) Mr Howard; (9) Dr Merriott; (10) Lady Keeling; (11) Alice Jordan; (12) Mr Spencer; (13) Mr Cozens; (14) Mr Stockdell; (15) Mr Bull; (16) Mr Wright; (17) Mr White; (18) Mr Kingsbury. C: (1) John Powell, counsel for p; (2) Henry Hatsell, counsel for ds1-2; (3) Richard Holford, counsel for ds3-5. Add: (1) Henry Newby the elder, woodmonger, London, deceased intestate, p's brother, H. Newby the Y's father; (2) Henry Newby the younger, deceased, H. Newby the E's son, p's nephew; (3) Sarah Newby, deceased, H. Newby the E's widow & administratrix, d1's mother. P (H. Newby the E's brother & administrator, and H. Newby the Y's uncle & administrator) seeks possession of leasehold premises H. Newby the E allegedly entrusted for his son H. Newby the Y & p before his marriage to S. Newby. H. Newby the E died intestate in 1681 and S. Newby became his administratrix, assigned some of the leasehold premises to ds3-5 in trust for herself & the rest to ds6-18, & died leaving d1 her son & executor.

1685, Easter	E 112/589	Bill. LMX 59.
1685, May 26	E 112/589	Answer. Swearing date of answer of ds3-5.
1685, May 30	E 112/589	Answer. Swearing date of answer of ds1-2.

83. Nichols v Villiers
P: (1) Mathew Nichols gent., Under Marshall of the king's household, St. Martin in the Fields, Midd. D: (1) Sir Edward Villiers, Knight Marshall of the king's household, judge of the King's Palace Court; (2) John Pim, merchant, London. C: (1) William Ettricke, counsel for p; (2) Rob. Merrett, counsel for d2. Add: (1) Thomas Gavell, vintner, London; (2) Christopher Lowman, keeper of King's Palace Court prison. P, Under Marshall of his Majesty's household, seeks inj ag ds' suit for payment of a £200 bond p had issued d1, Knight Marshall of the household, judge of the King's Palace Court, as security to perform his office. In 1685 d2 delivered p a writ ag T. Gavell for £60. C. Lowman (keeper of the prison of King's Palace Court) became surety for Gavell, who then failed to appear in Court. Though p had Gavell arrested at Lowman's suit, d2 persuaded d1 to sue p for the £200 bond, claiming p should have imprisoned Gavell in the first place.

| 1685, Mich | E 112/593 | Bill. LMX 272. |
| 1685, Nov 14 | E 112/593 | Answer. Swearing date of d2's answer. |

84. Osbaldeston v Wilson
P: (1) William Osbaldeston, linen draper, Westminster, London; (2) Thomas Jolley, tailor, Westminster, London; (3) John Lauthorne, joiner, Westminster, London. D: (1) Hannah Wilson, Westminster, London. C: (1) Henry Trinder, counsel for ps; (2) William Wogan, counsel for d. Ps seek relief from d's suit for payment of a £100 bond. P1 claims in 1682 d assigned him a messuage in Drury Lane with 18 months on the lease, promising to procure a further lease for him, which she then refused to transfer, & sued to eject p1 at KB. P1 brought a writ of Error in the Exchequer Chamber, & issued the £100 bond with ps2-3 as security to quit the premises by a certain date. P asserts d

allowed him a further 4 or 5 days to quit, but d now claims the bond is forfeit. D denies agreeing to assign p a further lease.

| 1685, Hil | E 112/590 | Bill. LMX 89; dated 7 February. |
| 1685, May 8 | E 112/590 | Answer. Swearing date. |

85. Padwicke v Scott

P: (1) John Padwicke, pavier, London. D: (1) Bartholomew Scott, lighterman, White Chapel, Midd. C: (1) Rich. Knapp, counsel for p; (2) Edward Couldinge, counsel for d. P seeks recovery of his house and goods which d seized using a warrant of attorney for a judgement for £50 which p had previously issued while extremely ill to d, allegedly as security for p's family. P also claims d pretends to have lent p's wife £30. D seeks relief from p's suit claiming they came to a full account and executed each other a general release.

| 1685, Mich | E 112/590 | Bill. LMX 124. |
| 1685, Dec 1 | E 112/590 | Plea. Swearing date of d's plea. |

86. Parsons v Grant

P: (1) Richard Parsons, carpenter, Twickenham, Midd. D: (1) John Grant, brewer, Kingston upon Thames, Surrey. C: (1) Francis Fuller, counsel for p's bill; (2) H. Trinder, counsel for d; (3) W. Williams, counsel for p's replication. Add: (1) John Weston gent., Isleworth, Midd, deceased; (2) Amy Parsons, Twickenham, Midd, deceased, p's mother; (3) John Forth esq., Hackney, Midd, deceased; (4) Sir William Hicke, Ruckholt, Essex, bart. P seeks possession of mortgage deeds or repayment of mortgage on p's cottage from d. P & his mother A. Parsons (deceased) had mortgaged the cottage in 1668 for £50 to J. Weston, who transferred the mortgage in 1672 to J. Forth (deceased). D claims he bought a brewery from Forth in 1675, whose stock included the mortgage. D claims he delivered up the mortgage deeds when Sir W. Hicke paid the mortgage for p in 1678, which p denies.

1685, Easter	E 112/588	Bill. LMX 25 (cf. E 112/589 LMX 38 Grant v Parsons).
1685, July 18	E 112/588	Answer. Swearing date of d's plea & answer.
1686, Hil	E 112/588	Replication. P's replication denies d delivered up the mortgage deeds.

87. Paul v Heber

P: (1) James Paul esq., London, Sir W. Paul's son & executor. D: (1) Reginald Heber, merchant, London; (2) Maurice Drady, merchant. C: (1) John Bernard, counsel for d1. Add: (1) Sir William Paul, Brawicke, Berks, knight, deceased, p's father, lessee of the prisage & butlerage of wines in English ports; (2) James Farrier, merchant, France. P, legatee from his late father, Sir W. Paul, of a lease of the prisage & butlerage of wines imported into the ports of England, seeks payment of duties for wine which ds allegedly imported through the port of Cowes, Isle of Wight, in May 1685. D1 claims J. Farrier imported the wine & asked d1 to pay the duties & receive the wine as security for repayment, which d1 did at the Custom House, London.

| 1685, Mich | E 112/594 | Bill. LMX 334 (lower part of the bill is truncated). |
| 1686, April 20 | E 112/594 | Answer. Swearing date of d1's answer. |

88. Payne v Grove

P: (1) Richard Payne gent., solicitor, Lincoln's Inn, Midd, attorney in the Court of Common Pleas. D: (1) Elizabeth Grove, J. Grove's widow & executrix, F. Wilkinson the E's daughter; (2) Francis Wilkinson the younger, F. Wilkinson the E's executor, d3's husband; (3) Mary Wilkinson, d2's wife. C: (1) W. Brookes, counsel for p; (2) John King, counsel for ds. Add: (1) John Grove, coal merchant, St. Mary Overs, Southwark, Surrey, deceased, d1's husband; (2) William Buckerfield, J. Grove's debtor; (3) James Cox, J. Grove's debtor; (4) Francis Wilkinson the elder, deceased, d1's father. P seeks payment of £40 fees which J. Grove allegedly owed p as his attorney. P claims in 1680 J. Grove hired him to negotiate with J. Grove's creditors to annul their commission of bankruptcy. P sued J. Grove in the Court of Common Pleas for the fees, but J. Grove died in 1682 leaving his widow & executrix d1. Ds claim J. Grove's estate is insufficient to pay debts as he owed £400 on a bond & judgement to d1's father F. Wilkinson the E, whose executor d2 is entitled to receive it.

1685, Trin	E 112/588	Bill. LMX 26.
1685, July 23	E 112/588	Answer (with attachments). Swearing date of ds' answer; 2 schedules attached of J. Grove's personal estate & debts repaid to it.
1686, Easter	E 112/588	Replication. P's replication asserts ds' answer is insufficient.

89. Pendleton v Keightley

P: (1) Edmund Pendleton, master card maker, London. D: (1) Thomas Keightley esq., London. C: (1) Daniell Foucault, counsel for p. P (one of the Masters of Co. of Cardmakers) seeks inj ag d's suit for payment of a £500 bond which p issued him in 1683 as security for an agreement d made to seal and stamp p's playing cards for 11 years. D reportedly claimed he had a patent to seal cards & receive duties thereon. The agreement allegedly stipulated p could only make cards for d, not exceeding 14 gross per week, & that p's name was inserted in place of d's name. D reportedly did not pay p for the cards, but had him arrested.

| 1685, Easter | E 112/589 | Bill. LMX 45; dated 6 April. |

90. Percivall v Webb

P: (1) Thomas Percivall gent., Chippenham, Cambs. D: (1) William Webb, merchant tailor, Hatton Garden, Midd; (2) Richard Shaw gent., Burwell, Cambs, Sir J. Russell's agent; (3) Dame Frances Russell, Sir J. Russell's widow; (4) Jeremiah White, d3's agent. C: (1) Edward Ward, counsel for p; (2) Samuel Dodd, counsel for ds1-2; (3) John Hely, counsel for d3. Add: (1) Sir John Russell, bart., deceased, d3's husband. P seeks relief ag d1's suit at cl for payment of a bond. P claims he & ds1-2 ran a malting trade from 1666-9, but that d2 lent the profits to his employer, Sir J. Russell, for which d2 issued d1 a bond. In 1675 p allegedly allowed d1 to draw bills upon him for debts owed by Sir J. Russell (then deceased), at d3's request. In 1680 p allegedly agreed to become security for the bond d2 owed d1. Now d1 is suing p for the bond. Ds1-2 claim they repaid p for sums owed, & that p issued d1 the bond for a loan.

| 1685, Mich | E 112/590 | Bill. LMX 88, dated 28 November. |
| 1686, April 21 | E 112/590 | Answer (with attachments). Swearing date of the answer of ds1-2; 3 schedules attached of |

		accounts of the malting trade between p & ds1-2.
1686, Easter	E 112/590	Plea. D3 requests the Court's judgement whether she must answer p's bill, as p has been outlawed for debt in a separate suit.
1686, Nov 8	E 112/590	Answer. Swearing date of d3's answer.
1687, Easter	E 112/590	Replication. P's replication maintains the answer of ds1-2 is insufficient.

91. Phillips v Dunnett

P: (1) Samuell Phillips, mealman, Upper Shadwell, Midd. D: (1) Barnaby Dunnett, yeoman, Woodbridge, Suff; (2) Henry Browne, solicitor, Barnards Inn, Holborn, London, d3's agent; (3) Edward Pratt, solicitor, Woodbridge, Suff. C: (1) Francis Winnington, counsel for p. P seeks relief ag ds' suit in the Court of Common Pleas for payment for corn. In 1681, p asked d1 by letter to send corn to London, then countermanded the request, finding corn to be cheap in London & expensive in the country. D1 claims he never received a countermand & sent the corn, which p refused to buy from d1's agent, who allegedly sold it elsewhere. D1 with ds2-3 got a judgement in the Court of Common Pleas ag p for the price of the corn.

1685, Easter	E 112/597	Bill. LMX 522.
1685, Easter	E 112/597	Copy bill.
1685, Oct 23	E 112/597	Answer. Swearing date of d2's answer.
1685, Nov 4	E 112/597	Commission. For the answers of d1 & d3.
1685, Nov 12	E 112/597	Answer. Swearing date of d1's answer.
1685, Nov 21	E 112/597	Answer. Swearing date of d3's answer.

92. Plukenett v Genew

P: (1) Leonard Plukenett gent., St. Margaret's in Westminster, Midd, R. & E. Plukenett's son & heir. D: (1) William Genew esq., E. Vangenew's son & executor; (2) Theodore Haacke gent., E. Vangenew's husband; (3) Thomas Lawrenson, d1's tenant; (4) John Rayly, d1's tenant. C: (1) Henry Trinder, counsel for p; (2) John Powell, counsel for ds1-2. Add: (1) Elizabeth Vangenew, deceased, d1's mother, d2's wife; (2) Robert Plukenett, deceased, p's father, E. Plukenett's husband; (3) Elizabeth Plukenett, deceased, p's mother, R. Plukenett's wife; (4) Fardinando Pew the elder, deceased, F. Pew the Y's father; (5) Fardinando Pew the younger, F. Pew the E's son. P, son of R. & E. Plukenett (both deceased), seeks repair of a messuage called the Helmet & buildings in King St., Westminster, which R. & E. Plukenett & F. Pew the E leased in 1655 for 31 years to E. Vangenew, who married d2 & died in 1668 leaving d1 her son & executor. Pew the E died leaving his son Pew the Y. D1 leased the premises to ds3-4, but claims the buildings were blown up by public authority to prevent the spread of fire. D1 also claims his brother Gerrard (deceased) bought Pew the Y's 1/2 of the premises, which d1 now owns.

1685, Hil	E 112/588	Bill. LMX 2.
1685, Easter	E 112/588	Demurrer. Ds1-2 deny this is a matter for equity.
1685, May 30	E 112/588	Answer. Swearing date of d2's answer.
1685, June 3	E 112/588	Answer. Swearing date of d1's answer.

1685, Trin   E 112/588   Replication. P asserts answers of ds1-2 are insufficient.

93. Plumer v Jeliffe

P: (1) Charles Plumer, mariner, London, employed by the Co. of Royal Adventurers of England. D: (1) John Jeliffe, factor, for the Co. of Royal Adventurers of England. C: (1) Will. Moses, counsel for p. Add: (1) Thomas Thurloe, chief agent, of the Co. of Royal Adventurers of England. P, hired in 1677 by the Co. of Royal Adventurers of England to the river Gambo & North Guinea as master of a yacht, the *St. Maria*, seeks payment of £21 5s 4d of a £71 5s 4d debt which d (the Co.'s factor) owed him for medical bills & debts incurred when the yacht was blown off course to Jamaica. D repaid p £50 in bills, & reportedly told p to collect the rest from the Co., which issued p 2 bills for £20 & £10. D sued p for the £10 bill in the Sheriff's Court in London, where p could not prove the debt.

1685, Mich   E 112/590   Bill. LMX 114; dated 4 November.

94. Powis v Turner

P: (1) Rt. Hon. William, Earl of Powis, lord of the manor of Hendon, Midd.. D: (1) Samuel Turner esq., Maudlin, Sussex; (2) Edward Hobart gent., solicitor, Gray's Inn, Midd, p's former agent; (3) Howard Brock the younger gent., St. Andrews, Holborn, Midd. C: (1) Anthony Weldon, counsel for p; (2) Edward Ward, counsel for ds; (3) W. Killingworth, counsel for d2's rejoinder. Add: (1) Benjamin Huling, p's tenant, executed for high treason; (2) William Huling, p's tenant, executed for high treason. P, lord of the manor of Hendon, seeks recovery of premises copyhold of the manor which his agent d2 demised to d3 for £2000 after the previous tenants B. & W. Huling were executed for high treason. P claims while he was imprisoned in the Tower of London accused of conspiring ag Charles II, he agreed to lease the manorial tithes & ordinary profits to d1 in trust for d2 for 7 years at £400 per annum. P claims d2 possessed the manor, cut timber & wrongfully demised the copyhold premises to d3. D2 asserts he is lessee also of the forfeitures & extraordinary profits, & that p allowed him to cut timber.

1685, Mich	E 112/591	Bill. LMX 134.
1686, Jan 25	E 112/591	Answer. Swearing date of d2's answer.
1686, Jan 27	E 112/591	Answer. Swearing date of d3's answer.
1686, April 7	E 112/591	Answer. Swearing date of d1's answer (wrongly dated 1685?).
1686, May 22	E 112/591	Further answer. Swearing date of d3's further answer.
1686, Easter	E 112/591	Replication. Dated 27 April; p asserts d2's answer is insufficient.
1686, Trin	E 112/591	Replication. P asserts d1's answer is insufficient.
1686, Trin	E 112/591	Rejoinder. D2 maintains his answer is sufficient.

95. Prettyman v Horne

P: (1) William Prettyman esq., Hatton Garden, London, remembrancer of his Majesty's first fruits and tenths in this Court. D: (1) Joseph Horne, merchant,

London, W. Wheatly's executor; (2) Mathias Cupper, linen draper, St. Martin in the Fields, Midd, W. Wheatly's executor. C: (1) Edward Ward, counsel for p. Add: (1) William Wheatly gent., London, deceased. P seeks relief from the suits of ds (the late W. Wheatly's executors) in Chancery and the office of Common Pleas in the Exchequer for payment of a mortgage or foreclosure on lands p mortgaged to W. Wheatly, and a £2000 bond p issued as security on the mortgage. P claims ds refused to accept payment only of the mortgage and interest arrears.

| 1685, Easter | E 112/589 | Bill. LMX 40; dated 11 April. |

96. Puckle v Pawlett

P: (1) Thomas Puckle, merchant, London, W. London's administrator. D: (1) Hon. Francis Pawlett, esq.; (2) Sir Andrew Henley the younger, bart., Sir A. Henley the E's son. C: (1) William Ettricke, counsel for p; (2) William Killingworth, counsel for d1; (3) C. Whitelocke, counsel for d2. Add: (1) William London, merchant, London, deceased; (2) Thomas Harewell gent., Westminster, Midd, W. London's executor & trustee; (3) Sir Andrew Henley the elder, Bramshill, Hants, bart., deceased, d2's father. P, administrator of W. London (deceased), seeks payment of a £50 debt London owed him, from a £600 penal bond (payable when d1 got married) which d1 issued W. London allegedly for £100 in gold. P claims London deposited the bond with d2's father Sir A. Henley the E, after whose death d2 transferred the bond back to d1, who then married. London's executor T. Harewell refused to execute his will. D2 denies ever having the bond & claims London transferred it to his father as security for a £100 loan. D1 denies borrowing £100 in gold, but claims 20 years ago while playing at dice London lent him £20 upon a bond, which should be cancelled as a gambling debt.

1685, Easter	E 112/588	Bill. LMX 27.
1685, Easter	E 112/588	Copy bill.
1685, Mich	E 112/588	Demurrer. D1's demurrer claims the bond is extortionate & not a matter for equity.
1686, Jan 16	E 112/588	Affidavit. P swears on this date he does not possess the bond.
1686, Feb 18	E 112/588	Answer. Swearing date of d2's answer.
1686, June 23	E 112/588	Commission. For d1's answer.
1686, Oct 15	E 112/588	Answer. Swearing date of d1's answer.

97. Purley v Willymot

P: (1) Francis Purley esq., barrister, Inner Temple, London, p2's husband; (2) Elizabeth Purley, p1's wife, R. Ball's daughter & executrix; (3) Hellen Ball the younger, infant of 10 years, R. Ball & H. Ball the E's daughter, represented by ps4-5; (4) Edward Brown, clerk, p3's next friend; (5) Anne Brown, p4's wife, R. Ball's executrix, p3's next friend. D: (1) James Willymot esq., Kelshall, Herts, H. Ball the E's brother, p3's uncle. C: (1) Robert Clowes, counsel for ps; (2) Robert Foalkes, counsel for d. Add: (1) Richard Ball, doctor in divinity, deceased, master of the Temple, father of ps2-3, H. Ball the E's husband; (2) Hellen Ball the elder, deceased, R. Ball's wife, d's sister, p3's mother. Ps seek inj ag d's suit for payment of a £2000 bond which R. Ball (deceased in 1684, father of ps2-3) issued d in 1670 as security to buy & settle lands upon his intended wife, d's sister, H. Ball the E (deceased in 1681, p3's mother) within 12 months of their marriage. R. Ball died without executing the agreement, leaving p2 & p5 as his executrixes.

| 1685, Mich | E 112/591 | Bill. LMX 143. |
| 1685, Nov 19 | E 112/591 | Answer. Swearing date. |

98. Pye v St. John

P: (1) Meliora Pye, widow, p2's mother, Jacob Drax's administratrix de bonis non, M. Drax's legatee, Sir J. Drax's daughter; (2) Elizabeth Pye, p1's daughter under 21 years, with p1 as next friend, M. Drax's legatee, Sir J. Drax's grandchild; (3) Meliora Gumeldon, under 21 years, M. Drax's legatee, Sir J. Drax's grandchild; (4) Richard Gumeldon, under 21 years, M. Drax's legatee, Sir J. Drax's grandchild. D: (1) Sir Walter St. John, bart., H. Drax's executor; (2) John Bawden, merchant, H. Drax's executor; (3) Abraham Jackson gent., H. Drax's executor; (4) Warwick Bampfield esq., M. Drax's brother & executor; (5) Drax Shatterden, M. Drax's legatee; (6) Dorothy Shatterden, M. Drax's legatee. N/f: (1) Thomas Gumeldon esq., father & next friend of ps3-4. C: (1) Edward Ward, counsel for ps; (2) John Heames, counsel for ps; (3) John Nowes, counsel for ds1-2. Add: (1) Jacob Drax, deceased, M. Drax's son; (2) Dame Margaret Drax, deceased, Jacob Drax's mother & administratrix; (3) Sir James Drax, London, knight, deceased, M. Drax's husband; (4) James Drax gent., deceased, Sir J. Drax's son; (5) Henry Drax gent., deceased, Sir J. Drax's son. Ps seeks payment of legacies left them by M. Drax. In 1661 p1's father Sir J. Drax left a £100 annuity each to his widow M. Drax & son Jacob Drax, payable from an estate in Barbados by his elder sons & executors James & H. Drax. James Drax died in 1663, & Jacob Drax died intestate in 1679. In 1682 M. Drax sued H. Drax in this Court for non-payment of the annuities to herself and Jacob. H. Drax died & the suit was revived ag ds1-3, his executors, who paid some of the debt. M. Drax died leaving d4 her executor and ps & ds5-6 her legatees of the remaining annuity arrears. Ds1-2 claim H. Drax's estate is insufficient to pay his debts.

| 1685, Mich | E 112/590 | Bill. LMX 102, dated 16 November. |
| 1686, June 9 | E 112/590 | Answer (with attachments). Swearing date of the answer of ds1-2; 3 schedules attached of accounts of H. Drax's estate. |

99. Raynalls v Ward

P: (1) Mathew Raynalls, R. Raynalls' administrator. D: (1) Thomas Ward, d2's husband; (2) Love Ward, d1's wife, A. Reynalls' administratrix; (3) Robert Mechum; (4) Phillis Mechum; (5) Isabell Holmes. C: (1) Edward Umfrevile, counsel for p; (2) John Ansell, counsel for ds1-2. Add: (1) Richard Reynalls, parish of St. Clement Danes, Midd, deceased intestate, spelled Reynolds in ds1-2's answer, A. Reynalls' husband; (2) Anne Reynalls, deceased intestate, R. Reynalls' widow. P seeks possession of R. Reynalls' personal estate from ds. In 1680 R. Reynalls died intestate whereupon p claims he became his administrator & allowed his widow A. Reynalls to use the personal estate until her death in 1684 in d4's house. P asserts ds clandestinely possessed R. Reynalls' household goods, money & securities. D2 (A. Reynalls' cousin & administratrix) & d1 claim p only became R. Reynalls' administrator in 1685.

| 1685, Easter | E 112/589 | Bill. LMX 39. |

1685, July 1   E 112/589   Answer. Answer of ds 1-2, sworn by d2 on this date, sworn by d1 on 2 July; schedule below answer of papers re. A. Reynalls' estate.

100. Robson v Jeyne

P: (1) William Robson gent., St. Margett Westminster, Midd, Sir Edward Villiers's agent. D: (1) Francis Jeyne, goldsmith, H. Jeyne's brother & administrator. C: (1) William Ettricke, counsel for p; (2) J. Viney, counsel for d. Add: (1) Henry Jeyne, captain of a regiment of foot soldiers, deceased, d's brother; (2) Sir Edward Villiers, Knight Marshall of his Majesty's Household. P, Sir E. Villiers's agent, seeks an inj ag d's suit at KB & payment of a £100 debt which H. Jeyne (deceased) owed his colonel, Sir E. Villiers, from 1677-9. D, H. Jeyne's brother & administrator, has had p arrested at KB for retaining H. Jeyne's pay, but p claims H. Jeyne had agreed to have his pay transferred to his creditors (including Sir E. Villiers) but then died.

1685, Mich   E 112/594   Bill. LMX 333.
1685, Nov 16   E 112/594   Answer. Swearing date.

101. Rogers v Coney

P: (1) Richard Rogers, merchant, London. D: (1) William Coney, merchant, London; (2) Edmond Wright, merchant, London. C: (1) Edward Ward, counsel for p; (2) William Cherry, counsel for ds. Add: (1) John Letchington. P seeks relief ag d1's suit for payment of a £140 bond p issued d1 (as d2's trustee), together with a mortgage on messuages in Edmonton, as security for £70 lent by d2 to enable p to buy 1/8 of the ship, *Elizabeth*, from J. Letchington. P claims he entrusted d1 to sell the 1/8 part, whose proceeds d1 then refused to transfer to p. Ds claim p had already sold the messuages before mortgaging them to d1, and deny p repaid the loan by the due date.

1685, Mich   E 112/590   Bill. LMX 98.
1686, May 10   E 112/590   Answer. Swearing date of d2's answer.
1686, May 21   E 112/590   Answer. Swearing date of d1's answer.
1686, June 14   E 112/590   Answer. Swearing date of another answer by d2.

102. Rogers v Grueber

P: (1) Peter Rogers, victualler, Stepney, Midd. D: (1) Daniell Grueber, merchant, London; (2) Thomas Stone, mariner, London, master of a ship, the *Charles*, in 1684. C: (1) Robert Rawlins, counsel for p. P seeks relief ag d1's suit in KB for payment of a £120 bond which d2 (master of a ship, the *Charles*) issued in 1684 to d1 with p as security for a loan to fit the ship out for a voyage to Limerick & Seville. D2 & p agreed to repay d1's agents 283 pieces of eight in Spain. D1 reportedly never paid them the loan, so d2 & p only paid d1's agents items in lieu of the pieces of eight. The ship was wrecked leaving Spain. P claims ds now conspire to compel him to pay the full bond.

1685, Mich   E 112/591   Bill. LMX 142.

103. Row v Buckle

P: (1) Anthony Row esq., purveyor to Charles II's stables, St. Giles in the Fields, Midd. D: (1) Robert Buckle. C: (1) Daniel Foucault, counsel for p; (2)

William Banistre, counsel for d. Add: (1) John Coling, deceased, p's servant. P, previously purveyor to Charles II's stables, seeks inj ag d's suit for payment of £178 19s 6d which d claims p owes him for oats. P asserts his servant J. Coling (deceased) bought oats & beans from d, for which he drew bills upon p in advance. When Charles II died, p's employment ceased, allegedly leaving d with bills for goods not delivered.

1685, Mich	E 112/589	Bill. LMX 77; dated 23 October; cf. E 112/589 LMX 78 Row v Moor.
1685, Nov 3	E 112/589	Answer (with attachments). Swearing date; account between p & d attached.
1685, Mich	E 112/589	Exception. P's exceptions concern J. Coling's dealings, & p's account with d.

104. Row v Moor

P: (1) Anthony Row esq., purveyor to Charles II's stables, St. Giles in the Fields, Midd. D: (1) George Moor, corn merchant, Minories, London. C: (1) Daniel Foucault, counsel for p; (2) William Banistre, counsel for d. Add: (1) John Coling, deceased, p's servant. P, previously purveyor to Charles II's stables, seeks inj ag d's suit for payment of £85 which d claims p owes him for oats. P asserts his servant J. Coling (deceased) bought oats & beans from d, for which he drew bills upon p in advance. When Charles II died, p's employment ceased, allegedly leaving d with bills for goods not delivered.

| 1685, Mich | E 112/589 | Bill. LMX 78; dated 23 October; cf. E 112/589 LMX 77 Row v Buckle. |
| 1685, Nov 3 | E 112/589 | Answer. Swearing date. |

105. Sawyer v Allan

P: (1) Sir Robert Sawyer, knight, Attorney General. D: (1) John Allan esq., Northants; (2) James Nelthrope esq., R. Nelthrope's father. C: (1) Edward Ward, counsel for d2. Add: (1) Richard Nelthrope esq., d2's son. P, Attorney General, seeks payment of d1's bond issued to d2, which p alleges was in exchange for £300 lent by d2's son R. Nelthrope. R. Nelthrope's estate is forfeit to the Crown as he conspired ag Charles II in the "late fanaticall plott" and absconded. D2 claims he lent his own money to d1, not his son's, so the bond should not be forfeit to the Crown.

| 1685, Easter | E 112/590 | Bill. LMX 91; dated 22 April. |
| 1685, June 13 | E 112/590 | Answer. Swearing date of d2's answer. |

106. Sawyer v Audley

P: (1) Sir Robert Sawyer, Attorney General, knight. D: (1) Edward Audley, broker, London, bankrupt, outlawed, d2's husband; (2) Anne Audley, d1's wife, T. Stretchley's sister; (3) Sir Robert Viner, knight, bart., president of Christ Church Hospital, London; (4) Sir John Moore, knight, executor of d3's place for him; (5) Nathaniell Hawes gent., treasurer of Christ Church Hospital; (6) John Farmer gent., steward of Christ Church Hospital. C: (1) Edward Ward, counsel for p; (2) Thomas Jenner, counsel for ds3-6. Add: (1) Thomas Stretchley gent., deceased, d2's brother; (2) George Witharidge. P seeks payment to the Crown of a £50 annuity T. Stretchley left to Christ Church Hospital, London, in trust for his sister d2, whose husband d1 was sued in

1683 in the Court of Common Pleas by G. Witharidge for a £100 bond, went bankrupt & was outlawed. P claims the annuity is forfeit to the Crown. Ds3-6 are willing to pay the annuity as the Court directs in return for indemnity.

| 1685, Hil | E 112/589 | Bill. LMX 63. |
| 1685, June 19 | E 112/589 | Answer. Swearing date of answer of ds3-6. |

107. Sawyer v Malthus

P: (1) Robert Sawyer, Attorney General, knight. D: (1) William Malthus; (2) Henry Pottenger; (3) John Butcher; (4) Thomas Weymondesold. C: (1) Edward Ward, counsel for p. Add: (1) Richard Peirce esq., grocer, London, His Majesty's farmer of scavage/shewage & portage duties. P, Attorney General, on behalf of R. Peirce, His Majesty's farmer of scavage/shewage & portage duties for alien ships entering the port of London, seeks payment of scavage/shewage & portage duties by ds who have imported goods into London but failed to pay the duties. In 1684 p leased the duties for 7 years from the mayor & aldermen of London at £1200 per annum. Ds reportedly claim they are Englishmen, not aliens.

| 1685, Mich | E 112/590 | Bill. LMX 90; dated 16 November. |

108. Sawyer v Mayor & Aldermen, London

P: (1) Sir Robert Sawyer, Attorney General, knight. D: (1) Mayor & Aldermen, London. P, Attorney General, seeks the cancellation of an indenture which ds, the Mayor & Aldermen of London (trustees of the orphans of freemen of London), entered into to mortgage and sell premises within London. P claims the indenture, intended to support the orphans, produced far fewer profits than intended.

| 1685, Trin | E 112/588 | Bill (with attachments). LMX 30; names of |
| | | signatories of the indenture attached. |

109. Sawyer v Slingsby

P: (1) Sir Robert Sawyer, knight, Attorney General, on behalf of the Moniers of his Majesty's Mint in the Tower of London. D: (1) Henry Slingsby esq., previously master & worker of his Majesty's gold & silver monies. C: (1) R. Lechmere, counsel for p; (2) Edward Warde, counsel for d. Add: (1) Thomas Anderson, Monier of his Majesty's mint in the Tower of London; (2) Daniell Robinson, Monier of his Majesty's mint in the Tower of London; (3) Matthias Harding, Monier of his Majesty's mint in the Tower of London; (4) James Wilder, Monier of his Majesty's mint in the Tower of London; (5) Thomas Hunt, Monier of his Majesty's mint in the Tower of London; (6) Edward Shirton, Monier of his Majesty's mint in the Tower of London; (7) Robert Seares, Monier of his Majesty's mint in the Tower of London; (8) Richard Collard, Monier of his Majesty's mint in the Tower of London; (9) Christopher Sutton, Monier of his Majesty's mint in the Tower of London; (10) John Nichols, Monier of his Majesty's mint in the Tower of London; (11) Sir Ralph Freeman, knight, deceased. P, Attorney General acting for the Moniers of his Majesty's Mint in the Tower of London, seeks payment of arrears of 3 shillings for coining each pound of gold & 8 pence for each pound of silver d allegedly owes the Moniers (totalling £1938 14s). In 1662, d & Sir R. Freeman (since deceased) were granted the office of master & worker of his Majesty's monies. D was suspended from the office in 1680. D claims he had to pay for the Moniers' negligence & mistakes in their work, & that they owe him money.

1685, Trin	E 112/588	Bill. LMX 8; dated 30 June; cf. E 112/588 LMX 6 Moniers v Slingsby & E 112/590 LMX 128 Slingsby v Anderson.
1685, Oct 23	E 112/588	Answer. Swearing date.
1686, Hil	E 112/588	Replication. P asserts d's answer is insufficient.

110. Sawyer v St. Paul's

P: (1) Sir Robert Sawyer, Attorney General, knight. D: (1) Dean & Chapter of St. Paul's; (2) William Bonnett, E. Bonnet's alleged husband; (3) John Perry esq.; (4) Francis Scott, d1's agent. Add: (1) Elianora Cabourne, or Bonnett, d2's alleged wife, convicted of high treason; (2) Abraham Harrison, goldsmith. P, Attorney General, seeks a writ of distringas ag d1, & payment to the Crown of £100 by A. Harrison & £200 by d3. P claims E. Cabourne or Bonnett (d2's alleged wife) had lent money in other people's names (eg., £100 to Harrison & £200 to d3), was convicted of high treason in 1684 for clipping money, & her estate became forfeit to the Crown. D2 now reportedly claims he lent the £100 & sues Harrison in the Court of Common Pleas. D1 (having a grant of traitors' goods in their bailiwick) & their agent d4 are suing d3 for the £200.

1685, Mich	E 112/590	Bill. LMX 127; dated 27 October.

111. Seys v Belwood

P: (1) Evan Seys, mariner, Ratcliffe, Midd. D: (1) William Belwood, merchant, London; (2) John Gibbons, merchant, London; (3) William Chevall gent.. C: (1) F. Fuller, counsel for p; (2) Sam. Dodd, counsel for d3. Add: (1) John Arderne, scrivener, d3's agent. P seeks inj ag ds' suit at the Sheriff's Court in London for payment of a £200 bond for which p claims he was only the security, and that d1 was the principal borrower from d2. P asserts d1 paid off the bond, but d2 claims he was not paid and transferred it to d3's agent, J. Arderne. D3 maintains p is the principal name on the bond and demands payment.

1685, Easter	E 112/589	Bill. LMX 36.
1685, June 18	E 112/589	Answer. Swearing date of d3's answer.

112. Simpson v Gray

P: (1) Isabella Simpson, wiredrawer, St. Martin in the Fields, Midd, widow, p2's partner; (2) Alice Edwards, wiredrawer, St. Martin in the Fields, Midd, widow, p1's partner. D: (1) John Gray, vintner, London, E. Coleman's administrator. C: (1) Lewis Morgan, counsel for ps; (2) William Ettricke, counsel for d. Add: (1) Elizabeth Coleman, deceased intestate, widow. Ps, wiredrawers, seek payment from d of £14 4d which E. Coleman (deceased intestate) owed them for gold & silver thread. D, E. Coleman's administrator, claims E. Coleman owed him a penal bond for £45 + interest, which E. Coleman's estate (in d's possession) is insufficient to repay, & that this is not a matter for equity.

1685, Easter	E 112/594	Bill. LMX 326.
1685, June 20	E 112/594	Answer (with attachments). Swearing date of d's answer & demurrer; inventory of E. Coleman's estate in d's possession attached.

113. Slingsby v Anderson

P: (1) Henry Slingsby esq., former master & worker of his Majesty's gold and silver monies. D: (1) Thomas Anderson, Provost of his Majesty's mint, Tower of London; (2) Daniell Robinson, Monier of his Majesty's mint, Tower of London; (3) Mathias Harding, Monier of his Majesty's mint, Tower of London; (4) James Wilder, Monier of his Majesty's mint, Tower of London; (5) Thomas Hunt, Monier of his Majesty's mint, Tower of London; (6) Edward Shirton, Monier of his Majesty's mint, Tower of London; (7) Robert Seares, Monier of his Majesty's mint, Tower of London; (8) Richard Collard, Monier of his Majesty's mint, Tower of London; (9) Christopher Sutton, Monier of his Majesty's mint, Tower of London; (10) John Nicholls, Monier of his Majesty's mint, Tower of London; (11) John Briant, apprentice to the Moniers; (12) Philip Apps, apprentice to the Moniers; (13) Michaell Garnett, apprentice to the Moniers; (14) John Russell, apprentice to the Moniers; (15) Robert Colborne, apprentice to the Moniers; (16) Sir Robert Sawyer, Attorney General, knight. C: (1) Edward Ward, counsel for p; (3) Samuel Dodd, counsel for ds. P, master & worker of his Majesty's monies from 1662-1680, seeks reimbursement for fines & relief from the suits in this Court of ds, the Provost & Moniers of his Majesty's mint & the Attorney General. P claims he employed the moniers to make gold & silver coins, but that he had to pay fines for negligence & errors in their work. P was suspended from his office in 1680. Ds are suing p for breach of an agreement he allegedly made in 1676 to pay the moniers 3 shillings for coining each pound of gold, & 8 pence for each pound of silver. Ds11-15 claim they were only apprentices to the moniers.

1685, Mich	E 112/590	Bill. LMX 128; dated 30 November. cf. E 112/588 LMX 6 Moniers v Slingsby & E 112/588 LMX 8 Sawyer v Slingsby.
1685, Dec 23	E 112/590	Answer. Swearing date of d11's answer & disclaimer.
1685, Dec 23	E 112/590	Answer. Swearing date of d12's answer & disclaimer.
1685, Dec 23	E 112/590	Answer. Swearing date of d13's answer & disclaimer.
1685, Dec 23	E 112/590	Answer. Swearing date of d14's answer & disclaimer.
1685, Dec 23	E 112/590	Answer. Swearing date of d15's answer & disclaimer.
1685, Dec 23	E 112/590	Plea. Swearing date of the plea of ds1-10, who request the Court's judgement whether they need answer as they have agreed accounts with p elsewhere.
1686, Feb 10	E 112/590	Answer (with attachments). Answer of ds1-4 & ds6-10; sworn by ds1-4, ds6-7 & ds9-10 on this date, and sworn by d8 on 23 February 1686. Schedule attached of accounts between ds1-10 & p.

114. Smith v Chudleigh

P: (1) John Smith, merchant, London. D: (1) Hugh Chudleigh gent., Westminster, London. C: (1) J. Hely, counsel for p; (2) William Ettricke, counsel for d. P seeks inj ag d's suit for payment of an £85 5s 6d bill and 2 bills for £106 6s each which p issued d 2 or 3 years ago, for which p was to receive those sums from d's debtors. P allegedly only received £100 which he transferred to d, who reportedly promised to cancel the bills. D asserts p received full payment for the bills.

| 1685, Trin | E 112/589 | Bill. LMX 57; dated 23 June. |
| 1685, July 3 | E 112/589 | Answer. Swearing date. |

115. Smith v Rigby

P: (1) Thomas Smith, butcher, Cookham, Berks; (2) George Smith, wheelwright, Maidenhead, Berks; (3) John Wray, yeoman, Cookham, Berks; (4) Thomas Austen, yeoman, Cookham, Berks; (5) John Smith, yeoman, Cookham, Berks. D: (1) Elinor Rigby, London, d2's mother; (2) Mary Rigby, d1's daughter. C: (1) M. Davies, counsel for ps; (2) Thomas Jenner, counsel for ds. Ps seek inj ag ds' suit at KB allegedly granting ds a judgement for payment of £100 bond issued in 1678 by p1 (principal borrower) and the other ps (securing the bond), plus interest and legal charges. Ds filed a previous suit in 1680 ag p5 who paid £10. Ps claim they agreed to pay only the principal of the bond at £10 per year.

| 1686, Hil | E 112/590 | Bill. LMX 93; dated 1 February. |
| 1686, Feb 10 | E 112/590 | Answer. Swearing date of ds' answer. |

116. Smith v Waters

P: (1) William Smith, Isleworth, Midd, T. Smith's brother & administrator. D: (1) Ann Waters, Buckingham, Bucks, T. Smith's sister & alleged trustee; (2) William Rice, J. Rice's husband. C: (1) S. Houghton, counsel for p; (2) Sam. Dodd, counsel for d2. Add: (1) Thomas Smith, Isleworth, Midd, deceased intestate, brother of p, d1 & J. Rice; (2) Joan Rice, d2's wife, T. Smith's sister. P, brother & administrator of T. Smith (deceased intestate in 1683), seeks possession of T. Smith's estate. P claims T. Smith got distemper 10 years ago & his sister d1 tried to gain custody of his estate. D2 (married to T. Smith's sister J. Rice) claims T. Smith lodged in his house & assigned his estate to him in return for a £400 bond d2 issued as security to d1 as trustee.

| 1685, Mich | E 112/589 | Bill. LMX 81; dated 22 November. |
| 1685, Nov 26 | E 112/589 | Answer (with attachments). Swearing date of d2's plea & answer; schedule attached of T. Smith's personal estate. |

117. Smyth v Child

P: (1) Sir James Smyth, knight, Lord Mayor of London; (2) Sir William Turner, London, knight, alderman; (3) Sir James Edwards, London, knight, alderman; (4) Sir John Moore, London, knight, alderman; (5) Sir William Prichard, London, knight, alderman; (6) Sir Henry Tulse, London, knight, alderman; (7) Sir Robert Geffery, London, knight, alderman; (8) Peter Rich esq., London, alderman, chamberlain. D: (1) Sir Josiah Child, merchant, London, bart.. C: (1) Thomas Jenner, counsel for ps. Ps seek d's acceptance of a new lease for Buttolph wharf and messuages issued by the City of London in 1672 adding 18 years and reducing the annual rent from £50 to £30 after d's houses were burnt in the 1666 fire. Ps sued d in

Chancery to compel him to accept the new lease and pay arrears of the reduced rent, but d sued ps at KB.
1685, Hil   E 112/588   Bill. LMX 11; dated 10 February.

118. Solby v Watker

P: (1) Thomas Solby gent., London, G. Solby's son, brother of d1 & d3. D: (1) Elizabeth Watker, G. Solby's daughter & executrix, sister of p & d3; (2) William Bowles, d3's husband; (3) Anne Bowles, d2's wife, G. Solby's daughter, sister of p & d1. C: (1) Edward Wynne, counsel for p. Add: (1) George Solby, apothecary, London, deceased, freeman of London, father of p, d1 & d3. P seeks 1/2 the personal estate of his father G. Solby (deceased in 1684) according to a custom that 1/2 the personal estate of a deceased wifeless freeman of London must go to his child who had received nothing from the estate, with the other 1/2 going to his executor for his other children who had benefitted from the estate. P claims G. Solby before his death issued d1 (his daughter & executrix) £200 to pay his debts, which she has not done.
1685, Trin   E 112/589   Bill. LMX 34; dated 30 June.

119. Soper v Fowler

P: (1) Charles Soper, draper, London, p2's husband; (2) Mary Soper, London, p1's wife. D: (1) Matthias Fowler, vintner, London. C: (1) William Dobbins, counsel for ps. Add: (1) Richard Weoly, barber, chirurgeon, London; (2) Stephen Crisp, mercer, Colchester, Essex. P seeks payment of rent from d for leasehold premises in Priest's Court, Foster Lane, London, which p bought from R. Weoly & S. Crisp in 1681. D had leased the premises for 21 years from Weoly in 1669 at £25 per annum. The leases were burnt by a fire in p's house in Carter Lane, and now d reportedly refuses to pay p rent, has converted the premises into the Half Moon Tavern, & claims Weoly had allowed him an abatement of £10 per annum.
1685, Mich   E 112/590   Bill. LMX 99; dated 7 November.

120. St. Peter's, Westminster v Acheson

P: (1) Dean & Chapter, St. Peter's, Westminster; (2) Elizabeth Dickenson, G. Dickenson's daughter & executrix; (3) ? Smith, (no forename given) E. Tresham's executrix; (4) John Clendon esq.; (5) Nicholas Fownes; (6) Ellen Davies. D: (1) Dame Martha Acheson, J. Moore's daughter, R. Atkins' widow; (2) Sir William Trumball, doctor of laws; (3) John Harboard; (4) Rowland Blackborne. C: (1) Henry Trinder, counsel for ps; (2) Edward Ward, counsel for d1. Add: (1) John Moore esq., St. Martin in the Fields, Midd, deceased, d1's father; (2) John Dickenson the elder, deceased, p2's grandfather; (3) George Dickenson, deceased, p2's father; (4) Richard Atkins, deceased, d1's husband. Ps (Dean & Chapter of St. Peter's, Westminster, and their tenants of 1/2 premises in the Strand) seek relief from the suits of d1 to eject ps. Ps claim d1 & her husband assigned 1/2 the leasehold premises to p2's father G. Dickenson in 1643 in satisfaction of a £2500 debt that d1's father J. Moore owed p2's grandfather J. Dickenson. D1 assigned the remaining 1/2 premises to ds2-4, & now claims she is entitled to the freehold of p2's 1/2 premises.
1685, Trin   E 112/588   Bill. LMX 22.
1685, Nov 20   E 112/588   Answer. Swearing date of d1's answer.

43

121. Stiles v Langham
P: (1) Thomas Stiles, grocer, St. Mary Overs, Surrey. D: (1) John Langham, grocer, London. C: (1) William Hewes, counsel for p; (2) William Killingworth, counsel for d. P seeks an inj ag d's suit at law for payment of a £20 promissory note. P claims he had hired d as his broker to buy goods in London on his behalf, & that he issued the note at d's request before finding he did not owe d the money. D denies he was p's broker, but alleges p issued the note for goods he sold p.

| 1685, Trin | E 112/597 | Bill. LMX 523. |
| 1685, July 3 | E 112/597 | Answer. Swearing date. |

122. Stoughton v Palmer
P: (1) Hannah Stoughton, H. Stoughton's widow & administratrix. D: (1) Matthew Palmer, d2's husband; (2) Clementia Palmer, T. Stanney's widow & administratrix, d1's wife; (3) Edward Stanney, T. Stanney's cousin & trustee. C: (1) Daniell ?, counsel for p (signature damaged); (2) Francis Browne, counsel for d3; (3) Appleton, counsel for ds1-2. Add: (1) Humphrey Stoughton, tailor, deceased, p's husband; (2) Timothy Stanney, Hammersmith, Midd, deceased, d2's previous husband; (3) Percivall Stanney gent., St. Martin in the Fields, Midd, deceased; (4) Richard Wheeler, hosier, T. Stanney's executor; (5) Charles Wheeler, goldsmith, T. Stanney's executor. P, widow & administratrix of H. Stoughton, seeks payment of £25 12s 5d which T. Stanney (d2's previous husband, deceased) owed H. Stoughton. In 1675 T. Stanney & P. Stanney (deceased) bought the office of messenger's place from the Crown during the reign of Charles II, & entrusted it to d3. Ds1-2 claim T. Stanney's estate is insufficient to pay debts & his executors R. & C. Wheeler were unwilling to execute his will.

1685, Hil	E 112/588	Bill. LMX 1.
1685, May 5	E 112/588	Answer. Swearing date of d3's answer.
1685, May 9	E 112/588	Answer (with attachments). Swearing date of answer of ds1-2; inventory attached of T. Stanney's personal estate & debts.

123. Strong v Ashby
P: (1) Joseph Strong, goldsmith, St. Katherine's near the Tower, Midd. D: (1) Champion Ashby, merchant, London, part owner of a ship, the *William and Betty*, d2's attorney; (2) Searne Williamson, Norway, R. Menlove's administrator. C: (1) Richard Knapp, counsel for p. Add: (1) Rowland Menlove, mariner, Ratcliffe, Midd, deceased; (2) John Clarke, merchant, London. P seeks payment of a £64 penal bond R. Menlove issued him in 1682 for a £33 5s loan. Menlove later issued a £250 bond with d1 (part owner of a ship, the *William and Betty*) to J. Clarke for the repayment of £127 10s to repair the ship, for which d1 indemnified Menlove & appointed him ship's master. In 1683 Menlove sailed the ship to Guinea & drowned. D2 (Menlove's administrator) issued d1 his power of attorney to receive debts owed to Menlove, & ds now refuse to repay p's bond.

| 1685, Easter | E 112/589 | Bill (with attachments). LMX 60; cf. E 112/589 LMX 68 Nelson v Williamson; inventory attached of R. Menlove's goods on board the ship. |

124. Symons v Watts
P: (1) Thomas Symons, merchant, London, part owner of a ship, the *Success*, lived in Montserrat. D: (1) Stephen Watts, merchant, Bristol, copartner with ds2-3, part owner of the *Success*; (2) Richard Gotley, merchant, Bristol, copartner with d1 & d3, part owner of the *Success*; (3) Edward Perrin, merchant, Bristol, copartner with ds1-2, part owner of the *Success*. C: (1) William Leigh, counsel for p. Add: (1) John Jones, mariner, Bristol, p's attorney; (2) Arthur Hart, merchant, Bristol, arbitrator between p & ds; (3) Robert Henley, merchant, Bristol, arbitrator between p & ds; (4) John Hine, merchant, Bristol, arbitrator between p & ds; (5) Robert Yate, merchant, Bristol, arbitrator between p & ds. P seeks reimbursement of £26 19s 10d from ds after J. Jones, acting on p's behalf, issued ds a general release and paid d2 £72 following arbitration by A. Hart, R. Henley, J. Hine & R. Yate of a dispute between p & ds. P (resident in Montserrat) & ds had sent their ship, the *Success*, to the Caribbean Islands, where p sold it as decayed & unprofitable. Ds threatened to sue for the ship, cargo & damages. P claims ds owe him £26 19s 10d, but ds claim the arbitrators awarded them less than their damages.
1685, Easter   E 112/589   Bill. LMX 62; dated 12 May.

125. Taylor v Bickerton
P: (1) Samuel Taylor, button seller, parish of St. Andrews, Holborn, Midd. D: (1) George Bickerton, merchant, London; (2) Peter Squoles, d3's husband; (3) Anne Squoles, d2's wife, E. Williams's widow & administratrix. C: (1) William Brooke, counsel for p; (2) Thomas Powys, counsel for ds. Add: (1) Edward Williams, tailor, St. Martin in the Fields, Midd, deceased intestate, d3's former husband. P seeks payment of a judgement for £1000 which he had obtained at KB ag E. Williams, who, before paying, died intestate in 1678, leaving his widow & administratrix, d3. P agreed with d3 that he & d1 (another creditor of E. Williams) would collect the debts. P now claims he deposited the articles of agreement with d1 & d3, but d1 conspires with d3 & her new husband d2 to receive the debts & defraud p of his £1000. D1 claims p went bankrupt & his creditors received his assets.

1685, Easter	E 112/598	Bill. LMX 577 (cf. E 112/598 LMX 578 Bickerton v Taylor).
1685, May 12	E 112/598	Affidavit. P swears on this date that he does not possess the articles of agreement he had made with d1 & d3.
1685, June 2	E 112/598	Answer. Swearing date of d1's answer.
1685, June 2	E 112/598	Answer (with attachments). Swearing date of the answer of ds2-3; accounts attached of sums received & paid by E. Williams's estate.

126. Temple v Clayton
P: (1) Thomas Temple, girdler, London, A. Temple's son & administrator; (2) John Temple the younger, vintner, London, A. Temple's son & administrator. D: (1) Sir Robert Clayton, knight, overseer of Lord Loughborough's will; (2) Francis Coles, Lord Loughborough's executor. C: (1) Whitlock Deane, counsel for ps; (2) Edward Ward, counsel for d1. Add: (1) Anne Temple, Ashby de la Zouche, Leics, deceased, ps' mother, widow & administratrix of John Temple

the E; (2) John Temple the elder, sadler, Aderstone, Warw, deceased, ps' father, A. Temple's husband; (3) Rt. Hon. Henry, Lord Hastings, Leics, deceased, Lord Baron of Loughborough. Ps, administrators de bonis non of their father, J. Temple the E (deceased & unadministered by their mother, A. Temple, also deceased), seek payment of £601 19s which Lord Loughborough owed J. Temple the E since the Civil War for goods. Loughborough died in 1666, appointing d2 executor & d1 overseer of his will. Ps got a judgement at KB in 1678 which outlawed d2. D1 claims the debt is old enough to be barred by the statute of limitations.

| 1685, Mich | E 112/594 | Bill. LMX 325. |
| 1685, Nov 25 | E 112/594 | Answer. Swearing date of d1's answer & demurrer. |

127. Thrompton v Gaell

P: (1) Susan Thrompton, Longborough, Leics, J. Monk's mother, sister of J. Ashton & E. Browne. D: (1) George Gaell, Hadley, Suff, W. Gaell's nephew & heir at law; (2) William Abell, W. Gaell's cousin & executor. C: (1) H. Kowes, counsel for p. Add: (1) Roger Gillingham esq., barrister, Middle Temple, London, d in original bill; (2) William Gaell gent., London, deceased, d1's uncle, d in original bill; (3) Henry Penton esq., barrister, Lincoln's Inn, Midd, d in original bill; (4) John Ashton gent., Westminster, London, p's brother; (5) John Monk, deceased, p's son, J. Ashton's nephew, executor & trustee of his realty; (6) Margaret Ashton, J. Ashton's widow; (7) Elizabeth Browne, sister of p & J. Ashton, J. Browne's wife; (8) John Browne, E. Browne's husband. P, a widow, seeks revival ag ds (W. Gaell's nephew & executor) of her 1682 suit in this Court ag R. Gillingham, W. Gaell & H. Penton, for possession of premises left by her brother J. Ashton (deceased in 1665) to his executor & trustee J. Monk (p's son, deceased) to pay an annuity to his widow Margaret (now deceased), & the reversion to go to p & her sister E. Browne (deceased). After the London fire of 1666, Monk conveyed the premises to his tenant R. Gillingham, to pay Margaret's annuity. J. Monk went bankrupt & his interest in the premises was sold to W. Gaell, who, with R. Gillingham & H. Penton, refused to assign p the premises. W. Gaell died & the suit was abated.

| 1685, Hil | E 112/588 | Replication. P's replication to (absent) answers of R. Gillingham & H. Penton (to original bill?). |
| 1685, Hil | E 112/588 | Bill of revivor. LMX 24; attached to E 112/588 LMX 23. |

128. Tooley v Tooley

P: (1) Jacob Tooley, woodmonger, parish of St. Sepulchres, London, d1's son, d2's brother. D: (1) Jane Tooley, mother of p & d2; (2) Elizabeth Tooley, p's sister, d1's daughter. C: (1) John Rowe, counsel for p; (2) Gi. Duncombe, counsel for d2. Add: (1) Ralph Harrupp; (2) Isabell Watson, J. Watson's wife; (3) Joseph Watson, hotpresser, I. Watson's husband; (4) Thomas Lilbourne, Offerton, Durh, deceased, d1's brother, uncle of p & d2. P seeks relief ag d2's suit at KB for payment of a £200 bond. P claims d1 (mother of p & d2) authorised him to receive £300 from R. Harrupp, retain £50 of it, & transfer the rest to I. Watson. D1 intended the £300 for d2's marriage portion, & lent £200 in I. Watson's possession to her husband J. Watson. D2 obtained from J. Watson a bond for the £200. P then borrowed the £200 from J. Watson, which d1 forbids him to pay to d2. D2 claims she inherited the £300 from T. Lilbourne, but d1 had her arrested for the bond.

1685, Trin   E 112/589   Bill. LMX 61; dated 26 June.
1685, July 3   E 112/589   Answer. Swearing date of d2's answer.

129. Troughton v Glenne

P: (1) John Troughton esq., Middle Temple, London, p2's husband; (2) Judith Troughton, Middle Temple, London, p1's wife, W. Zouch's daughter & administratrix; (3) Dorothy Duncombe, St. Pauls, Covent Garden, Midd, J. Wayne's daughter & executrix. D: (1) Mary Glenne, Chesthunt, Herts, T. Glenne's widow & executrix; (2) Edward Mihill, married to a daughter of d1 & T. Glenne. C: (1) Jo. Clapham, counsel for ps. Add: (1) William Zouch gent., solicitor, Lincoln's Inn, Midd, deceased, p2's father; (2) John Wayne, merchant tailor, London, deceased, p3's father; (3) Ralph Thorne, brewer, Hoddesdon, Herts, deceased, son in law of d1 & T. Glenne; (4) Thomas Glenne, brewer, Chesthunt, Herts, deceased, d1's husband. Ps seeks payment of a bill for £77 12s 2d + interest which T. Glenne (deceased) issued J. Wayne (W. Zouch's trustee, deceased) to redeem the goods of his son in law R. Thorne (deceased), who Wayne had sued in 1665 for a £100 bond Thorne owed Zouch (p2's father, deceased) since 1661. P3 (Wayne's daughter & executrix) sued d1 (T. Glenne's widow & executrix) in the Court of Common Pleas, but d1 & her son in law d2 claim T. Glenne had paid Zouch for the bill.

1685, Trin   E 112/589   Bill. LMX 56.
1685, Trin   E 112/589   Copy bill.
1685, Nov 28   E 112/589   Commission. For ds' answer.
1686, Jan 6   E 112/589   Answer. Swearing date of ds' answer.

130. Walbridge v Sparke

P: (1) John Walbridge, St. Hellens within Bishopsgate, London. D: (1) Edward Sparke, vicar, Tottenham Highcross, Midd, doctor in divinity; (2) John Baseley, Tottenham Highcross, Midd, p's tenant. C: (1) Ste. Crimet, counsel for p; (2) Giles Duncombe, counsel for d1. Add: (1) Sir Robert Hanson, Mayor of London, knight, deceased, sold premises to p. P seeks inj ag the suit in this Court of d1 (vicar of Tottenham Highcross) for payment of arrears of tithes from p's premises in the parish. P claims d1 possessed a strip of his land adjoining the vicarage, for which d1 promised to exempt him and his tenants from tithes. D1 denies possessing the strip or exempting p. P claims d1 conspires with d2, p's tenant, to make p pay tithes.

1685, Trin   E 112/598   Bill. LMX 582.
1685, July 21   E 112/598   Answer. Swearing date of d1's answer.

131. Waldrone v Goldsbrough

P: (1) William Waldrone, London, p2's husband; (2) Faith Waldrone, London, p1's wife. D: (1) Robert Goldsbrough, W. Goldsbrough's administrator. C: (1) Giles Duncombe, counsel for ps. Add: (1) William Goldsbrough esq., clerk of parliament, deceased. Ps seek payment of £25 which W. Goldsbrough

47

(deceased) owed p1 for loans, board & lodging in 1683, and £20 which W. Goldsbrough owed p2 from before her marriage to p1. R. Goldsbrough became W. Goldsbrough's administrator, and reportedly claims the estate is insufficient to pay debts, or is now fully administered.

1685, Trin   E 112/591   Bill. LMX 152; dated 11 July on reverse of bill.

132. Walk v White
P: (1) Gregory Walk, merchant, London. D: (1) Bithia White, J. White's widow & administratrix; (2) Thomas Hull, attorney. C: (1) John Goodfellow, counsel for p. Add: (1) John White, scrivener, London, deceased intestate, d1's husband; (2) James Plumer. P seeks inj ag ds' suit for payment of £69 p allegedly owed J. White (deceased intestate in 1683). P claims J. White owed him £150 but that d1, J. White's widow & administratrix, sued him in 1684 in KB for payment for goods. P hired d2 as his attorney, and p & d1 issued each other general releases. P claims at d1's request he paid off a £100 bond J. White owed J. Plumer, but that d1 now sues him to avoid repaying the bond.

1685, Mich   E 112/589   Bill. LMX 75.

133. Walker v Banister
P: (1) Rebecca Walker, T. Walker's sister & administratrix. D: (1) George Banister gent., Leeds, Yorks, T. Walker's executor; (2) William Sawyer, merchant, Leeds, Yorks, T. Walker's executor; (3) Astruphus Danby; (4) William Pocock, merchant; (5) Giles Mathews; (6) James Windus, scrivener, spelled Windows in bill; (7) Robert Stamper, scrivener, spelled Stampert in bill; (8) Robert Christmas; (9) James Hutchenson; (10) Eden Spencer; (11) Elizabeth Hutchenson; (12) Thomas Burbury. C: (1) John Herle, counsel for p; (2) Will Helson ?, counsel for d4; (3) Thomas Fletcher, counsel for ds6-7. Add: (1) Thomas Walker, deceased, bankrupt, p's brother. P, sister & administrator of T. Walker (deceased in 1683) & a spinster, seeks T. Walker's personal estate, money & securities which she claims were entrusted to and possessed by ds. T. Walker appointed ds1-2 his executors, who refused to execute his will, claiming he had failed to pay his creditors a composition agreed in 1674. D4 claims he paid T. Walker's debt, & with d5 became bound for his bail. Ds6-7 deny being entrusted with T. Walker's money.

1685, Mich	E 112/589	Bill. LMX 76.
1685, Mich	E 112/589	Copy bill.
1685, Nov 28	E 112/589	Commission. For answer of ds1-2.
1686, Jan 16	E 112/589	Answer. Swearing date of answer of ds1-2.
1686, Jan 21	E 112/589	Answer. Swearing date of d4's answer.
1686, Jan 23	E 112/589	Answer. Swearing date of answer of ds6-7.

134. Walker v Hind
P: (1) William Walker gent., solicitor, Staple Inn, London. D: (1) Thomas Hind; (2) Thomas Reeve; (3) Anthony Warman; (4) Edward Warman; (5) James Belt, spelled Belke in his answer; (6) William Holland; (7) John Collett; (8) Charles Gilbert; (9) Edward Adams; (10) John Tilton; (11) Thomas Brinde; (12) Richard Blanchard. C: (1) Giles Duncombe, counsel for p; (2) N. Croft, counsel for ds3-7 & d11; (3) William Ettricke, counsel for d12. P, lessee of an ordinance of the Company of the Master, Wardens and Commonalty of the Mystery of Making

Playing Cards to receive fees from the makers of pasteboard, seeks discovery of quantity of pasteboard made by the ds (members of the Company), and appropriate payment. Ds claim payment cannot be exacted from members themselves.
Alternative titles: Walker v Blanchard.

1685, Easter	E 112/589	Bill. LMX 35; dated 13 May.
1685, May 21	E 112/589	Demurrer. D12's demurrer.
1685, Easter	E 112/589	Demurrer. Demurrer of ds3-7 & d11.

135. Watts v Goddard
P: (1) Tomas Watts, blacksmith, London, p2's husband; (2) Joane Watts, London, p1's wife. D: (1) John Goddard, Boxtead, Suff, T. Windle's administrator. C: (1) William Martyn, counsel for ps. Add: (1) Thomas Windle, Long Melford, Suff, deceased. Ps seek payment of a £10 bond which p2 issued to the Crown (with other bonds between 1681-3) as security that T. Windle would pay an annual 50 shilling rent for a wine licence. Windle died without paying the licence so p2 was compelled to pay the £10 bond. D, Windle's administrator, reportedly now refuses to repay p2.

1685, Mich	E 112/590	Bill. LMX 130.

136. Watts v Tilliard
P: (1) John Watts, butcher, Westham, Essex. D: (1) William Tilliard the elder, Colebrooke, Midd, R. Tilliard's executor; (2) Robert Augur, butcher, Westham, Essex; (3) Alice Grane, d2's mother in law, also spelled Gray; (4) John Stone, attorney at law, New Inn, London, d1's attorney; (5) Richard Harvey, Westham, Essex; (6) John Browne, d7's husband; (7) Mary Browne, d6's wife. C: (1) Mo. Bramston, counsel for p. Add: (1) Richard Tilliard, Wansted, Essex, deceased. P seeks relief from the suit of d1 (R. Tilliard's executor) for payment of d2's debt for which p became liable when he (at d3's request) paid d2's bail after d1 had d2 arrested at KB for a debt to R. Tilliard, but d2 absconded without paying the debt. D2 later paid part of the debt with d5, but p claims the ds are conspiring to make him pay the rest.

1685, Easter	E 112/588	Bill. LMX 21.

137. Weston v Adson
P: (1) William Weston gent., Thistleworth, Midd. D: (1) Thomas Adson, vintner, innkeeper, Thistleworth, Midd, d2's husband; (2) Mary Adson, Thistleworth, Midd, d1's wife. C: (1) Paul Pulling, counsel for p. P seeks repayment of £20 which ds borrowed from him in 1683. D1 reportedly promised to issue p a bond as security, which ds now refuse to do, or deny they ever borrowed the money.

1685, Easter	E 112/589	Bill. LMX 69; dated 6 April.

138. Whitehall v Peake
P: (1) Gilbert Whitehall, goldsmith, London. D: (1) Benjamin Peake, merchant, London. C: (1) Robert Brent, counsel for p; (2) G. Evan, counsel for d. Add: (1) Isaac Meynell, goldsmith, London, deceased; (2) John Grimes, goldsmith, London, deceased. P seeks inj ag d's suit for payment of remainder of £2000 bond issued in 1671 by p, I. Meynell and J. Grimes (both deceased). P claims

he had only paid back £400 in 1684, but d promised not to sue for a year if p paid another £100. D claims p was also supposed to pay quarterly interest on the bond, and that p is well able to pay the bond.

| 1685, Easter | E 112/588 | Bill. LMX 28. |
| 1685, Oct 21 | E 112/588 | Answer. Swearing date of d's answer. |

139. Whitfield v Rackett

P: (1) Nathaniell Whitfield gent., parish of St. James, Westminster, Midd; (2) John Cove, jeweller, parish of St. Bridget, London, p3's husband; (3) Sarah Cove, parish of St. Bridget, London, p2's wife; (4) John Morgan gent., Cashalton, Surrey; (5) Walter Tandy, refiner, Cripplegate, London; (6) John Hinson, yeoman, St. Ives, Hunts; (7) John Halstead the elder gent., Woodhurst, Hunts; (8) Job Halstead gent., Woodhurst, Hunts; (9) Samuell Urhn, goldsmith, Cambs; (10) Robert Rawlins, yeoman, Cashalton, Surrey; (11) William Sallis, victualler, St. Dunstans in the West, Midd. D: (1) Michael Rackett, glassman, White Chapel, Midd, J. Rackett's nephew. C: (1) John Richardson, counsel for ps' bill; (2) Edward Ward, counsel for ps' replication. Add: (1) Robert Gregory, goldsmith, St. Giles without Cripplegate, London, deceased, J. Gregory's husband; (2) Jane Gregory, deceased intestate, R. Gregory's widow & executrix, previously J. Rackett's widow & executrix; (3) John Rackett, deceased, J. Gregory's previous husband, d's uncle. Ps seek payment of legacies willed to them by R. Gregory (deceased in 1684), who left J. Gregory (deceased intestate in 1685) his widow & executrix. J. Gregory lodged & died in d's house. D claims J. Gregory's estate came not from R. Gregory but from her previous husband, d's uncle, J. Rackett (deceased), who left her executrix of his estate in trust for his relatives. D asserts J. Gregory demised her estate to him.

1685, Mich	E 112/589	Bill. LMX 74.
[1685, undated]	E 112/589	Answer. D's answer, undated, incomplete.
1685, Mich	E 112/589	Replication. Ps' replication maintains R. Gregory's estate is sufficient to pay their legacies.

140. Wigan v Kerton

P: (1) William Wigan, clerk, vicar, parish of Kensington, Midd. D: (1) Richard Kerton, Kensington, Midd; (2) William Kerton, Kensington, Midd. C: (1) Edm. Gyles, counsel for p. P, vicar of the parish of Kensington entitled to small tithes & 1/2 the great tithes, seeks payment for arrears of tithes from ds who occupy parish land but have not paid tithes.

| 1685, Mich | E 112/591 | Bill. LMX 132; dated 27 October. |

141. Wilkins v Webster

P: (1) William Wilkins, innholder, London; (2) Anthony Langford, victualler, London. D: (1) Grace Webster, E. Webster the E's widow & executrix; (2) William Brookes esq.; (3) Samuel Dodd esq.; (4) Matthew Petley; (5) John Johnson; (6) Thomas Foster; (7) Thomas Stoakes; (8) Joseph Anger, d9's agent; (9) Thomas Anger; (10) Ralph Bowes, E. Webster the E's brother & overseer of his will; (11) Uriah Bowes, E. Webster the E's brother & overseer of his will; (12) Samuel Webster, E. Webster the E's son; (13) Edward Webster the younger, E. Webster the E's son; (14) Ralph Webster, E. Webster the E's son; (15) William Webster, E. Webster the E's son; (16) Martha Webster, E. Webster the E's daughter; (17) Elizabeth Webster, E. Webster the E's daughter; (18) John Hill. C: (1) William Abell, counsel for ps; (2) Francis Browne, counsel for ds10-11 & d18; (3) William Brooke, counsel for ds8-9 & ds13-17; (4) E. Farnham, counsel for ds2-7. Add: (1) Edward Webster the elder, goldsmith, London, deceased, d1's husband. Ps seek payment of bonds totalling £400 owed to them by E. Webster the E, who died in 1675 leaving legacies to his children ds12-17, with d1 as his widow & executrix, & ds10-11 as overseers of his will. Ps claim d1 was to pay E. Webster the E's debts from a brewhouse, which she mortgaged to d18 instead. D1 went bankrupt at the suit of her creditors ds8-9, & a commn was awarded ag her to ds2-7, who seized the estate. Ds10-11 claim E. Webster the E owed them debts; ds13-17 deny receiving their legacies & claim the estate was small.

1685, Easter	E 112/589	Bill. LMX 49.
1685, Oct 27	E 112/589	Answer. Swearing date of d18's answer.
1685, Nov 20	E 112/589	Answer. Swearing date of d11's answer.
1686, Jan 29	E 112/589	Answer. Swearing date of answer of ds8-9, & ds13-17 by Mathias Holtropp, their guardian.
1686, Feb 1	E 112/589	Answer (with attachments). Swearing date of d10's answer; inventory attached of d1's goods seized by commissioners for excise owed by the brewhouse.
1686, June 20	E 112/589	Answer. Answer of d2, d5 & d7 & the disclaimer of ds3-4 & d6; sworn by d2, ds4-5 & d7 on this date, by d6 on 21 June 1686, & by d3 on 27 November 1686.
1686, Oct 25	E 112/589	Further answer. Swearing date of d18's further answer.

142. Williams v Cusson

P: (1) Elizabeth Williams, J. Williams's daughter and executrix. D: (1) Alexander Cusson gent., d2's husband; (2) Mary Cusson, d1's wife, H. Wells's widow and executrix. C: (1) Richard Holford, counsel for p. Add: (1) John Williams, stationer, St. Paul's Church yard, London, deceased, p's father; (2) Hugh Wells gent., deceased, d2's former husband; (3) Phillip Brace gent., solicitor, Furnivall Inn, London, H. Wells's trustee & overseer of his will. P, executrix of J. Williams (deceased) & a spinster, seeks cancellation of a £50 bond allegedly owed by Williams to H. Wells (deceased), whose widow and executrix d2 and her new husband d1 have obtained a verdict in the Court of Common Pleas ag p for payment. P claims the bond is 30 years old and has already been paid off.

1685, Trin	E 112/589	Bill. LMX 53.
1685, Oct 16	E 112/589	Answer. Swearing date of ds' answer.

143. Wilson v Walker

P: (1) Thomas Wilson, cordwainer, parish of St. Clements Dane, Midd. D: (1) Alexander Walker, distiller, St. Giles in the Fields, Midd, J. Beane's brother in law & administrator; (2) Alice Ryder, St. Pauls, Covent Garden, Midd; (3) Mary Hargrave. C: (1) John Twisleton, counsel for p; (2) E. Sabbs, counsel for ds. Add: (1) John Beane, cordwainer, St. Martin in the Fields, Midd, deceased. P seeks inj ag any suit of the ds for possession of goods & chattels p claims J. Beane (deceased) gifted to him. P, Beane's apprentice, claims he cared for Beane on his deathbed. D1, Beane's brother in law & administrator, claims Beane made a nuncupavit will leaving everything to d1 to pay his debts to ds2-3, & denies Beane was of sound mind if he made p such a deed of gift.

| 1685, Easter | E 112/589 | Bill. LMX 33. |
| 1685, June 19 | E 112/589 | Answer. Swearing date of ds' answer. |

144. Winchester v Pigott

P: (1) William Winchester, porter, Serjeant's Inn, Fleet St., London. D: (1) Elizabeth Pigott, A. Pigott's widow & administratrix; (2) Nathaniell Pigott gent., St. Clement Danes, Midd, A. Pigott's son & heir; (3) Edward Griffin gent., Drury Lane, Westminster, London. C: (1) Edward Ward, counsel for p. Add: (1) Adam Pigott, cutler, London, deceased intestate, d1's husband, d2's father; (2) Richard Audley gent., Hammersmith, Midd, insolvent. P seeks payment of £100 bond that R. Audley & A. Pigott issued p in return for a £50 loan in 1682. Audley went insolvent & absconded, and A. Pigott died intestate leaving d1 his widow & administratrix and d2 his son & heir, who claim A. Pigott settled his realty on d2 before p's debt, or that the bond is fraudulent, or the estate is insufficient to pay debts. P also asserts d3 conducted business in trust for A. Pigott.

| 1685, Easter | E 112/589 | Bill. LMX 51; dated 25 April. |

145. Wolstenholme v Turner

P: (1) Sir Thomas Wolstenholme, Sir J. Wolstenholme's son & executor; (2) Thomas Wolstenholme esq., barrister, Inner Temple, London, Dr L. Wright's administrator. D: (1) Sir Edmund Turner, husband of Sir J. Harrison's daughter, farmer of the customs; (2) Richard Harrison esq., Balls, Herts, Sir J. Harrison's son & executor. C: (1) Henry Trinder, counsel for ps. Add: (1) Sir John Wolstenholme, deceased, p1's father, member of the House of Commons, farmer of the customs; (2) Sir John Harrison, deceased, bankrupt, d2's father, member of the House of Commons, farmer of the customs; (3) Sir Paul Pinder, member of the House of Commons, farmer of the customs; (4) Sir Thomas Dawes, member of the House of Commons, farmer of the customs; (5) Sir John Jacob, member of the House of Commons, farmer of the customs; (6) Lady Vere; (7) Dr Lawrence Wright, deceased, Lady Vere's trustee. Ps seek reimbursement of sums p1's father Sir J. Wolstenholme (farmer of the customs under Charles I, bankrupt & imprisoned during the Commonwealth) was compelled to pay as a signatory of bonds issued by Sir J. Harrison, Sir P. Pinder, Sir T. Dawes & Sir J. Jacob (also farmers of the customs) for £150,000 fine to the Crown. In addition, J. Harrison borrowed £50,000 from Sir J. Wolstenholme, who also repaid the farmers' £2000 debt to Lady Vere & her trustee Dr L. Wright (deceased). Charles II issued £200,000 compensation to the farmers, who refused to reimburse Sir J. Wolstenholme, who died leaving p1 as executor. P2 became L. Wright's administrator.

| 1685, Trin | E 112/588 | Bill (with attachments). LMX 23; mistakenly attached to E 112/588 LMX 24; schedule |

attached of Sir J. Wolstenholme's creditors; cf. E 112/589 LMX 58 Harrison v Wolstenhome.

146. Wolstenholme v Turner
P: (1) Sir Thomas Wolstenholme, bart., Sir J. Wolstenholme's son; (2) Thomas Wolstenholme esq., solicitor, Inner Temple, London. D: (1) Sir Edmund Turner, knight, Sir J. Harrison's son-in-law; (2) Richard Harrison esq., Sir J. Harrison's son & executor. C: (1) Henry Trinder, counsel for ps; (2) F. Panton, counsel for ds. Add: (1) Sir John Harrison, deceased, farmer of the customs, d2's father, d1's father in law; (2) Sir John Wolstenholme, deceased, p1's father, farmer of the customs; (3) Sir Paul Pindar, deceased, farmer of the customs. Ps seek payment of sums allegedly owed to p1's father, Sir J. Wolstenholme, farmer of the customs. In 1641 Sir J. Harrison (with others) lent Parliament £50,000, with p1's father & Sir P. Pindar as surety. P1's father also acted as surety for bonds issued by the other farmers of the customs, who (with others) took out a commn of bankruptcy in 1653 ag p1's father for the bonds & seized his estate. Ps also claim the farmers retained Sir J. Wolstenholme's share of the reimbursement for the customs from Parliament. Ps have got a judgement at cl ag Sir J. Harrison's son & executor d2 for the sums. Ds claim Sir J. Wolstenholme was justly liable for the customs.

1685, Mich	E 112/590	Bill (with attachments). LMX 109; list attached of commissioners for the bankruptcy of p1's father.
1686, Feb 8	E 112/590	Answer (with attachments). Swearing date of ds' answer; schedule attached of bonds owed by the farmers of the customs.

147. Wordell v Chipp
P: (1) John Wordell gent., Totnam, Midd. D: (1) Thomas Chipp, chirurgion, Totnam, Midd; (2) Margaret Haynes, Christchurch, Hants, d1's mother in law. C: (1) John Danyell, counsel for p; (2) Edward Ward, counsel for ds. Add: (1) Elizabeth Bryant, Totnam, Midd. P seeks relief ag d2's suit for possession of p's mortgaged premises in Suffolk & payment of an £800 judgement. P, a prisoner in KB on a separate issue, claims d1, his former partner in the malt trade, retained p's profits & persuaded p to issue d2 (d1's mother in law) the mortgage & an £800 judgement in KB as security for a £400 loan. Ds allegedly never paid the loan, sold p's goods to E. Bryant & now sue p for the mortgage & judgement. Ds claim d2 paid p the loan, & that p owed d1 debts.

1685, Mich	E 112/591	Bill. LMX 136 (cf. E 112/591 LMX 135 Bryant v Wordell).
1686, Jan 27	E 112/591	Answer (with attachments). Swearing date of d1's answer; account of p's debts to d1 attached.
1686, April 17	E 112/591	Answer. Swearing date of d2's answer.

148. Worrall v Austin
P: (1) William Worrall gent., St. Giles without Cripplegate, Midd. D: (1) Jonathan Austin, husband of d5's mother; (2) Isaac Tayler, d5's next friend in

53

answer; (3) Robert Clerke, d4's husband; (4) Frances Clerke, d3's wife; (5) Cressey Eaton, W. Eaton's nephew, under 21 years, with d2 as next friend; (6) William Bellamy, attorney, in the Sheriff's Court of London; (7) Leonard Scott, scrivener. C: (1) Ambrose Phillipps, counsel for d1. Add: (1) William Eaton gent., Luton, Beds, deceased, intestate, d5's uncle, M. Burton's brother; (2) Margaret Burton, W. Eaton's sister & administratrix; (3) William Foster, doctor of laws, judge of Bedford Ecclesiastical Court. P seeks relief ag any suits of ds for payment of bonds & a counter bond. In 1677 W. Eaton died intestate leaving M. Burton his sister & administratrix, & nephew d5 (a minor). D1, d5's stepfather, hired p to sue M. Burton in the Bedford Ecclesiastical Court for d5's share of W. Eaton's estate. P & ds1-2 issued W. Foster (the judge) 2 £100 bonds, & d1's indemnity of M. Burton ag future creditors of W. Eaton, in return for £102 (d5's share). £50 of the share was deposited with p, who issued d2 a £200 counter bond, & d5 a £100 bond. P claims ds threaten to sue him for the bonds.

1685, Easter	E 112/588	Bill. LMX 17; documents damaged.
1685, April 20	E 112/588	Answer. Swearing date of answer of d2, d4 & d5 (with d2 as next friend).
1685, May 26	E 112/588	Answer. Swearing date of d1's answer.

149. Yardley v Say

P: (1) William Yardley, infant under 21 years, p2's son; (2) John Yardley, parish of St. Andrews Holborn, Midd, p1's father and guardian. D: (1) Robert Say, doctor of divinity, provost of Oriel College, Oxford; (2) Anne Hopkins, W. Hopkins's sister. C: (1) Paul Pullein, counsel for p. Add: (1) William Hopkins, city of Oxford, Oxon, deceased, A. Hopkins's brother. P1, under 21 years, seeks payment of £200 & an estate copyhold of St. John's College, Oxford, (left for him by W. Hopkins, deceased to his father & guardian p2 until p1's majority). W. Hopkins left d1 his executor & d2 his sister, who ps claim refuse to pay the legacy. D1 claims he is willing to lend the £200 at interest for p1 if this Court approves security to indemnify him ag any loss of the sum.

1685, Easter	E 112/589	Bill. LMX 71; dated 1 June.
1685, Easter	E 112/589	Copy bill.
1685, June 1	E 112/589	Commission. For d1's answer.
1685, June 25	E 112/589	Answer. Swearing date of d1's answer.

150. Yoakley v Dandy

P: (1) Michael Yoakley, mariner, St. Katherine's near the Tower, London, T. Yoakley's brother. D: (1) Elizabeth Dandy, A. Dandy's widow; (2) Susanna Yoakley, T. Yoakley's widow; (3) John Rowse; (4) Margaret Coleburne; (5) Jacob Grove; (6) John Milward; (7) Hester Neflock. C: (1) Geo. Fetteplace, counsel for p; (2) Ro. Blayney, counsel for d1 & d7. Add: (1) Thomas Yoakley, deceased, p's brother, d2's husband; (2) Andrew Dandy, merchant tailor, London, deceased, d1's husband. P seeks relief from payment of a £25 annuity or £400 bond. In 1668 p's brother T. Yoakley (deceased) & his wife d2 demised a leasehold messuage in Debtford and a 1/2 share of a leasehold messuage in Stepney to A. Dandy (deceased) & his wife d1. A. Dandy leased the premises back to T. Yoakley & d2 for a £25 annuity with security of a £400 bond issued with d3. P owned the other 1/2 of the Stepney messuage & claims since

T. Yoakley's death in 1677 he has mistakenly paid d1 the annuity. D1 claims d2 assigned T. Yoakley's premises to p in trust to pay d1 the annuity, & d1 has instructed p's tenants ds4-7 to pay the rent to her.

1685, Mich   E 112/590   Bill. LMX 105.

1685, Nov 16   E 112/590   Answer. Swearing date of answer of d1 & d7.

151. Young v Maggott

P: (1) Henry Young, St. Buttolphs, Bishopsgate, London. D: (1) George Maggott, brewer. C: (1) John Fisher, counsel for p. Add: (1) Mary Young, St. Buttolphs, Bishopsgate, London, p's wife. P seeks inj ag d's suit at the Court of Common Pleas for payment of an alleged £20 debt p owes d. P claims while he was overseas in his late Majesty's service, his wife Mary ran a victualling house, and bought beer from d for which she paid in full.

1685, Easter   E 112/589   Bill. LMX 32.

INDEX TO PLEADINGS, 1685–6
NAMES

Beck, John, merchant, 71
Bellamy, William, attorney, 148
Belt, James, 134
Belwood, William, merchant, 111
Bennett
  –, 77
  Elizabeth, 9
  George, 10
  James, 9
  John, tanner, 9
  Mary, 9
  Richard, 10
  Thomas the elder, tanner, 9
  Thomas the younger,
    cheesemonger, 9
Berkeley, Hon. George, Earl of, 70
Bernard, John, 87
Berry, Samuell, carpenter, 82
Bertie
  Nicholas, 11
  Peregrine, 11
Beverley
  Anthony, 57
  John, vintner, 57
Bickerton, George, merchant, 12, 125
Biggs, William, carpenter, 34
Bignall, Michael, scrivener, 34
Birkhead
  Edward, timber merchant, 76
  Thomas, 5
Birt, Richard, mariner, 13
Bishopp, Richard, carpenter, 34
Blackam, Richard, clothworker, 1
Blackborne, Rowland, 120
Blacke, John, pipe borer, 34
Blackerby, Samuel, 30
Blanchard, Richard, 134
Bland, John, merchant tailor, 18
Blaney, Isaac, mariner, 14
Blayney, Ro., 150
Bonham
  Ann(e), 72, 73
  Margaret, 72
  Thomas, 72, 73
Bonifield, Daniell, 5
Bonnett, William, 110
Bonwicke, Benjamin, 39
Boone
  Mary, 63
  Richard, vintner, 63
  William, 63
Booth, Richard, merchant, 15, 16
Bostock, Frances, 1
Bowd
  Adlord the elder, draper, 17
  Adlord the younger, draper, 17
  Isaac, draper, 17
Bowes,
  Ralph, 141
  Uriah, 141

Bowles
  Anne, 118
  William, 118
Bowring, Ranulph, 65
Brace, Phillip, solicitor, 142
Bradford, William, 48, tailor, 82
Brailsford, Peter, 1
Bramston, Mo., 136
Brandon, John, framework knitter, 18
Brattell, Sir John, essay master of the Royal
  Mint, 113
Brees, Underhill, 66Brent, Robert, 138
Brereton
  Ralph, 19
  Richard, 19
Brewster, Samuel, solicitor, 65
Briant, John, 113
Brinde, Thomas, 134
Brock, Howard the younger, 94
Brooke, Brookes, W., William, 12, 19, 88,
  125, 141
Brooker, Joseph, pewterer, 20
Broome, John, 21
Brown(e)
  Anne, 97
  Edward, clerk, 97
  Elizabeth, 21, 127
  Francis, 13, 19, 30, 32, 52, 74, 122, 141
  Henry, solicitor, 91
  John, 127, 136
  Mary, 136
  Thomas, 21, scrivener, 59
Bryant, Elizabeth, 22, 147
Buckerfield, William, 88
Buckle, Robert, 103
Buckmaster, Joseph, 66
Bucknall
  John, 23
  Ralph, 23
Buckworth, Sir John, 113
Bull
  –, 82
  Richard, 54
Bullock
  Elizabeth, 48
  Joseph, 48
Burbury, Thomas, 133
Burt, Thomas, 34
Burton
  Deborah, 65
  Francis, milliner, 65
  Margaret, 148
Butcher, John, 107

Cabourne, Elianora, 110
Caple, Edward, goldsmith, 58
Carlisle, Rt. Hon. Edward,
  Earl of, 65
Carlton, Edward, 65
Cary, Nicholas, goldsmith, 58

Castle
 Mary, 25
 Richard, yeoman, 25
Catlyn, Richard, 39
Chace, Robert, 24
Chancellor
 Jane, 25
 Marke, joiner, 25
 Rebecca, 25
Chandler, John, goldsmith, 62
Charl(e)ton
 Stephen, barrister 34
 Susanna, 34, 36
Cherry
 Richard, vintner, 26
 William, 21, 59, 101
Chevall, William, 111
Chickley, Sir John, 82
Child, Sir Josiah, merchant, 117
Chipp, Chipps, Thomas, chirurgion, 22, 147
Chizard, James, attorney at law, 65
Christmas, Robert, 133
Chudleigh, Hugh, 114
Church
 –, 74
 Henry, 74
Clapham, Jo., 129
Clarke
 John, looking-glass maker, 3
 John, merchant, 81, 123
 Mary, 27
 Richard, wire drawer, 27
 Samuel, 5
Clayton, Sir Robert, 126
Clements, Mathew, 5
Clendon, John, 120
Clerke
 Frances, 148
 Robert, 148
Clowes, Robert, 97
Coape
 Henry, mercer, 28
 Samuell, mercer, 28
Cocke, Mary, 2, 4
Colborne, Robert, 113
Cole, Nicholas, 1
Coleburne, Margaret, 150
Coleman
 Elizabeth, 112
 John, merchant, 67
Coles, Francis, 126
Coling, John, 103, 104
Collard, Richard,109. Monier of his
 Majesty's mint, 113
Collett
 –, 21
 John, 134
Collier, Thomas, 5
Coney, William, merchant, 101
Coningsby, Humphry, 34

Cook
 Arthur, currier, 58
 John, labourer, 34
 R., 76
 Thomas, goldsmith, 58
Cooper, Thomas, fishmonger, 26
Coopestake, John, 46
Cope
 Mary, 44
 William, ship's captain, 44
Copley, Lionell, 69
Couldinge, Edward, 85
Courtney
 Nicholas, 39
 Peter, attorney, 60
Cove
 John, jeweller, 139
 Sarah, 139
Cox, James, 88
Cozens, 82
Craske, William, victualler, 62
Crawford, P., 1, 11
Crawford?, F., 50
Craycroft, Henry, 45
Crimet, Ste., 130
Crisp, Stephen, mercer, 119
Croft, N., 134
Crouch, Edward, 5
Cupper, Mathias, linen draper, 95
Cusson
 Alexander, 142
 Mary, 142

Dallow
 Edward, glassware maker, 29
 John, glassware maker, 29
 Phillip, glassware maker, 29
Danby, Astruphus, 133
Dandy
 Andrew, merchant tailor, 150
 Elizabeth, 150
Daniel(l), Danyell
 Anne, 30
 Jo., 22
 John, 147
 Sir Peter, 50
Dann, John, scrivener, 1
Darbyshire
 John, 74
 Martha, 74
Darnall, Ra., 6
Davis, Davies
 Benjamin the elder, 31
 Benjamin the younger, chirurgeon, 31
 Ellen, 120
 M., 115
 Richard, 31
Dawes
 Nicholas, merchant, 32
 Sir Thomas, 145

Harwell
 Edward, 74
 Elizabeth, 74
 John, 74
 Mary, 74
Hasler, Peter, 7
Hastings, Rt. Hon. Henry, Lord, 126
Hatchett, Ann, 38
Hathersich, Job, mercer, 56
Hatsell, Henry, 12, 48, 50, 58, 82
Hatton, George, tiler, bricklayer, 34
Haughton, John, attorney at law, 26
Hawes, Nathaniell, 106
Hawles, John, 75
Hayes, William, bailiff for St. Clements
  Danes, 60
Haynes, Margaret, 147
Hayter, Charnell, 15
Heames, John, 15, 98
Heath, Isaac, merchant, 32
Heber, Reginald, merchant, 87
Hell, William, 65
Helson ?, Will, 133
Hely,
 –, 20
 J., Jo., John, 33,
  67, 90, 114
Henley
 Sir Andrew the elder, 96
 Sir Andrew the younger, 96
 Robert, merchant, 124
Hensley, Joseph, cooper, 57
Herle, John, 133
Hewes, William, 121
Hick(e)s
 Sir Michael, 59
 Dame Susannah, 59
 Sir William, 59, 86
Hiett, William, merchant, 1
Higgins, Baldwin, 73
Hildegard, Edward, 1
Hill
 Daniell, linen draper, 44
 John, 141
Hilliard, Thomas, merchant, 58
Hind, Thomas, 134
Hine, John, merchant, 124
Hinson, John, yeoman, 139
Hoare, James, comptroller of the Royal Mint,
  113
Hobart, Edward, solicitor, 94
Holford, Richard, 52, 56, 82, 142
Holland, William, 134
Hollis, John, 32
Holmes, Isabell, 99
Hopkins
 Anne, 149
 William, 149
Hordesnell, J, 14
Horne, Joseph, merchant, 95
Houghton, S., 116

How
 Sir Richard, 59
 Dame Sarah, 59
Howard
 –, 82
 Edward, mariner, 14
 John, smith, farrier, 62
 Mary, 14
 Valentine, 53
Howes, Timothy, carpenter, 34
Hoyle, Samuel, scrivener, 64
Hughes, John, draper, 60
Huling
 Benjamin, 94
 William, 94
Hull, Thomas, attorney, 132
Humphry(e)s
 Edward, broker, 42
 Mary, 139
Hunt
 John, tobacco-pipe maker, 37
 Thomas, 109, Monier of his Majesty's
  mint, 113
Huntingford, John, 5
Hutchenson
 Elizabeth, 133
 James, 133

Ironsides
 Margaret, 10
 Ralph, doctor in physic, 10
Isaacson, Radolph, 61

Jackson, Abraham, 98
Jacob, Sir John, 145
Jansen, Piter, smith at the Royal Mint, 113
Jeffryes, Robert, bricklayer, 51
Jeliffe, John, factor, 93
Jenings
 Sarah, 62
 William, 62
Jenkins, John, 96
Jenner, Thomas, 10, 68, 106, 115, 117
Jephson, Thomas, girdler, 65
Jeyne
 Francis, goldsmith, 100
 Henry, captain of a regiment of foot
  soldiers, 100
Jobson, William, 40
Johnson
 John, 141
 Sa., 55
Johnston, John, 65
Jolley, Thomas, tailor, 84
Jollife, William, merchant, 1
Jones
 Edm., 20
 Dr. Henry, 10
 John, mariner, 124
 Thomas, 46

Jordan, Alice, 82

Keck, Samuel, 54
Keeling
  Lady, 82
  Thomas, barber surgeon, 63
Keightley, Thomas, 89
Kerton
  Richard, 140
  William, 140
Kettlewell
  Bridget, 53
  Robert, bookseller, 53
Kewids
  Abraham, dyer, 74
  Mary, 74
Kift, Henry, stationer, 1
Kilboe, William, 31
Kilburne, Thomas, goldsmith, 58
Killingworth, W., William, 1, 47, 67, 94, 96, 121
King
  David, clothworker, 34
  John, 88
  Sarah, 64
Kingsbury, 82
Kingsman, Jason, 17
Kinsey, Thomas, vintner, 69
Knapp,
  Nicholas, 25
  Nicholas the elder, 25
  Nicholas the younger, 25
  Rich. Richard, 25, 81, 85, 123
Knowles, Israel, carpenter, 34
Kowes, H., 127

Lambert, Edward, scrivener, 46
Lambly, John, mariner, 91
Langford, Anthony, victualler, 141
Langham, John, grocer, 121
Langrish
  Barrell, milliner, 65
  Gilbert, 65
Lattimer, John, cook, 43
Launder, James, 5
Lauthorne, John, joiner, 84
Lawrenson, Thomas, 92
Lechmere, R., 18, 109
Lee, Abraham, 49
Leigh, William, 124
Letchington, John, 101
Lewin
  Daniel, 66
  Edmund, 66
  Margaret, 66
Lewis, Francis, 139
Lightfoot, William, 138
Lilb(o)urne
  George, druggist, 67
  Thomas, 128
Lindsay, John, goldsmith, 24

Lister
  Frances, 68
  Mathew, 68
Litton, Rowland, 69
Lloyd, Edward, solicitor, 1
London, Mayor and Aldermen, 108
London, William, merchant, 96
Love
  Barnaby, clerk, 70
  Edward, 70
  William, merchant, 1
Lowe, John, merchant, 32
Lowfield, Thomas, mercer, 59
Lowman, Christopher, keeper of King's
  Palace Court prison, 83
Ludlam, George, salter, 1
Ludlie, Theophilus, carpenter, 34
Ludlow,
  Edmund, 71
  Dame Elizabeth, 71
  Nathaniell, 71
Luffton, Edmund, brewer, 5
Lumley, Lady, 82
Lyford
  Anne, 80
  Robert, 29
  Thomas, 80
Lyng, Thomas, 40

Maggott, George, brewer, 151
Major, Thomas, mercer, 72
Malthus, William, 107
Mann, Nicholas, solicitor, 13
Manning
  Edward, 72, 73
  Mary, 82
  Thomas, 48, 82
Markham, Christopher, bailiff for St. Clement
  Danes, 60
Martin, Joseph, merchant, 53
Martyn, William, 135
Mason, Cawen, 56
Massey, Elias, glass maker, 139
Mathew
  Elizabeth, 74
  John, 74
  Nathaniell the elder, 74
  Nathaniell the younger, 74
  Thomas, 74
Mathews, Giles, 133
Maynard
  Gabriel, 75
  John, 75
  Thomas, yeoman, 75
Mechum
  Phillis, 99
  Robert, 99
Menlove, Rowland, mariner, 81, 123
Merrett, Rob., 83
Merriott, Dr, 82

Sawyer
  (Sir) Robert, Attorney General, 32, 105, 106. 107, 108, 109, 110, 113
  William, merchant, 133
Say, Robert, doctor of divinity, 149
Scott
  Bartholomew, lighterman, 34, 85
  Francis, 110
  Leonard, scrivener, 148
  Thomas, carpenter, 34
Seares Robert, 109, Monier of his Majesty's mint, 113
Searne
  Mary, 13
  Richard, boatswain, 13
Selby, James, 63
Seys, Evan, mariner, 111
Shatterden
  Dorothy, 98
  Drax, 98
Shaw
  Sir John the elder, 61
  Sir John the younger, 6
  Jonathan, scrivener, 82
  Richard, 90
Sheffield, Richard, armourer, 34
Shenton
  Alexander, 113
  William, 113
Shepley, Daniel, clothworker, 1
Shipman, William, apothecary, 1
Shirton, Edward, 109. 113
  (Monier of his Majesty's mint)
Short
  Alice, 72
  William, cheesemonger, 72
Shute
  Margaret, 56
  Zachary, linen draper, 56
Shuttleworth, George, 23
Silk, Robert, gunmaker, 139
Simpson, Isabella, wiredrawer, 112
Skipwith, Thomas, 11
Slingsby,
  Anthony, 113
  Henry, 79, 109, 113
Smallpeece, Giles, sadler, 38
Smith
  –, 120
  Dennis, merchant, 37
  George, wheelwright, 115
  James, 80
  John, baker, 139
  John, merchant, 114
  John, yeoman, 115
  Richard, apothecary, 8
  Thomas, 5, 116
  Thomas, butcher, 115
  William, 116

Smyth
  Edward, 23
  Sir James, 117
Snapp, Richard, 75
Solby
  George, apothecary, 118
  Thomas, 118
Soper
  Charles, draper, 119
  Mary, 119
Sparke, Edward, vicar, 130
Spencer
  –, 82
  Eden, 133
Spicer
  David, 50
  Elizabeth, 50
Squoles
  Anne, 12, 125
  Peter, 12, 125
Stamper, Robert, scrivener, 133
Stanney
  Edward, 122
  Percivall, 122
  Timothy, 122
Sterling
  James, 24
  Mary, 24
Stevens, Anne, 70
Stiles, Thomas, grocer, 121
Stoakes, Thomas, 141
Stockdell, 82
Stone
  John, attorney 76, 136
  Thomas, mariner, 102
Stor(e)y, Samuel, merchant, 15, 16
Stoughton
  Hannah, 122
  Humphrey, tailor, 122
Stretchley, Thomas, 106
Strong, Joseph, goldsmith, 123
Studd
  Ralph, 50
  Rebecca, 50
Suckley, Francis, innholder, 57
Sutton
  Christopher, 109, Monier of his Majesty's mint, 113
  Thomas, 47
Swallow, Thomas, 113
Symons, Thomas, merchant, 124

Tandy, Walter, refiner, 139
Tanner
  John, merchant, 19
  Richard, baker, 62
Tasker, John, salter, 34
Tayler, Taylor
  Isaac, 148
  Samuel, button seller, 12, 125
  Thomas, 70

Samuel, 141
William, 141
William, dyer, 1
Weldon, Anthony, 94
Wells, Hugh, 142
Weoly, Richard, barber,
    chirurgeon, 119
Weston
    John, 86
    William, 137
Weymondesold, Thomas, 107
Wheatly, William, 95
Wheeler
    Charles, goldsmith, 122
    Richard, hosier, 122
Whichcot, Jeremy, merchant, 1
Whiddon, Jacob, 65
White
    –, 2
    Bithia, 132
    Henry, merchant tailor, 139
    Jeremiah, 90
    John, scrivener, 132
Whitehall, Gilbert, goldsmith, 138
Whitelocke, C., 96
Whitfield
    Mary, 68
    Nathaniell, 139
    Timothy, barrister, 68
Wickins, Stephen, 34
Wigan, William, clerk, vicar, 140
Wightman, Thomas the younger, 1
Wilder, James, 109, Monier of his Majesty's
    mint, 113
Wilkins, William, innholder, 141
Wilkinson
    Francis the elder, 88
    Francis the younger, 88
    John, 65
    Mary, 88
William
    Edward, tailor, 12, 125
    Elizabeth, 142
    Frances, 35
    John, stationer, 142
    Nathaniel, clerk, 35
    W., 36, 37, 86
Williamson, Searne, 81, 123
Willymot, James, 97
Wilson
    Charles, attorney, 78

Hannah, 84
Orlebar, solicitor, 69
Thomas, cordwainer, 143
Winchcombe, J., 78
Winchester, William, porter, 144
Windle, Thomas, 135
Windus, James, scrivener, 133
Winnington, Francis, 48, 91
Winter, Daniel, 47
Wise, John, clockmaker, 1
Witharidge, George, 106
Wittewronge, Ja., 31
Wogan, William, 84
Wolstenholme
    Sir John, 52, 145, 146
    Sir Thomas, 52, 145, 146
    Thomas, 52
    Thomas, barrister, 145
    Thomas, solicitor, 146
Wordell, John, 22, 147
Worrall, William, 148
Wray, John, yeoman, 115
Wright
    –, 82
    Edmond, merchant, 101
    Lawrence, 52, 145
Wyatt, Edwin, 72, 73
Wybourne
    Elizabeth, 16
    Isaac, 16
Wymondesold, Richard, tobacconist, 16
Wynne, Edward, 118

Yalden, John, 26, 56, 65, 66, 69
Yarbury, Richard, dry salter, 1
Yardley
    John, 149
    William, 149
Yarner, Abraham, 28
Yate, Robert, merchant, 124
Yoakley
    Michael, mariner, 150
    Susanna, 150
    Thomas, 150
Yoatly, Thomas, merchant, 58
Young
    Henry, 151
    Mary, 151

Zouch, William, solicitor, 129

INDEX TO PLEADINGS, 1685–6
SUBJECTS

King's Palace Court (Court of the Verge), 83
Lancaster, Duchy Court, 60
White Chapel (Marshalsea), 14
Compter's Court (City of London), 26
Sheriff's Court (City of London), 93, 111
Bedford, church court, 148
Cowes (Isle of Wight), 87
Cowley Hall (Hillingdon, Middlesex), 55
Crown, 7, 32 (charter), 40, 56, 71, 79, 89 (patent), 106, 109, 110, 113, 122, 135, 145, 151
Customs, 52
Customs, farmers of, 52, 61, 145, 146

Damages (court-ordered), 6, 15, 60
daughter, 25, 72, 118, 129
Debtford (Deptford, Kent), 150
debts, 3, 4, 5, 12, 16, 18, 22, 25, 26, 28, 35, 37, 43, 56, 57, 60, 65, 81, 93, 96, 100, 118, 120, 125, 136, 151
deed, of gift, 143
deeds, 45, 64, 86, 119
deposit, 20, 47
Devon, 5
discovery (judicial), 58
distemper, 116
distringas, writ of, 32, 110
drowning, 81, 123
duel, 28
duties *(see also* taxes), 50, 87 (prisage and butlerage), 89, 107

East Indies, 30
ejectment, 66; action of, 84, 120
Ely (Cambs.), 11
endorse (a bond or note), 7, 67
equity, not a matter of (plea), 15, 112
error, writ of *(see also* courts), 84
estate, 9, 18, 27, 38, 41, 53, 61, 63, 88, 98, 105, 112, 116, 131, 141, 144, 148
excises, 56
executor, executrix *(see also* will), 5, 9, 13, 16, 24, 36, 38, 39, 50, 53, 56, 61, 62, 65, 66, 71, 72, 73, 74, 80, 88, 92, 95, 96, 97, 98, 118, 122, 126, 127, 129, 133, 136, 141, 142, 146

Factor, 37, 93
farmers, of taxes *(see also* Customs, farmers of, and Hearth Duties, farmers of), 107
farrier, 61
father, 9, 11, 17, 27, 31, 36, 50, 52, 59, 74, 75, 87, 96, 97, 98, 126, 129
fines, 113, 145
fire *(see also* London), 92, 119
footpath, 54
forfeiture*(see also* Crown), 71, 94, 105, 106, 110
fraud, alleged, 12, 26, 38, 63, 64, 125, 144
freehold, 120

Gambling, 96
glasshouses, 29
glassware makers, 29
glazier, 51
gold, 32, 44, 79, 96, 109, 112 (thread), 113
goods, household: 2, 4, 85, 99
goods (sold, contracted for), 8, 12, 15, 16, 18, 20, 28, 29, 37, 42, 46, 49, 57, 60, 61, 76, 77, 78, 91, 103, 104, 112, 121, 126, 132, 147, 151
grandchildren, 74
grandfather, 9, 25, 50
grandmother, 10
guardian, 31, 80, 149
Guinea, 44, 81, 93

Hearth duties, 56; farmers of, 5
heir (at law), 17, 144
'Helmet', the, 92
horses, 54, 62
Household, royal, officers of, 83
House of Commons *(see also* Parliament), 52
houses, 34, 36, 76, 85, 117
husband *(see also* remarriage), 12, 30, 34, 50, 62, 68, 125, 128, 139, 142, 151

Imprisoned, 17, 20, 22, 46, 94, 145
indemnity (judicial), 41, 59, 106, 149
infants *(see also* children, guardian, minors, next friend), 25, 41, 80
injunction *(see also* relief), 13, 14, 17, 19, 30, 40, 42, 44, 45, 46, 51, 60, 67, 70, 76, 78, 80, 83, 89, 97, 100, 111, 114, 115, 121, 130, 132, 138, 143, 151
innkeeper, 62
insanity, 25, 31, 64
insolvent, 19, 27, 144
interest, 10, 95, 112, 115, 129, 138
intestacy, 6, 7, 12, 27, 30, 34, 35, 36, 41, 59, 63, 72, 73, 82, 98, 99, 112, 116, 125, 132, 139, 144, 148
Ireland, 28
Ivelchester (Som.), 58

Jamaica, 13, 93
judge, 148
judgement, 5, 6, 12, 29, 38, 40, 60, 61, 65, 70, 85, 88, 91, 115, 125, 126, 145, 146, 147

Katherine, Queen (of Braganza), 40
Kent, 50
King's Palace Court prison *(see also* courts), 83

Land *(see also* copyholds, deeds, houses, leases, manors, messuages, mortgages, premises), 6, 9, 10, 18, 25, 48, 56, 64, 75, 94, 95, 97, 98, 120, 130, 144, 147, 149
lease, leasehold, 8, 20, 21, 23, 51, 54, 59, 64, 66, 82, 84, 87, 92, 119, 120, 150
legacy, legacies, 72, 74, 97, 139, 141, 149

license, licensee, 23, 135
lighthouses, 50
Limerick, 102
limitations, statute of (plea), 126
Lincolnshire, 11
loans (*see also* bills, bonds, notes, securities), 7, 14, 26, 63, 70, 75, 85, 90, 96, 101, 105, 110, 123, 128, 131, 137, 144, 147
lodger, lodging, 14, 42, 55, 61, 116, 139
logwood, 61
London (*and see* Bedlam), 34, 36, 91, 119, 121
  custom of, 118
  Fire of 1666, 34, 36, 117, 127
  freemen, 118
  Mayor and Aldermen, 107, 108, 117
  orphans, 108
  scavage, duties of, 107
London, places in
  Aldersgate, 64
  Buttolph (St. Botolph) Wharf, 117
  Carter Lane, 119
  Christ's Hospital, 106
  Custom House, 87
  Half Moon Tavern, 119
  Leadenhall St., 20
  London Bridge Waterhouse, 8
  Priest's Court, Foster Lane, 119
  Tower of, 79, 94, 109, 113
looking-glasses, 3
looking-glass maker, 3

Malting, 90, 147
manor, 10, 55, 75, 94
marriage, arrangement for, 77, 97, 128
marshes, 11
master, of a ship: 49, 81, 102, 123
Master and Worker of His Majesty's monies, 109, 113
mate, of a ship, 44
mercers, 28
merchants, 17
Messenger (royal), 122
messuage, 25, 48, 51, 55, 64, 84, 92, 101, 117, 150
Middlesex (*see also* Westminster)
  Drury Lane, 84
  Edmonton, 101
  Harrow, 75
  Hendon, manor of, 94
  Hillingdon, 55
  Kensington, 140
  St. Clement Danes, 60
  Stepney, 150
  Tottenham High Cross (parish), 130
  Well Close, Whitechapel, 29
  York House Garden, 23
millinery, 78
minors (*see also* children, infants), 68, 149
Mint, minting, 79, 109, 113
Moniers, Provost and Corporation of, 79, 109, 113

Monmouthshire, 40
Monserrat, 124
mortgage, 6, 10, 22, 45, 58, 59, 63, 86, 95, 101, 108, 141, 147
mother, 25, 27, 65, 86, 126, 128
mother-in-law, 147

Navarre, 42
nephew, 17
New Hampshire, 17
'next friend', 80
niece, 50
Northamptonshire, 40
notes (promissory), 67, 121

Oats, 103, 104
orphans, *see* London
outlawry, 106, 126
overseers (of will), 126, 141

Parents, 35, 68
Parliament (*see also* House of Commons), 146
partners, partnership, 17, 24, 28, 29, 147
patent, 89
pawn, 2, 48
payment, in instalments, 6
personal estate, personalty, 16, 18, 30, 33, 35, 39, 48, 56, 99, 118, 133, 143
pewter, 20
pipes, water, 8, 23
pirates, 32
plot, 105
premises (*see also* houses, land, messuage), 25, 31, 34, 36, 58, 59, 66, 68, 75, 80, 82, 84, 92, 108, 119, 120, 127
Purveyor, royal, 103, 104

Relief, from suit or judgement (*see also* courts, injunction), 1, 11, 15, 29, 37, 45, 49, 52, 59, 65, 67, 69, 84, 90, 91, 95, 101, 113, 120, 128, 136, 147, 148
remarriage, remarried, 12, 16, 36, 53, 62, 125, 139, 142
rents, 8, 21, 23, 34, 36, 39, 42, 66, 68, 80, 117
replevin, action of, 15
right of way, 54
rooms, 55
Royal African Company, 32, 93

St. John's College, Oxford, 149
St. Peter's, Westminster, Dean and Chapter, 120
scavage, duties of, *see* London
security (*see also* bonds, notes, surety), 4, 22, 26, 40, 51, 53, 63, 69, 85, 87, 89, 90, 95, 96, 97, 111, 135, 137, 150
servants, 70, 103, 104
Seville, 102
ships, 17, 101, 102, 107
  Charles, 102

CALENDAR OF EXCHEQUER EQUITY PLEADINGS 1784-5

152. Alexander v Sands

P: (1) Thomas Alexander, coffee house keeper, Cornhill, London; (2) Henry Pace, printer, Southwark, Surrey. D: (1) David Sands, upholder, Russell St., Bloomsbury, Midd; (2) James Wyatt gent., Queen Ann St. East, Midd; (3) Thomas Wyatt gent., New Inn; (4) Philip Astley gent., Lambeth, London; (5) John Astley gent., Lambeth, London; (6) Robert Johnson, stock broker, Pope's Head Alley, London; (7) Solomon De Medina, stock broker, Newington Green, London; (8) John Thorold Darwin, hatter, The Poultry, London; (9) James Richardson, stock broker, Bank Buildings, London; (10) John Carvick, stock broker, Bank Buildings, London; (11) James Branscomb, stock broker, Holborn, London; (12) John Wyatt, merchant, Walbrook; (13) James Ansell, auctioneer, Pall Mall, Midd. C: (1) Thomas Lowes. Add: (1) Edward Eagleton, bankrupt; (2) James Neatby. Ps seek payment of alleged debts from ds. In 1780, ps & ds became proprietors of the *Noon Gazette*; with p1 (treasurer), d4, d12, E. Eagleton (since bankrupt) & J. Neatby as the governing committee. The proprietors leased premises where p2 could print the newspaper. P1 quit the paper & claims ds owe him for rent he paid for p2's premises. P2 claims ds owe him for printing. Ds allegedly deny being indebted to ps.
1785, Hil   E 112/1706   Bill. LMX 3846.

153. Allan v Brown

P: (1) James Allan, merchant & underwriter, London; (2) Robert Sinclair, merchant & underwriter, London; (3) Joseph Nailer, merchant & underwriter, London; (4) William Herries, merchant & underwriter, London; (5) Robert Christie, merchant & underwriter, London; (6) Thomas Fraser, merchant & underwriter, London; (7) William Atkinson, merchant & underwriter, London; (8) Charles Kensington, merchant & underwriter, London; (9) Gavin Elliot, merchant & underwriter, London; (10) Henry Pierson, merchant & underwriter, London; (11) James Margetson, merchant & underwriter, London; (12) Robert William Halked, merchant & underwriter, London; (13) Hananel Modigliani, merchant & underwriter, London; (14) George Curling, merchant & underwriter, London; (15) Thomas Gildart, merchant & underwriter, London; (16) Robert Vigne, merchant & underwriter, London; (17) Harry Thompson, merchant & underwriter, London; (18) George Henckell, merchant & underwriter, London; (19) John Whitmore, merchant & underwriter, London; (20) Henry William Guyon, merchant & underwriter, London; (21) Jacob Wilkinson, merchant & underwriter, London; (22) Nathan Modigliani, merchant & underwriter, London; (23) Arthur Edie, merchant & underwriter, London. D: (1) Peter Brown, merchant, St. Thomas, West Indies; (2) John Stevenson, merchant, St. Thomas, West Indies; (3) Henry Kelly, merchant, St. Thomas, West Indies; (4) David Milligan, merchant, London, d5's partner; (5) Grant Allen, merchant, London, d4's partner; (6) William Manning, merchant, London, d7's partner; (7) Benjamin Vaughan, merchant, London, d6's partner; (8) William Davis, merchant, London, d9's partner; (9) James Strachan, merchant, London, d8's partner. C: (1) J. Bicknell, counsel for ps; (2) John Lloyd, counsel for ds8-9; (3) Thomas Nedham, counsel for ds6-7. Ps seek inj ag ds' suits for payment of insurance policies. In 1783, ds4-5 took out a policy apparently on a cargo of indigo laden on a ship, the *Altona* (owned by ds1-3), bound from the West Indies to Amsterdam. Ps1-11 underwrote the policy for £1600. Ds6-7, on behalf of ds1-3, also took out a policy on indigo on the same ship, underwritten by p4, p6 & ps12-17 for £1500. Ds8-9 also took out a policy for cargo on the ship, underwritten by p6, ps18-22 & p23 for £1200. The ship was lost, & ps claim that it did not contain indigo. Ds are suing ps for payment of the policies. Ds8-9 claim their policy was for general goods, not just indigo.

1785, Easter	E 112/1704	Bill. LMX 3779; mistakenly attached to part of E 112/1704 LMX 3784.
1787, April 1	E 112/1704	Answer. Swearing & filing date of the answer of ds8-9; schedule below answer of the £1200 policy.
1788, Easter	E 112/1704	Replication. Ps assert answer of ds8-9 is insufficient.
1788, Easter	E 112/1704	Rejoinder. Ds8-9 maintain their answer is sufficient.
1788, Nov 28	E 112/1704	Answer. Swearing & filing date of the answer of ds6-7; schedule below answer of the £1500 policy.

154. Allen v Morgan

P: (1) John Allen gent., parish of St. Bride, London. D: (1) John Morgan gent., Deptford, Kent; (2) James Hicks gent., Kennington Lane, Surrey. C: (1) J. Bicknell, counsel for p; (2) S. C. Cox, counsel for d1. P seeks inj ag d1's suit in the Court of Common Pleas for payment of a bill of exchange. P claims in 1784 he allowed d2 to draw a £69 bill of exchange upon him, which d2 promised to pay by the due date, but failed to do so. D2 endorsed the bill to d1, who has obtained a judgement in the Court of Common Pleas ag p for the bill.

1785, Easter	E 112/1694	Bill. LMX 3529.
1785, May 11	E 112/1694	Answer. Swearing date of d1's answer.

155. Angerstein v Middleton

P: (1) John Julius Angerstein, insurance broker, Throgmorton St., London; (2) Thomas Lewis, insurance broker, London; (3) James Mather, merchant, London. D: (1) Sir Charles Middleton, officer & commissioner of the navy, bart.; (2) Sir John Williams, officer & commissioner of the navy, knight; (3) Edward Hunt esq., officer & commissioner of the navy; (4) George Marsh esq., officer & commissioner of the navy; (5) George Rogers esq., officer & commissioner of the navy; (6) William Palmer esq., officer & commissioner of the navy; (7) Sir Richard Temple, officer & commissioner of the navy, bart.; (8) Edward Le Cras esq., officer & commissioner of the navy; (9) Samuel Wallis esq., officer & commissioner of the navy. C: (1) James Ibbetson, counsel for ps; (2) John Lloyd, counsel for ds; (3) Samuel Wallis, counsel for ds' answer to further amended bill. Add: (1) George Teer, navy captain, Deptford, Kent, ds' agent for transports, aged 53 years, ps' deponent. Ps seek payment for lost profits after ds discharged ps' ship from naval service. In 1780, ps bought a ship, the *George III*, repaired it & hired it for 12 months to ds, officers & commissioners of the navy. Ps claim in 1782, ds' agent G. Teer insisted ps repair & restock the ship again at Deptford, & ds witheld £8000 arrears for the ship's hire until p1 signed a new rental agreement with no stipulated time limit, promising p1 the ship would be sent on a 12 month voyage to the West Indies. Ds then dismissed the ship from service. Ps sued ds at KB for £10,000 lost profits. Ds deny promising to send the ship to the West Indies.

1785, Hil	E 112/1704	Bill. LMX 3784.
1785, April 20	E 112/1704	Commission. For ds' answer.
1785, April 22	E 112/1704	Answer. Swearing date of ds' answer, filed 26 April.
1785, Trin	E 112/1704	Exception. Ps' exception concerns whether G. Teer ordered the ship to be repaired & restocked for a 12 month voyage to the West Indies.
1785, Nov 7	E 112/1704	Amended bill. Ps reassert ds promised to send the ship to the West Indies.
1785, Nov 28	E 112/1704	Commission. For ds' answer to amended bill.
1786, Jan 20	E 112/1704	Answer (with attachments). Ds' answer to amended bill sworn on this date by d1 & ds3-9, and by d2 on 11 January; filed 23 January. Schedule attached of ds' instructions to G. Teer.
1786, Trin	E 112/1704	Replication. Ps assert ds' answer to amended bill is insufficient.
1786, Trin	E 112/1704	Rejoinder. Ds maintain their answer to amended bill is sufficient.
1787, May 12	E 112/1704	Amended bill. Further amended bill, mistakenly attached to E 112/1704 LMX 3779.
1787, Nov 16	E 112/1704	Answer. Answer to further amended bill of d1, ds4-6 & d8-9 (mistakenly attached to E 112/1704 LMX 3779), sworn by d9 & filed on this date, sworn by d1, ds4-6 & d8 on 7 November.
1788, Easter	E 112/1704	Replication. Ps assert ds' answer to the further amended bill is insufficient.
1788, Easter	E 112/1704	Rejoinder. Ds maintain their answer to the further amended bill is sufficient.

156. Appleby v Luttrell

P: (1) Ann Appleby, Queen Ann St. East, Marylebone, Midd. D: (1) Hon. John Luttrell, Kimpston, Hants. C: (1) James Agar, counsel for p; (2) E. King, counsel for d. Add: (1) Partridge, p's alleged fiancé (no forename given). P, a spinster, seeks payment of child support from d. P claims in 1784, when she was pregnant with d's child, d issued her a £600 bond as security to pay for the delivery & child support. P allegedly bore a daughter, but d requested the bond back & destroyed it. D claims p's fiancé, a Mr Partridge, demanded the bond to indemnify Partridge ag the child's upkeep, but that p miscarried & voluntarily returned the bond.

| 1785, Easter | E 112/1706 | Bill. LMX 3845. |
| 1785, Oct 27 | E 112/1706 | Answer. Swearing date. |

157. Arnold v Holker

P: (1) Benedict Arnold esq., Bryanstone St., Portman Sq., Midd, formerly of Philadelphia, America. D: (1) John Holker, Philadelphia, America; (2) Edward Bancroft, doctor of physic, Duke St., Westminster, Midd; (3) Richard Oxley, linen draper, Bread St., London. C: (1) E. King, counsel for p; (2) W. Scafe, counsel for ds2-3. P seeks inj ag ds' suit at KB for payment of a bond. P claims on 11 May 1779, he issued d1 a penal bond for £16,480 to secure the repayment of £8,204, the remainder of a £12,000 loan from d1. P claims d1 had advanced him the loan in the form of bills issued by the General Assembly of the Commonwealth of Pennsylvania. P asserts by May 1779, the remaining £8,204 bills were only worth £340 15s because of currency depreciation. In 1780, p fled America where his estates were seized & put to the use of the United States. D1 transferred the bond to his creditors ds2-3, who now sue p for the bond in d1's name, asserting the bills were worth their face value at the time of issue, & only depreciated afterwards.

1784, Mich	E 112/1713	Bill. LMX 4031.
1785, Feb 12	E 112/1713	Commission. For d1's answer.
1785, April 25	E 112/1713	Answer. Swearing date of d3's answer, filed 27 April.
1785, Aug 25	E 112/1713	Answer. Swearing date of d1's answer, filed 3 February 1786.
1786, Feb 27	E 112/1713	Answer. Swearing & filing date of d2's answer.
1786, May 10	E 112/1713	Amended bill. P denies the bills were worth their face value at the time of issue.
1786, July 5	E 112/1713	Commission. For d1's further answer.
1788, April 25	E 112/1713	Further answer. Swearing date of d1's further answer.

158. Askew v Thompson

P: (1) Leonard Askew gent., Liverpool, Lancs, previously resident in Charlestown, N. Carolina, N. America. D: (1) William Thompson, glazier, Duchess St., Portland Pl., Midd, J. Thompson's executor; (2) Elizabeth Thompson, d3's mother, J. Thompson's wife; (3) Peter Tisdale Lane, d2's son; (4) John Earl, J. Thompson's executor. C: (1) W. Alexander, counsel for p. Add: (1) John Thompson, deceased, d2's husband. P seeks payment of annuities from ds. In 1781, p shipped goods aboard a ship, the *Resolution*, from Charlestown to be sold in England, & issued power of attorney to ds2-3 to receive the profits for him. D2's husband J. Thompson tried to claim the profits, then died leaving d1 & d4 his executors. P claims ds1-3 agreed to invest the profits in bank annuities in their names in trust for p, but now ds allegedly deny the annuities belong to p.

1785, Trin   E 112/1706   Bill. LMX 3844.

159. Atkinson v Hartley

P: (1) William Atkinson, merchant, London; (2) John Wilson, merchant, London, J. Fletcher's assignee; (3) Alexander Champion, merchant, London, J. Fletcher's assignee; (4) Abraham Hake, merchant, London, J. Fletcher's assignee; (5) William Grove, merchant, London, J. Listard's assignee; (6) Peter De La Rive, merchant, London, J. Listard's assignee; (7) George Ernst De Hahn, merchant, London; (8) Thomas Bell, merchant, London, R. Bruce's assignee; (9) James Crabb, merchant, London, R. Bruce's assignee; (10) James Potts, merchant, London; (11) Thomas Wilson, merchant, London, T. Rowley's assignee; (12) Arthur Edwards, merchant, London, T. Rowley's assignee; (13) John Walker, merchant, London, T. Rowley's assignee; (14) William Atkinson, merchant, London, T. Rowley's assignee; (15) Hodgson Atkinson, merchant, London, T. Rowley's assignee; (16) George Farquhar Kinlock, merchant, London; (17) Thomas Carter, merchant, London, G. Cawthorn's assignee; (18) John Walker, merchant, London, G. Cawthorn's assignee. D: (1) Samuel Hartley, merchant, London; (2) Robert Beaver, ship's captain. C: (1) William Waller, counsel for ps; (2) J. Stanley, counsel for ds. Add: (1) John Fletcher, merchant, London, bankrupt; (2) John Listard, merchant, London, bankrupt; (3) Richard Bruce, merchant, London, bankrupt; (4) Thomas Rowley, merchant, London, bankrupt; (5) George Cawthorn, merchant, London, bankrupt; (6) Alexander Anderson the younger, broker, d1's employee. Ps, underwriters, seek repayment of an insurance policy. In 1779, d1's broker A. Anderson prepared a £1700 insurance policy upon d1's cargo on a ship, the *Juno*, bound for Africa and the West Indies, with d2 as captain. P1, J. Fletcher, J. Listard, p7, R. Bruce, p10, T. Rowley, p16 & G. Cawthorn underwrote the policy, which included a warranty that the ship was armed, but on the voyage the ship was captured by French frigates, & they had to pay d1. J. Fletcher went bankrupt with ps2-4 as his assignees; J. Listard went bankrupt with ps5-6 as assignees; G. Cawthorn went bankrupt with ps17-18 as assignees; R. Bruce went bankrupt with ps8-9 as assignees; & T. Rowley went bankrupt with ps11-15 as assignees. Ps now claim the warranty rendered the policy void, but ds assert ps were still liable for payment.

1785, Trin	E 112/1701	Bill. LMX 3693; filed 5 July 1785.
1785, Nov 7	E 112/1701	Answer (with attachments). Swearing date of d1's answer; schedules attached of the policy & d1's letters concerning the ship.
1786, Feb 13	E 112/1701	Commission. For d2's answer.
1786, May 3	E 112/1701	Answer (with attachments). Swearing date of d2's answer, filed 10 May; schedule attached of d2's instructions for the voyage.

160. Aylett v Welford

P: (1) Edward Aylett gent., Haymarket, Midd. D: (1) Mary Welford, Petty France, Midd; (2) William Langmore, steward of the manor of Stepney. C: (1) Thomas Lowes, counsel for p. P seeks inj to prevent ds from transferring d1's premises away. P claims in 1782, d1 mortgaged her messuage copyhold of the manor of Stepney or Stebunheath to p for £81 19s 3d, plus a further £20 in 1783, but did not execute a deed of mortgage. In 1785 p sought repayment or the deed to be drawn up, but d1 allegedly conspired with d2, steward of the manor of Stepney, in claiming the premises are subject to a prior mortgage or are to be sold.

1785, Trin   E 112/1723   Bill. LMX 4299.

161. Baldwin v Bourke

P: (1) Christopher Baldwin, merchant, London. D: (1) John Bourke esq., I. Foster's administrator; (2) Edmund Pitts esq., I. Foster's administrator; (3) Thomas Foster, I. Foster's administrator; (4) James Bogle French esq., London, R. Christian's executor; (5) Justinian Casamajor esq., London, R. Christian's executor; (6) Mainswete Walrond, planter, Antigua. C: (1) J. Bicknell, counsel for ps; (2) J. Stanley, counsel for ds1-3; (3) Charles Abbot, counsel for ds4-5. Add: (1) Ingham Foster, ironmonger, Clements Lane, Lombard St., London, deceased; (2) Robert Christian, deceased. P seeks inj ag the suit of ds1-3 at KB for payment of bills of exchange. P claims in 1777 d6 (a plantation owner in Antigua) was indebted to R. Christian, who died, leaving ds4-5 as his surviving executors. D6 drew bills of exchange upon p totalling £6200 5s 11d with which to pay ds4-5 the debt. D6 issued p security of d6's plantation & regular consignment of sugar, with ds4-5 as trustees. In 1779, d6 stopped sending p sugar, so p refused payment of some of the bills. Ds4-5 sued p, ag which p got an inj in this Court. Now ds1-3, I. Foster's administrators, are suing p at KB for some of the bills, which ds4-6 had endorsed to I. Foster.

1784, Mich	E 112/1720	Bill. LMX 4203.
1784, Nov 27	E 112/1720	Answer. Answer of ds4-5, sworn by d4 on this date, sworn by d5 & filed on 30 November.
1784, Dec 11	E 112/1720	Answer. Swearing date of answer of ds1-3, filed 13 December.
1785, Hil	E 112/1720	Exception. P's exceptions to the answer of ds4-5 concern the compliance of ds4-6 with the trust deeds.

162. Barber v Taylor

P: (1) Miles Barber, merchant, London. D: (1) Robert Taylor, merchant, ship owner, London. C: (1) J. Stanley, counsel for p; (2) J. Pippard, counsel for d. P seeks relief from his indenture to compensate d, ship owner, for loss of vessel, its cargo of slaves and various supplies (after shipwreck). P claims he is overcharged, that ship's capacity was less than represented, and seeks proof of actual damages. D is suing at KB.

1785, Easter	E 112/1701	Bill. LMX 3699.
1785, May 27	E 112/1701	Answer. Filing date.

163. Barrett v Dixon

P: (1) William Barrett, mariner, parish of St. George, Midd, father & executor of G. Barrett. D: (1) John Dixon, merchant, Magpie Alley, Fenchurch St., London, d2's partner; (2) William Eames, merchant, Sherborne Lane, London, d1's

partner; (3) George Whitlock, clerk, Magpie Alley, Fenchurch St., London, d1's employee. C: (1) Thomas Nedham, counsel for p. Add: (1) George Barrett, seaman, deceased, p's son. P, father & executor of G. Barrett, seeks payment of his son's wages. P claims in 1781, his son was a seaman aboard a ship owned by ds1-2, the *Empress of Russia*, which sank. Ds1-2 apparently never paid G. Barrett his wages of £27. G. Barrett died in 1782, leaving p his executor. Ds allegedly deny having employed G. Barrett, or claim he was already paid.
1785, Trin   E 112/1720   Bill. LMX 4209.

164. Barrett v Parker
P: (1) Mary Barrett, St. Mary White Chapel, Midd, N. Gamson's executrix. D: (1) James Parker, stationer, Chancery Lane, Midd, E. Parker's administrator. C: (1) William Waller, counsel for p. Add: (1) Nicholas Gamson, parish of St. Luke, Midd, deceased; (2) Edward Parker esq., Tooks Court, Holborn, Midd, deceased. P seeks to revive ag d her suit filed in this Court in 1783 ag E. Parker, seeking to redeem mortgaged premises. The suit abated when E. Parker died intestate in 1784, leaving d his administrator.
1785, Easter   E 112/1719   Bill of revivor. LMX 4191.

165. Barron v Brest
P: (1) Thomas Barron gent., Salisbury St. in the Strand, Midd. D: (1) William George Brest, St Martin's Court, Midd. C: (1) Charles Shuter, counsel for p; (2) Thomas Lewis, counsel for d. Add: (1) William Mercer, Midd, d's partner. P seeks inj ag d's suit at KB for payment of a bond. P claims he issued d the bond for debts incurred while betting on the lottery at the office of d and his partner W. Mercer. P claims the bond is therefore invalid as a gambling debt. D asserts the bond was issued in exchange for a loan.
1785, Hil   E 112/1708   Bill. LMX 3897.
1785, Feb 25 E 112/1708   Answer. Swearing date.

166. Bean v English
P: (1) Samuel Bean, merchant, Richmond, Surrey, bankrupt. D: (1) Thomas English, merchant, London; (2) Francis Roper. C: (1) J. Stanley, counsel for p; (2) J. Bicknell, counsel for d1; (3) J. Pippard, counsel for d2. Add: (1) Arthur Eddie, merchant, London, p's assignee; (2) Colin Mackenzie, merchant, London, p's assignee. P seeks inj ag ds' suit at KB for payment of a bill of exchange. In 1776, ds issued p a promissory note for £378 14s 2d, which p endorsed away, but was unable to pay by the due date. P allowed ds to draw a bill of exchange upon him as security for the note. P went bankrupt in 1779, with A. Eddie & C. Mackenzie as his assignees. Ds got a verdict at KB that p is liable to pay the bill of exchange, claiming the promissory note was presented to them for payment long after p's bankruptcy.
1784, Mich   E 112/1693   Bill. LMX 3514.
1784, Dec 3   E 112/1693   Answer. Swearing & filing date of d1's answer.
1785, Jan 22   E 112/1693   Answer. Swearing & filing date of d2's answer.

167. Bickhaffer v Williams
P: (1) Henry Bickhaffer, tailor, Covent Garden, Midd, p2's husband; (2) Mary Bickhaffer, Covent Garden, Midd, p1's wife, C. Williams's granddaughter. D:

(1) David Williams, C. Williams's son & executor. C: (1) William Waller, counsel for ps. Add: (1) Catherine Williams, Llandovery, Carm, deceased, p2's grandmother. Ps seek payment of a £50 legacy. Ps claim that in 1783 p2's grandmother C. Williams died, leaving her son d as executor, & bequeathing p2 £50. Ps claims d refuses to pay the legacy, allegedly denying C. Williams's estate was sufficient to pay her debts.

1785, Easter	E 112/1718	Bill. LMX 4146.

168. Billingham v Merrett

P: (1) Thomas Billingham, corn chandler, Goswell St., Midd, J. Billingham's husband. D: (1) Mary Merrett. C: (1) E. King, counsel for p; (2) R. Richards, counsel for d. Add: (1) Jane Billingham, late of Goswell St., Midd, deceased, p's wife, niece of d's first husband Charles Wall. P seeks inj ag d's suit at KB for repayment of a loan d allegedly made to p's late wife, Jane. D claims Jane borrowed the money on p's behalf for his new business. P denies any such loan was made, and asserts d owes him debts instead.

1785, Trin	E 112/1700	Bill. LMX 3686.
1786, Feb 3	E 112/1700	Answer. Swearing date, filed 4 February.
1786, Hil	E 112/1700	Exception. P's exception to d's answer concerns the alleged loan.

169. Blackaby v Jones

P: (1) John Blackaby, porter, White Lyon Court, Birchin Lane, London. D: (1) Griffith Jones, porter, Gloster Row, Newington Butts, Surrey; (2) Russell Laugher, porter, Labour in Vain Hill, London; (3) Samuel Young, porter, Wagstaffs Buildings, Maiden Lane, Surrey; (4) Harris Rich, porter, Wagstaffs Buildings, Maiden Lane, Surrey. C: (1) John Fonblanque, counsel for p; (2) E. King, counsel for ds. P seeks disability payment from the society of porters. P claims in 1781, he & ds, partners as porters carrying goods for 20 years, formed a society to provide assistance for members who fell ill. P claims since 1783 he has been lame & unable to work, & the society paid him until 1784, but not thereafter. Ds claim p's illness is caused by heavy drinking, invalidating his claim upon the society.

1785, Trin	E 112/1720	Bill. LMX 4204.
1785, Nov 1	E 112/1720	Answer. Swearing date of ds' answer, filed 7 November; schedule below answer of accounts between ds & p.
1786, Easter	E 112/1720	Replication. P asserts ds' answer is insufficient.
1786, Easter	E 112/1720	Rejoinder. Ds maintain their answer is sufficient.

170. Bliss v Beldon

P: (1) James Bliss gent., solicitor, Tooley St., Southwark, Surrey; (2) Michael Swan gent., solicitor, Tooley St., Southwark, Surrey, p1's common law agent. D: (1) Thomas Beldon the elder, Harn Lane, London; (2) Thomas Beldon the younger; (3) Elizabeth Holloway. C: (1) Charles Thompson, counsel for ps. Ps seek inj ag ds' suit at KB. Ps claim in 1774 d3 sought their help because ds 1–2 were suing her for a £26 debt. Ps claim d3 was uncooperative in defending the

suit, & a verdict was awarded ag her in 1784 for £51 damages & costs, which she could not pay, & so was imprisoned. Ds1-2 allegedly conspired with d3 to sue ps in KB for negligence in conducting the suit.
1785, Trin   E 112/1696   Bill. LMX 3566.

171. Boddam v Cracraft

P: (1) Thomas Boddam esq., Fore St., London, d's assignee; (2) Michael Bourke esq., Compton St., Midd, d's assignee. D: (1) Richard Cracraft, money scrivener, Philpot Lane, bankrupt. C: (1) Richard Hollist, counsel for ps; (2) J. Bicknell, counsel for d. Add: (1) Oliver Toulmin, merchant, Crutched Friars, London, deceased, d's assignee; (2) Alexander Stewart esq., Ballintry, Ireland. Ps seek inj ag d's suit in the Exchequer of Pleas for non-payment of d's salary. In 1779, d went bankrupt with ps & O. Toulmin (now deceased) as his assignees, who hired d to make an account of his own estate. A. Stewart got a verdict at KB for £1000 ag d for criminal conversations with Stewart's wife, to which d filed a writ of error, with ps as bail. Stewart agreed with ps not to proceed if his debts to d were set off ag the £1000 verdict. Toulmin died, & d has now got a judgement ag ps in the Exchequer of Pleas for £477 9s, arrears of his salary for drawing up his accounts. Ps claim they received few of d's debts, & could not pay the salary.

1785, Easter	E 112/1703	Bill. LMX 3772.
1785, May 27	E 112/1703	Answer. Swearing date, filed 28 May.
1786, Hil	E 112/1703	Replication. Ps assert d's answer is insufficient.
1786, Hil	E 112/1703	Rejoinder. D maintains his answer is sufficient.

172. Boucher v Ogle

P: (1) Jonathan Boucher, clerk, Paddington, Midd. D: (1) Anne Ogle, Annapolis, Maryland, N. America, widow of Samuel Ogle, the late Governor of Maryland. C: (1) Charles Abbot, counsel for p. P seeks inj ag d's suit at KB for repayment of a bond. P had issued d the bond in return for a loan, with which p bought property in the colony of Maryland, N. America. P claims he repaid the bond to d's representative. In the ensuing War of Independence, p fled the colony and was dispossessed while d became a citizen of the new state. P claims he should have immunity from the suit.
1784, Mich   E 112/1700   Bill. LMX 3666.

173. Bouvilla v Mortimer

P: (1) Elias Bouvilla gent., New Bond St., Hanover Sq., Midd; (2) Victor D'Hancarville gent., Queen Ann St., Westminster, Midd. D: (1) Peter Mortimer, New Bond St., Midd; (2) Robinson, J. J. A. Brunet's agent & attorney. C: (1) William Almack, counsel for ps. Add: (1) Jean Jacques Antonio Brunet, moneylender, d2's employer. Ps seek inj ag d1's suit in KB ag p1 for payment of 2 bills of exchange. In 1783, p2 drew 2 bills of exchange for £110 each upon p1, in order to get them discounted by d2, the agent of J. J. A. Brunet, moneylender. D2 never paid p2 the money, concealed himself when p2 got a warrant for his arrest, & endorsed the bills to d1, who is suing p1. D1 asserts d2 paid him the bills in exchange for goods.

81

1785, Hil   E 112/1698   Bill. LMX 3637.

1785, April 6   E 112/1698   Answer. Swearing date of d1's answer; schedule below answer of goods d2 bought from d1 with the bills.

174. Bowden v Corry

P: (1) Joseph Bowden, currier, Chelsea, Midd. D: (1) James Corry, yeoman, Chelsea, Midd. C: (1) R. Richards, counsel for p; (2) W. Ainge, counsel for d. P seeks inj ag d's suit for payment of debts incurred when d, p's lodger, allegedly replaced furniture seized by p's creditors from his house, on the understanding that p would repay d. P claims d's rent was in arrears and that d owed him other debts also.

1785, Easter   E 112/1700   Bill. LMX 3663.

1785, April 21   E 112/1700   Answer. Filing date; 2 schedules of accounts included below answer.

175. Brassett v Brassett

P: (1) John Brassett, yeoman, St. Catherine's, Tower of London, Midd. D: (1) Charles Brassett gent., East Smithfield, Midd. C: (1) Thomas Nedham, counsel for p; (2) John Lloyd, counsel for d. P seeks discovery of debts d allegedly owes p. P claims since 1780 he had business dealings with d, who owes him several debts for goods. D denies he owes p, and asserts p only made this allegation after d sued p in this Court in 1784 for debts p apparently owes d.

1784, Mich   E 112/1719   Bill. LMX 4192.

1785, Jan 26   E 112/1719   Answer. Swearing & filing date.

1785, Hil   E 112/1719   Replication. P asserts d's answer is insufficient.

1785, Hil   E 112/1719   Rejoinder. D maintains his answer is sufficient.

176. Bristow v Ewer

P: (1) John Bristow, engine maker, Ratcliff Highway, Midd. D: (1) Francis Ewer, carpenter, Princes Sq., Midd. P seeks inj ag d's suit at KB for non-payment of bills of exchange, drafts, and promissory notes which p issued d. P claims d asked to borrow the bills etc and promised to pay them off before the due date. D refused to return the bills etc, claiming p issued them in exchange for goods and loans.

1785, Trin   E 112/1708   Bill. LMX 3906; no record of p's counsel.

177. Brown v Brown

P: (1) George Brown gent., attorney at law, Crane Court, Fleet St., London, brother of ds1-2. D: (1) Jane Brown, servant, Combermere, Ches, p's sister and d3's servant; (2) Sarah Brown, Hankelow, Ches, p's sister and d4's fiancee; (3) Thomas, Colonel D'Avenant esq., Market Drayton, Salop, d1's employer; (4) Philip Gregory, Wapping, Midd, d2's fiance. C: (1) F. E. Tomlins, counsel for p; (2) R. Richards, counsel for ds1-2. Add: (1) Thomas Pengree gent., Shoreditch, Midd, deceased. P seeks inj ag ds' suit at KB for payment of bonds p had issued as a result of a transaction in which p claims ds1-2, his sisters, (at his advice) lent money to T. Pengree, with Pengree's estate as security. Ds1-2 claim they lent the money not to Pengree but to p. Pengree went bankrupt and died. P claims d3 (d1's employer) blackmailed him into issuing his own bonds to cover his sisters' losses.

| 1784, Mich | E 112/1705 | Bill. LMX 3799. |
| 1784, Nov 16 | E 112/1705 | Answer. Swearing and filing date of the answer of ds1-2. |

178. Brown v Thackray

P: (1) George Brown gent., attorney at law, Crane Court, Fleet St., London. D: (1) William Thackray the elder, father of d2 & d17; (2) William Thackray the younger, d1's son, d17's brother; (3) Thomas Cornwall; (4) Francis Foster; (5) Robert Duckrell, pastry cook, Bond St., Midd, insolvent; (6) William Parker; (7) King, (no forename given); (8) Joseph Jellett, haberdasher, 2 Wimpole St., Marylebone, Midd, insolvent; (9) Henry Cox, innkeeper, Mitre Tavern, Fleet St., London; (10) Thomas Hill, sheriff's officer; (11) William Robertson; (12) Thomas Cooper; (13) Joseph Hedges; (14) Robert Lloyd; (15) Robert Nugent; (16) William Garrison; (17) Robert Thackray, Staple Inn, London, now imprisoned at KB, d1's son, d2's brother. C: (1) T. E. Tomlins. P seeks inj ag the suit of ds6-7 for payment of bills, & p also seeks payment of legal fees. P claims that in 1784 d17 hired p as attorney for ds4-5. P allowed d4 to draw 2 bills for £15 & £20 upon him for d5's use. D5 transferred the bills to ds6-7, then went insolvent. D5 issued p power of attorney to sell d5's estate. D5's estate was sold by d1 & the proceeds paid to d17. D8 agreed to buy d5's house, & part-paid p promissory notes, which p paid to ds9-10 at d5's request. D8's notes were not accepted because d8 was insolvent. Ds6-7 are suing p for the bills. Ds1-2 persuaded p to work for d11, who was in debt to ds12-14, with d3 as witness. D16 drew a draft for debts owed to p upon d17, which has not been paid.

| 1785, Trin | E 112/1718 | Bill. LMX 4145. |

179. Brown v Wiltshire

P: (1) William Brown, cabinet maker, Turnstyle, Holborn, Midd. D: (1) Richard Wiltshire, victualler, Red Lion Passage, High Holborn, Midd, amended bill alters address to Blackfriars Rd., & occupation to lottery office keeper; (2) William Clark gent., St. James's Place, Midd; (3) Joseph Lee, sheriff's officer, parish of St. Clement Danes, Midd, added to supplementary bill. C: (1) William Waller, counsel for p; (2) Henry Boulton, counsel for p in supplementary bill; (3) J. Johnson, counsel for d1. P seeks inj ag the suits of ds1-2 in the Palace Court & at KB for a £60 debt. P claims he & ds1-2 were partners in a lottery business, from which ds1-2 owed him debts. Ds1-2 denied owing p, & instead sued him in 1784 for a £60 debt p allegedly owed them. As a supplement, p adds that when his bail bonds were not accepted, d3, sheriff's officer, also brought actions ag him.

1785, Hil	E 112/1701	Bill. LMX 3708.
1785, Jan 31	E 112/1701	Answer. Swearing date of d1's answer, filed 1 February.
1785, Trin	E 112/1701	Replication. P asserts d1's answer is insufficient.
1785, Trin	E 112/1701	Rejoinder. D1 maintains his answer is sufficient.

1785, May 9	E 112/1701	Amended bill. Alters d1's address & occupation.
1785, Nov 18	E 112/1701	Answer. Swearing & filing date of d1's answer.
1786, Easter	E 112/1701	Supplementary bill. Includes d3.

180. Brownell v Lambert

P: (1) Robert Christian Brownell the elder esq., shipwright, St. James's St., Midd, P. Brownell's husband, father of ds2-3. D: (1) Lewis Lambert, d2's assignee; (2) Robert Christian Brownell the younger gent., Southwark, Surrey, son of p & P. Brownell, insolvent; (3) John Brownell gent., Hammersmith, Midd, son of p & P. Brownell. C: (1) W. Scafe, counsel for p; (2) William Waller, counsel for ds. Add: (1) Thomas Horn, shipwright, Stepney, Midd, deceased, P. Brownell's father; (2) Phillis Brownell, p's wife, T. Horn's daughter, mother of ds2-3; (3) Mary Fenwick, T. Horn's executrix, deceased; (4) Henry Fourt, T. Horn's executor, deceased; (5) John Seacombe, T. Horn's executor, deceased. P seeks inj ag ds' suit for payment of £1000. In 1753, T. Horn entrusted £1000 to be paid after his death to his daughter Phillis, p's wife. T. Horn died in 1757, leaving M. Fenwick, H. Sourt & J. Seacombe his executors, who paid p £1000 in annuities in 1764. Ds2-3 (the sons of p & Phillis) & d1 (assignee of the estate of d2, who is insolvent) assert p was paid the £1000 immediately after T. Horn's death, & that the annuities were later paid for the benefit of ds2-3. Ds are suing p for the money.

1784, Mich	E 112/1720	Bill. LMX 4206.
1784, Nov 19	E 112/1720	Answer. Swearing date of d3's answer.
1784, Nov 20	E 112/1720	Answer. Swearing date of d1's answer.
1784, Nov 27	E 112/1720	Amended bill. P claims he received the annuities in payment for the trust and no other payment for ds2-3.
1784, Dec 11	E 112/1720	Answer. Swearing date of d1's answer to amended bill, filed 13 December.
1784, Dec 11	E 112/1720	Answer. Swearing date of d3's answer to amended bill, filed 13 December.
1784, Dec 16	E 112/1720	Exception. P's exceptions to the answers of d1 & d3 concern p's alleged use of the annuities to support ds2-3.
1785, Feb 8	E 112/1720	Answer. Swearing date of d2's answer to amended bill.

181. Burdett v Lillyman

P: (1) Thomas Francis Burdett esq., Bartlett's Buildings, Holborn, London, formerly T. F. Pritchard, before marrying E. Burdett. D: (1) William Lillyman, Midd, d5's assignee; (2) Joseph Fenemore, Midd, d5's assignee; (3) George Hanxwell, Midd, d5's assignee; (4) William Freeman, merchant, Bath, Som; (5) John Ellis, butcher, Glanville St., Marylebone, Midd, bankrupt. C: (1) William Mellish, counsel for p; (2) R. Richards, counsel for ds1-3 & d5; (3) Thomas Evance, counsel for d4. Add: (1) Elizabeth Burdett, p's wife. P seeks inj ag ds' suit at KB for payment of a bond. P claims in 1781, he issued a bond for £195 16s 9d to d5 as security for debts owed by himself & his wife E. Burdett. D5

84

transferred the bond to his creditor d4. In 1782, d5 went bankrupt, with ds1-3 as his assignees. Ds have got a judgement at KB ag p for the bond, claiming p has never paid the debt for which the bond was issued as security.

1785, Hil	E 112/1710	Bill. LMX 3975.
1785, Feb 10	E 112/1710	Answer. Swearing date of d5's answer, filed 11 February; schedule below answer of accounts between p & d5.
1785, Feb 10	E 112/1710	Answer. Swearing date of the answer of ds1-3, filed 11 February.
1785, June 15	E 112/1710	Commission. For d4's answer.
1785, Sept 9	E 112/1710	Answer. Swearing date of d4's answer, filed 9 November.

182. Burkitt v Robarts

P: (1) Alexander Sheafe Burkitt gent., St. Mary Abbas, Kensington, Midd. D: (1) John Chapman Robarts, hosier, Newgate St., London. C: (1) J. Bicknell, counsel for p; (2) Thomas Nedham, counsel for d. P seeks inj ag d's suit for payment of a £160 bond. P claims in 1783, he issued d a £160 bond as payment of a debt to d, who agreed to pay off bills & notes which p had endorsed since 1781 for d's benefit. P allegedly since discovered he owes very little to d, who did not pay off the bills & notes, but is instead suing p for the bond. D denies p ever issued bills & notes for his benefit.

1785, Hil	E 112/1734	Bill. LMX 4538.
1785, June 15	E 112/1734	Answer. Swearing & filing date.
1785, Trin	E 112/1734	Exception. P's exceptions concern bills & notes he allegedly issued for d.
1785, Nov 16	E 112/1734	Amended bill. Further concerns the bills & notes p allegedly issued for d.
1786, May 29	E 112/1734	Further answer (with attachments). Swearing & filing date of d's further answer; 6 schedules attached of accounts between d & p.

183. Burnsall v Williams

P: (1) David Burnsall esq., Lawrence St., Chelsea, Midd, G. Burnsall's executor. D: (1) Robert Williams gent.. C: (1) W. Ainge, counsel for p; (2) J. Bicknell, counsel for d. Add: (1) George Burnsall gent., St. Mary le Bone, Midd, deceased. P, executor of G. Burnsall (deceased), seeks repayment of alleged loans made by the deceased to d. D claims the money was given as a present.

1785, Trin	E 112/1700	Bill. LMX 3684.
1786, Jan 20	E 112/1700	Answer. Swearing date, filed 21 January.

184. Butcher v Menham

P: (1) Robert Holt Butcher, clerk, Milbank, Westminster, Midd. D: (1) Thomas Menham, merchant, Newcastle upon Tyne, Northumb; (2) Alexander Fordyce esq.. C: (1) J. Bicknall, counsel for p. P seeks inj ag d1's suit in the Court of Durham for payment of a £500 bill of exchange. P claims in 1780 he issued the bill of exchange to d2, who agreed to pay it off by the due date. D2 allegedly deposited the bill with d1, as security for debts for which d1 was suing d2. D2 apparently asserts that p issued him the bill in return for cash. D1 is suing p for the bill.

1784, Mich   E 112/1697   Bill. LMX 3586.

185. Butler v Ashton

P: (1) Jane Butler, Countess Dowager of Lanesborough, Ireland; (2) William Gardiner esq., colonel of ? regiment, Queen St., Mayfair, Midd. D: (1) William Ashton, shoemaker, Oxford St., Midd; (2) John Richardson, grocer, South Molton St., Midd. C: (1) Thomas Nedham, counsel for ps; (2) Richard Hollist, counsel for d2; (3) J. Bicknell, counsel for d1. Ps seek inj ag ds' suit at KB for payment of a £250 bill of exchange. In 1784 p1 drew the bill upon p2, agreeing to pay it off by the due date. P1 claims she received only £120 for the bill from d2, who promised to advance her the balance later. Now ds are suing ps at KB for the full £250, claiming d2 paid p1 the full value of the bill, & that d1 paid d2 likewise.

1785, Hil   E 112/1696   Bill. LMX 3568.
1785, Feb 9   E 112/1696   Answer. Swearing date of d1's answer, filed 10 February.
1785, April 26 E 112/1696   Answer. Swearing date of d2's answer, filed 27 April.

186. Byron v Thompson

P: (1) Rt. Hon. William, Lord Byron. D: (1) Robert Thompson, coach maker, Drury Lane, Midd. C: (1) F. P. Stratford, counsel for p. Add: (1) Robert Ansell, picture dealer, parish of Marylebone, Midd. P seeks inj ag d's suit at KB for payment of a promissory note. In 1779 bespoke & bought a phaeton from d, who agreed to receive payment of £35 & p's vis à vis carriage. P endorsed to d a £50 promissory note issued by R. Ansell in 1779 in return for pictures p sold him. D issued p £15 change & a receipt. D is now suing p at KB, allegedly claiming that R. Ansell went bankrupt in 1780 & could not pay the note. P claims d should have sought payment from Ansell before 1780, & thereafter should have sought payment from p, but instead failed to inform p of the problem until 1784.

1785, Hil   E 112/1704   Bill. LMX 3791.

187. Caesar v Charnock

P: (1) Carlos Caesar, grocer, Holborn, London. D: (1) Robert Charnock, merchant, Lewes, Sussex. C: (1) Charles Shuter, counsel for p. P seeks inj ag d's suit at the Surrey Assizes for payment of 2 bills of exchange. P claims in 1784, d sent him 2 parcels of goods & drew 2 bills of exchange for £55 4s 6d & £86 11s upon p in payment. P accepted the bills, but the parcels were lost. P claims the bills should have been cancelled, but d had p arrested & obtained a verdict ag him for the amount of the bills + costs. D allegedly asserts that he drew the bills in return for money he lent p.

1785, Easter   E 112/1717   Bill. LMX 4135.

188. Caesar v Hankey

P: (1) Carlos Caesar, grocer, tea dealer, Holborn Bridge, London. D: (1) Thomas Hankey, banker, Fenchurch St., London, partner of other ds; (2) Joseph Chaplin Hankey, banker, Fenchurch St., London, partner of other ds; (3)

86

Stephen Hall, banker, Fenchurch St., London, partner of other ds; (4) Robert Hankey, banker, Fenchurch St., London, partner of other ds. C: (1) H. Scafe, counsel for p. P seeks inj ag ds' suit at KB for payment of p's alleged overdrawing of his account at ds' bank. P claims he lodged money in his account sufficient to cover his cheques, but because his deposits were not actually recorded, he had not been credited with them and subsequently ds had him arrested.

| 1785, Easter | E 112/1708 | Bill. LMX 3908; cf. E 112/1705 LMX 3816 Riley v Caesar. |

189. Capper v Hickey

P: (1) James Capper esq., Mortimer St., Midd. D: (1) Joseph Hickey, d4's trustee; (2) Joseph Watts, d4's brother & trustee; (3) David Sands, d4's trustee; (4) John Watts, upholsterer, Compton St., Soho, Midd, insolvent, d2's brother. C: (1) J. Campbell, counsel for p; (2) J. Bicknell, counsel for d1 & d4; (3) J. Johnson, counsel for d2. P seeks inj ag d1's suit at KB for a £200 bill of exchange. P claims in 1777 he hired d4 to furnish his house, for which he paid d4. P also allowed d4 to draw bills of exchange upon p, which d4 allegedly agreed to pay off by the due date. In 1778, d4 went insolvent & assigned his estate to ds1–3 in trust for his creditors. D1 then had p arrested in KB for a £200 bill p had issued d4, who had endorsed it to d1. Ds assert p issued d4 the bill as payment for furniture, not as a loan.

1784, Mich	E 112/1698	Bill. LMX 3630.
1785, Jan 24	E 112/1698	Answer. Swearing & filing date of d1's answer.
1785, Jan 27	E 112/1698	Answer. Swearing date of d4's answer, filed 28 January.
1785, Feb 4	E 112/1698	Exception. P's exceptions concern d1's acquisition of the bill of exchange.
1785, Feb 8	E 112/1698	Answer. Swearing date of d2's answer, filed 11 February.

190. Carver v Keele

P: (1) Edward Carver esq., Birmingham, Warw. D: (1) Daniel Mayo Keele; (2) Thomas Prichard, Parsonage Farm, Horsham, Sussex; (3) Ralph Jackson, Snow Hill, Midd. C: (1) R. Richards, counsel for p; (2) Maurice Bernard, counsel for d1. Add: (1) Thomas Hayter, merchant, London, prisoner in the Fleet for debt. P seeks inj ag d1's suit at KB for payment of bills of exchange. P claims in 1782 he drew bills of exchange totalling £250 upon T. Hayter, in payment of debts Hayter owed p. P endorsed the bills to d2 to be discounted, but d2 only paid p £60 & endorsed the bills to d3. D1 now sues p, claiming d3 paid him the bills in exchange for goods.

1785, Easter	E 112/1699	Bill. LMX 3650; cf. E 112/1699 LMX 3649 Carver v Prichard.
1785, June 6	E 112/1699	Answer. Swearing & filing date of d1's answer; schedule below answer of an account between d1 & d3.
1786, Hil	E 112/1699	Replication. P asserts d1's answer is insufficient.

1786, Hil   E 112/1699   Rejoinder. D1 maintains his answer is sufficient.

191. Carver v Prichard

P: (1) Edward Carver esq., Birmingham, Warw. D: (1) Thomas Prichard, Parsonage Farm, Horsham, Sussex; (2) James Willis, Threadneedle St., London; (3) John Footman, salt merchant, Pudding Lane, London; (4) Alexander Guest, glazier & huckster, Madeley Wood, Salop; (5) James Gibbons, iron manufacturer, Coalbrook Dale, Salop, partner with ds6-9; (6) William Ferriday, iron manufacturer, Coalbrook Dale, Salop, partner with d5 & ds7-9; (7) William Goodwin, iron manufacturer, Coalbrook Dale, Salop, added when bill was amended, partner with ds5-6 & ds8-9; (8) Thomas Botfield, iron manufacturer, Coalbrook Dale, Salop, partner with ds5-7 & d9; (9) George Turner Watkiss, iron manufacturer, Coalbrook Dale, Salop, renamed from George Farmer Wallis when bill was amended; partner with ds5-8. C: (1) R. Richards, counsel for p; (2) Thomas Plumer, counsel for ds4-8; (3) Thomas Pippard, counsel for ds2-3. Add: (1) Thomas Hayter, merchant, London, prisoner in the Fleet for debt. P seeks inj ag ds' suits at KB for payment of bills of exchange. P claims in 1782 he drew bills of exchange totalling £1000 upon T. Hayter, in payment of debts Hayter owed p. P endorsed the bills to d1 to be discounted, but d1 endorsed the bills away & never paid p. Now ds2-9 are severally suing p at KB for the bills, claiming they have given value for them.

1785, Trin   E 112/1699   Bill. LMX 3649, amended 14 June 1785; cf. E 112/1699 LMX 3650 Carver v Keele.
1785, June 15   E 112/1699   Commission. For the answers of ds4-8.
1785, Nov 14   E 112/1699   Answer. Swearing date of the answer of ds2-3, filed 15 November.
1785, Nov 26   E 112/1699   Answer. Swearing date of the answer of ds5-8.
1785, Nov 26   E 112/1699   Answer. Swearing date of d4's answer, filed 28 November.

192. Cecil v Reilly

P: (1) Ann Cecil, Upper Brook St., Grosvenor Sq., Midd, J. Cecil's widow & administratrix. D: (1) Peter Reilly. C: (1) E. King. Add: (1) John Cecil, apothecary, Bond St., Midd, deceased intestate, p's husband; (2) George Reynolds, prisoner in KB; (3) Isaac Narbell; (4) Thomas Massey, Ludlow, Salop; (5) Alexander Wallis, Oxon. P, a widow, seeks inj ag d's suit at KB for alleged debts. P claims in 1778, G. Reynolds persuaded p's husband J. Cecil to become a partner in a business with him & I. Narbell to manufacture Egyptian Bitumen. In 1780, Reynolds, together with d, persuaded T. Massey & A. Wallis to become partners. P claims the partners discovered the business was a scheme for Reynolds & d to extort money. J. Cecil died in 1782, & d has since sued p at KB for debts allegedly owed him by her husband.

1785, Trin   E 112/1709   Bill. LMX 3959.

193. Christie v Rich

P: (1) James Christie, auctioneer, Westminster, Midd, A. P. Warren's administrator, p2's partner; (2) James Ansell, auctioneer, Westminster, Midd, p1's partner; (3) Shadrack Venden, A. P. Warren's administrator; (4) David

McCullock, A. P. Warren's administrator. D: (1) Peter Rich, J. Warren's executor. Add: (1) Alport Peter Warren esq., Battersea, Surrey, deceased, J. Warren's nephew; (2) John Warren esq., Kensington Gore, Midd, deceased, A. P. Warren's uncle. Ps seek inj ag d's suit at KB for payment of an alleged debt. Ps claim J. Warren died in 1776, leaving his executor d1 under p1's direction to sell his estate & buy securities for his nephew & residual legatee, A. P. Warren. D & A. P. Warren each claimed the other owed them debts. In 1782, A. P. Warren died, leaving p1 & ps3-4 his administrators. D is suing ps at KB for payment of A. P. Warren's alleged debt, & ps claim d has not paid A. P. Warren's legacy from J. Warren.

1785, Trin   E 112/1723   Bill. LMX 4276.

194. Clark v Roper
P: (1) Henry Clark, cheesemonger, White Chapel Rd., Midd, S. Clark's son. D: (1) William Roper, pattern maker, White Chapel Rd., Midd, S. Clark's executor. C: (1) John Fonblanque, counsel for p; (2) E. King, counsel for d. Add: (1) Sibella Clark, White Chapel, Midd, deceased, p's mother. P seeks payment of the residual estate of his mother, S. Clark, from d. S. Clark died in 1784, leaving d as her executor & p her son as residual legatee. P claims d has not paid any of the legacies, & that p has had to pay his mother's debts himself. D alleges he cannot fully administer the estate because p witholds part of it, but d claims to be willing to act as this Court directs.

1785, Trin	E 112/1716	Bill. LMX 4107.
1785, Nov 24	E 112/1716	Answer (with attachments). Swearing & filing date of d's answer; inventories attached of S. Clark's effects received & sold by d.
1786, Easter	E 112/1716	Replication. P asserts d's answer is insufficient.
1786, Easter	E 112/1716	Rejoinder. D maintains his answer is sufficient.
1790, July 8	E 112/1716	Answer. D's answer to a supplemental bill (missing) filed by Elizabeth Clark, p's widow & administratrix.

195. Clarke v Laing
P: (1) John Clarke, coal factor, London, p2's partner; (2) Ralph Clarke, coal factor, London, p1's partner. D: (1) Robert Laing, master mariner, Dockwray Square, Northumb. C: (1) E. King, counsel for ps. Add: (1) Nathaniel Green gent., Seething Lane, London, ps' trustee. Ps, for themselves & other part-owners of a ship, the *William & Robert*, seek discovery of the profits from the ship. In 1782, d, captain & part-owner of the ship, sold a 16th share in the ship & cargo to p1 for £250. In 1783, p1 assigned the share to N. Green in trust for himself & p2. Ps assert d has never paid them any profits, but d allegedly claims the ship's expenses have outweighed its earnings.

1785, Trin   E 112/1718   Bill. LMX 4147.

196. Clarke v Simmons
P: (1) John Clarke, coalfactor, London. D: (1) Ann Simmons, Dockwray Sq., nr North Shields, Northumb, E. Simmons's widow. C: (1) Thomas Nedham,

counsel for p. Add: (1) Edward Simmons, mariner, North Shields, Northumb, deceased intestate, d's husband. P seeks inj ag d's suit at KB for payment of proceeds from the sale of a ship. D's husband E. Simmons drew bills of exchange upon p to buy the ship. After d's husband died intestate, d gave p power of attorney to sell the ship. Upon the sale, p retained part of the proceeds to cover his original outlay. D denies p paid for original bills of exchange.

1784, Mich   E 112/1705   Bill. LMX 3811; schedule of d's account with p below bill.

197. Clarkson v Ford

P: (1) Thomas Clarkson, Edward St., Berkeley Sq., Midd. D: (1) Arthur Ford, J. Ford's father & administrator. C: (1) John Lloyd, counsel for p. Add: (1) Elizabeth Purvis, deceased, otherwise Ford; (2) Joseph Hunt; (3) Sarah Peele, deceased insolvent; (4) Robert Patterson; (5) William Silver, deceased insolvent; (6) James Lowe, J. Ward's executor; (7) Joseph Ward, insolvent; (8) John Ford, deceased, E. Purvis's husband. P, creditor of J. Ward (deceased insolvent in 1779), seeks revival of his supplemental bill filed in 1782 in this Court ag E. Purvis or Ford, J. Hunt, S. Peele, R. Patterson, W. Silver & J. Lowe, seeking repayment of a debt from J. Ward's residual estate decreed in 1771 to be returned to J. Ward by his assignees. The suit abated when E. Purvis died leaving her husband J. Ford, who died leaving d his administrator. S. Peele & W. Silver also died, insolvent. P now seeks revival ag d.

1785, Easter   E 112/1706   Bill of revivor. LMX 3830; cf. E 112/1703 LMX 3759 Lowe v Frord.

198. Collet v Green

P: (1) Jonathan Collet, glassman, Cockspur St., Charing Cross, Midd. D: (1) James Green, watchmaker, Fenchurch St., London, J. Brockbank's assignee; (2) Albert Innes, merchant, Crutched Friars, London, J. Brockbank's assignee; (3) Richard Hollier, refiner, Falcon St., London, J. Brockbank's assignee. C: (1) E. King, counsel for p. Add: (1) John Brockbank, merchant, Cowpers Court, Cornhill, London, bankrupt; (2) James Junod, goldsmith & enameller, Frith St. Westminster, Midd. P, by way of supplement to his 1782 bill in this Court seeking payment of a £27 bill of exchange from J. Brockbank, informs that in 1783 J. Brockbank went bankrupt, with ds as his assignees. P claims that in 1781, J. Junod owed p debts, for which he issued p the bill, drawn upon J. Brockbank. J. Brockbank allegedly refused to pay the bill, so p sued him.

1785, Hil   E 112/1697   Supplementary bill. LMX 3585.

199. Cruger v Hurst

P: (1) Henry Cruger, merchant, London, and partners. D: (1) John Hurst, hosier, London. C: (1) F. P. Stratford, counsel for p; (2) E. King, counsel for d. Add: (1) Mr Donaldson, merchant, partner to Mr Cox, Philadelphia, N. America; (2) Mr Reid, merchant, partner to Mr Ford, Philadelphia, N. America; (3) Charles Hurst, d's brother. Ps seek relief ag a debt to d, a hosier, whose goods ps sold to Philadelphia merchants in America. Ps claimed d gave credit for 12 months, which d denies. D's brother in America had ps' receipts attached there, allegedly on d's behalf (though defendant does not acknowledge any receipt). Ps seek inj ag d pursuing the debt.

| 1785, Easter | E 112/1701 | Bill. LMX 3697. |
| 1785, June 6 | E 112/1701 | Answer. Filing date. |

200. Davies v Austin

P: (1) John Davies esq., parish of Mary le Bone, Midd. D: (1) Sarah Austin, maidservant. C: (1) Robert Ledlie, counsel for p. P seeks inj ag d's suit for payment of arrears of wages. P claims that while d was a maidservant in his house, he advanced to her sums of money, but upon her failure to account for them, he fired her. She then sued him for non-payment of wages.

| 1784, Mich | E 112/1708 | Bill. LMX 3910. |

201. Davis v Farmer

P: (1) David Davis, jeweller, artificial flower maker, Moorfields, Midd, p2's partner; (2) Joshua Jonas, jeweller, artificial flower maker, late of Moorfields, Midd, allegedly now overseas; p1's partner. D: (1) Cam Farmer, feather and fur manufacturer, Oxford St., Midd. C: (1) J. Pippard, counsel for ps; (2) Arthur Onslow, counsel for d. Ps seeks inj ag d's suit for full payment of debts. D claims that a settlement for partial repayment agreed between ps and their creditors, including d, fraudulently portrayed ps to be in worse financial difficulties than was the case. D demands full repayment of this and a later debt.

| 1785, Easter | E 112/1700 | Bill. LMX 3661. |
| 1785, June 4 | E 112/1700 | Answer. Swearing date; 2 schedules of accounts included below bill. |

202. Deane v Kaye

P: (1) Arthur Deane, hosier, Shoreditch, Midd. D: (1) Joseph Kaye gent., Hanover Square, Midd; (2) Thomas Plumer Byde esq., Ware Park, Heref, bankrupt; (3) Rev. Benjamin Round, clerk, White Horse St., Ratcliff H'way, Midd, d2's assignee; (4) Robert Woodgate esq., Golden Square, Midd, d2's assignee; (5) John Feakins, carpenter, parish of St. Marylebone, Midd; (6) James Bradley, carpenter, parish of St. Marylebone, Midd. C: (1) J. A. Stainsby, counsel for p; (2) W. Scafe, counsel for ds3-4. Add: (1) Peter Calmel esq., parish of St. James, Westminster, Midd; (2) Martha Andrews, Edgeware, Midd. P seeks payment of a £2000 debt, or foreclosure on mortgaged premises. In 1766, ds5-6 leased 13 parcels of ground in the parish of St. Marylebone from P. Calmel. Ds5-6 mortgaged 10 of the parcels of ground to d1, & 3 to M. Andrews. In 1770, M. Andrews transferred her mortgage to d1. In 1777, d1 borrowed £2000 on the security of the mortgages from d2, who then borrowed £2000 on the security of the mortgages from p. D2 did not repay the £2000, so p's interest in the mortgaged premises allegedly became absolute. In 1779 d2 went bankrupt with ds3-4 as his assignees. D1 & ds5-6 allegedly refuse to assign p the premises. Ds3-4 claim to be willing to act as this Court directs, in return for indemnity.

| 1785, Hil | E 112/1707 | Bill. LMX 3878. |
| 1785, May 12 | E 112/1707 | Answer. Swearing & filing date of answer of ds3-4. |

203. Douglas v Prescott

P: (1) Peter Douglas esq., ship's captain, East India Co., St. Martin in the Fields, Midd. D: (1) George Prescott, banker, London, defendant with his partners. C: (1) E. King, counsel for p; (2) Robert Steele, counsel for ds. P seeks relief ag d's suit for payment of respondentia bond + full interest for fixed term which p claimed to have sought to pay before due date to avoid full interest, allegedly by prior agreement with d. Refusing partial payment, d had had p arrested for debt. P seeks inj ag d's legal proceedings elsewhere.

1785, Easter	E 112/1701	Bill. LMX 3703.
1785, April 23	E 112/1701	Answer. Filing date.

204. Doves v Alsager

P: (1) James Doves, mariner, Chelsea, Midd, bankrupt. D: (1) Richard Alsager, packer, Bearbinder Lane, London, d3's assignee; (2) Silvanus Greville, bankrupt, lives abroad, formerly d3's assignee; (3) Edward Ryan, Swithin's Lane, London, bankrupt, p's creditor. C: (1) J. Pippard, counsel for p. Add: (1) John Kent gent., Maidstone, Kent, deceased, p's assignee; (2) Philip Detillon the elder gent., Maidstone, Kent, deceased, p's assignee. P seeks inj ag ds' suit at KB for payment of a £50 promissory note. P went bankrupt in 1776, was imprisoned in KB, & his assignees, J. Kent & P. Detillon (now both deceased) possessed his estate. In 1778, d3, p's creditor, went bankrupt with ds 1-2 as his assignees. In 1779, d2 went bankrupt & absconded abroad. P claims while imprisoned in KB he issued d3 a £50 promissory note, now held by ds 1-2, for which d3 never paid him. Ds allegedly now seek payment of the note, contrary to the 1731-2 Act of Parliament stating that notes issued by bankrupts are void.

1784, Mich	E 112/1691	Bill. LMX 3482.

205. Edie v Dwyer

P: (1) Arthur Edie, merchant & underwriter, London; (2) Alexander Anderson the younger, merchant & underwriter, London; (3) Thomas Kett, merchant & underwriter, London; (4) Joseph Crump, merchant & underwriter, London; (5) Thomas Hobbs, merchant & underwriter, London. D: (1) Henry Dwyer esq., South Moulton St., Midd. C: (1) J. Bicknell, counsel for ps; (2) Joseph Stacpoole, counsel for d. Add: (1) James Russell, cornet, Lyons, France, deceased, 9th Regiment of Dragoons. Ps seeks inj ag d's suits at KB for payment of an insurance policy. In 1784, J. Russell instructed G. Dwyer by letter to draw up a life insurance policy to cover an alleged £5600 debt Russell owed d. Ps underwrote £200 each of the policy, which included a warranty that Russell was in good health. Russell died, & ps then apparently discovered that he had been in poor health, & was not indebted to d. D has filed several suits at KB ag ps for the policy, claiming Russell owed him a promissory note for £5600 in loans.

1785, Hil	E 112/1704	Bill. LMX 3776.
1786, April 6	E 112/1704	Answer. Swearing date.
1786, Mich	E 112/1704	Exception. Ps' exceptions to d's answer concern the circumstances under which Russell issued d the promisory note.
1788, Feb 4	E 112/1704	Further answer. Swearing & filing date of d's further answer, claiming Russell issued the note for loans, not gambling debts.

| 1788, Easter | E 112/1704 | Replication. Ps assert d's answers are insufficient. |
| 1788, Easter | E 112/1704 | Rejoinder. D maintains his answers are sufficient. |

206. Edwards v Blackburn

P: (1) William Edwards, watchmaker, Cornhill, London. D: (1) William Blackburn, watchmaker, Aldersgate St., London; (2) Edward Johnson, broker, Ludgate Hill, London. C: (1) Maurice Bernard, counsel for p. P seeks inj ag ds' suit at KB for payment of a bill of exchange bearing p's acceptance. P claims he accepted the bill drawn by d1 (p's colleague) on the basis that this was a means to tide d1 over temporarily. However, d1 transferred the bill to d2, who now claims payment from p.

| 1785, Trin | E 112/1708 | Bill. LMX 3903. |

207. Evans v Haffey

P: (1) Evan Evans, merchant, Leadenhall St., London. D: (1) John Haffey gent., merchant, Wood St., Walthamstow, Essex; (2) Christopher Corrall, laceman, Lombard St., London. C: (1) E. King, counsel for p; (2) J. Pippard, counsel for d1; (3) W. Scafe, counsel for d2. Add: (1) Gilbert Ross, merchant, London, arbitrator between p and d1; (2) John Barns, merchant, London, arbitrator between p and d1. P seeks inj ag ds' suit at KB for payment of bonds and bills of exchange. D1 claims he lent money to p, his partner in a hopselling business, for which p issued a bond. D1 also claims p issued him another bond for a half share of profits. D1 transferred the bonds to d2, who drew bills of exchange on p for interest on the bonds. P refused to accept the bills, and asserts that the arbitrators who refereed the dissolution of the partnership determined that d1 had already received profits sufficient to cancel p's debts to him.

1784, Mich	E 112/1705	Bill. LMX 3817.
1784, Dec 11	E 112/1705	Answer. Swearing and filing date of d2's answer.
1785, Jan 22	E 112/1705	Answer. Swearing date of d1's answer, filed 24 January.

208. Eyre v Cooper

P: (1) Charles Eyre esq., King's printer, Clapham, Surrey, J. Eyre's son & executor; (2) William Strahan esq., King's printer, London. D: (1) James Cooper, bookseller, Yarmouth, Norf. C: (1) John Lloyd, counsel for ps. Add: (1) John Eyre gent., King's printer, Putney, Surrey, deceased, p1's father; (2) John Baskett, King's printer, London, bankrupt. Ps, King's printers, seek inj to prevent d from printing certain prayers. In 1731 J. Eyre lent sums amounting to £32,000 to J. Baskett (since bankrupt), in return for an assignment of the office of King's printer. In 1750 J. Eyre died, & p1, his son & executor, assumed the office, selling 1/3 to p2. Ps claim d has lately printed & sold prayers to which ps have exclusive printing rights. D allegedly denies ps' office grants them sole rights to print the prayers.

| 1784, Mich | E 112/1693 | Bill. LMX 3510; cf. E 112/1693 LMX 3511 Eyre v Mowbray, & E 112/1693 LMX 3512 Eyre v Gaines. |

209. Eyre v Gaines

P: (1) Charles Eyre esq., King's printer, Clapham, Surrey, J. Eyre's son & executor; (2) William Strahan esq., King's printer, London. D: (1) James Gaines, printer, Yarmouth, Norf. C: (1) John Lloyd, counsel for ps. Ps, King's printers, seek inj to prevent d from printing certain prayers. Ps claim d has lately printed & sold prayers to which ps have exclusive printing rights. D allegedly denies that ps' office grants them sole rights to print the prayers.

1784, Mich	E 112/1693	Bill. LMX 3512; cf. E 112/1693 LMX 3510 Eyre v Cooper, & E 112/1693 LMX 3511 Eyre v Mowbray.

210. Eyre v Mowbray

P: (1) Charles Eyre esq., King's printer, Clapham, Surrey, J. Eyre's son & executor; (2) William Strahan esq., King's printer, London. D: (1) Walter Mowbray, printer, Portsmouth, Hants. C: (1) John Lloyd, counsel for ps. Ps, King's printers, seek inj to prevent d from printing certain prayers. Ps claim d has lately printed & sold prayers to which ps have exclusive printing rights. D allegedly denies that ps' office grants them sole rights to print the prayers.

1784, Mich	E 112/1693	Bill. LMX 3511; cf. E 112/1693 LMX 3510 Eyre v Cooper, & E 112/1693 LMX 3512 Eyre v Gaines.

211. Finch v Greenhill

P: (1) Thomas Finch gent., Harlesdon Green, Wilsdon, Midd, J. Finch the E's son, executor & devisee in trust; (2) Joseph Finch the younger gent., Dollis Hill, Wilsdon, Midd, J. Finch the E's son & devisee in trust. D: (1) James Greenhill gent., solicitor, Lincolns Inn, Midd. C: (1) Thomas Nedham, counsel for p. Add: (1) Joseph Finch the elder gent., Harlesdon Green, Wilsdon, Midd, deceased, ps' father. Ps add a supplement to their bill filed in 1782 ag d in this Court seeking absolute foreclosure of d's mortgaged premises. Ps, devisees in trust of the estate of their father, J. Finch the E (deceased), claimed d had failed to repay several mortgages totalling £560 of his chambers in Lincolns Inn made to ps' father in 1763, 1770 & 1774. By way of supplement, ps add that the chambers have since burnt down, & ps received £500 insurance. D has rebuilt the chambers, & ps now seek payment of the balance of the mortgage arrears.

1785, Hil	E 112/1718	Supplementary bill. LMX 4159; schedule below bill of d's mortgage arrears, & insurance ps received.

212. Fitch v Andrews

P: (1) Ann Fitch, Cecil St., The Strand, Midd. D: (1) Richard Andrews the younger, R. Andrews the E's son & administrator. C: (1) Alexander Popham, counsel for p; (2) E. King, counsel for d. Add: (1) Richard Andrews the elder, wine merchant, Wood St., London, deceased intestate, d's father. P seeks payment of a bond. In 1769, p lent £3000 to R. Andrews the E, who issued p a bond for £3000 + interest & a mortgage of premises, the Devil Tavern, as security. Andrews the E died intestate in 1780, leaving d, his son & administrator. P claims d paid her interest on the loan, but none of the principal, so she sued him at KB. D alleges his father's estate is fully administered, & was insufficient to pay his debts.

1785, Trin	E 112/1723	Bill. LMX 4260; amended 19 December 1785 to claim R. Andrews the E's estate was sufficient to pay his debts.
1785, Nov 23	E 112/1723	Answer. Swearing & filing date.
1785, Mich	E 112/1723	Exception. P's exceptions concern the extent of d's father's estate.

213. Flight v Wadham

P: (1) Thomas Flight esq., Hackney, Midd, d's trustee; (2) Banister Flight gent., Queen St., Cheapside, London. D: (1) James Wadham, linen draper, Southwark, Surrey. C: (1) William Waller, counsel for ps; (2) John Fonblanque, counsel for d. Add: (1) Stephen Williams, linen draper, The Poultry, London, arbitrator between p2 & d; (2) William Prescott, linen draper, Bow Church Yard, London, arbitrator between p2 & d; (3) John Withers, linen draper, Cheapside, London, arbitrator between p2 & d; (4) Robert Wylie, merchant, Abchurch Lane, London, d's trustee, aged 45 years, ps' deponent. Ps seek inj ag any suit of d for payment of a £20,000 bond. In 1783, p2 became d's business partner as a scotch factor. A dispute arose, & p2 & d agreed to arbitration of S. Williams, W. Prescott & J. Withers, who dissolved the partnership. In 1784, d went insolvent, claiming he owed no more than £500, & entrusted his estate to pay his creditors to R. Wylie & p1, who issued d a £20,000 bond as security in return. Ps claim d actually owed far more than £500, & that d has directed his creditors to seek payment from p1, & threatens to sue p1 for payment of the £20,000 bond. D alleges ps knew his debts exceeded £500.

1784, Mich	E 112/1718	Bill. LMX 4157; amended 7 June 1785 to add that ps have been compelled to pay some of d's creditors; mistakenly attached to another suit Fielder v Leigh; cf. E 112/1718 LMX 4163 Flight v Wadham.
1785, Feb 19	E 112/1718	Answer. Swearing date of d's answer; schedule below answer of d's accounts.
1786, May 3	E 112/1718	Answer. Swearing date of d's answer to amended bill.
1786, Easter	E 112/1718	Replication. P denies D's answer is sufficient.
1786, Easter	E 112/1718	Rejoinder. D maintains his answer is sufficient.

214. Flight v Wadham

P: (1) Thomas Flight esq., Hackney, Midd, d's trustee; (2) Robert Wylie, merchant, Abchurch Lane, London, d's trustee; (3) Banister Flight gent., Queen St., Cheapside, London. D: (1) James Wadham, linen draper, Southwark, Surrey; (2) James Knight, d1's creditor; (3) John Wheeler, d1's creditor. C: (1) William Waller, counsel for ps. Ps, for themselves & other creditors of d1 except ds2-3, seek inj ag the suit of ds2-3 for payment of dividends from d1's estate. In 1784, d1 (p3's previous business partner) went insolvent & assigned his estate in trust to p1 & R. Wylie to pay his creditors. D1's creditors ds2-3 also signed the indenture of assignation, & issued d1 power of attorney to receive payment of their debts. Ps claim d1 did not transfer leasehold premises in Gracechurch St., London, to them as part of the assignation. Ds2-3 are now suing ps for payment of dividends which ps have witheld from d1. Ds assert the premises are of no value, & earn no income.

1785, Hil	E 112/1718	Bill. LMX 4163; cf. E 112/1718 LMX 4157 Flight v Wadham.
1785, May 9	E 112/1718	Answer. Swearing date of ds' answer, filed 10 May; schedule below answer of accounts of d1's debts & creditors.

215. Fontaine v Smith

P: (1) Elias Benjamin De la Fontaine esq., Bath. D: (1) Walter Smith, linen draper, Oxford St., London, d2's partner, bankrupt; (2) William Turner, linen draper, Oxford St., London, d1's partner, bankrupt; (3) Thomas Wooloton, linen draper, Oxford St., Midd, assignee of ds1-2; (4) Charles Miller, linen draper, King St., Cheapside, London, assignee of ds1-2; (5) William Salte, linen draper, The Poultry, London, assignee of ds1-2. C: (1) E. King, counsel for p; (2) J. Stanley, counsel for ds. Add: (1) John Henry Aickles, Nassau St., Soho, Midd, imprisoned for theft; (2) John Knight. P seeks inj ag ds' suit at KB for payment of a bill of exchange. P claims in 1783 he asked J. H. Aickles to draw a £200 bill of exchange upon him in return for the cash. Aickles never paid p the money, endorsed the bill away, & was imprisoned on a separate charge of theft. Ds1-2 went bankrupt with ds3-5 as assignees. Ds now sue p, claiming J. Knight bought goods from ds1-2 with the bill.

1785, Trin	E 112/1701	Bill. LMX 3704.
1786, Jan 23	E 112/1701	Answer. Swearing date of answer of ds3-5, filed 9 February.
1786, Jan 24	E 112/1701	Answer. Swearing & filing date of answer of ds1-2; schedule below answer of goods ds1-2 sold J. Knight in return for the bill.

216. Forbes v Mott

P: (1) Alexander Forbes, innholder, Wood St., London; (2) Edward Gilbert, innholder, Staines, Midd; (3) John Boxall, innholder, Farnham, Surrey; (4) John Leaver. D: (1) John Mott, innholder, Aldersgate St., London; (2) Thomas Harris, innholder, Aldersgate St., London; (3) William Hanks, innholder, Brentford, Midd, cf. also E 112/1708 LMX 3911; (4) Joseph White, innholder, Staines, Midd; (5) Peter Harvey, innholder, Bagshot, Surrey; (6) John Stevens, innholder, Farnham, Surrey; (7) James Over, innholder, Alton, Hants; (8) Joseph Hall, innholder, Wickham, Hants; (9) William Crease, innholder, Gosport, Hants. Ps seek enforcement of contract allegedly agreed between ps and ds. Ps, proprietors of the Heavy Coaches to and from London and Gosport, claim they agreed with ds, proprietors of the Light Coaches to and from London and Gosport, to join and share profits. Ds allegedly deny making any such agreement.

1784, Mich	E 112/1705	Bill. LMX 3812; no counsel named; cf. E 112/ 1907 OXFORDSHIRE 54 Costar v Harder, & E 112/1708 LMX 3911 Grave v Harder.

217. Forth v Cordukes
P: (1) John Forth gent., Holborn, St. Giles in the Fields, Midd. D: (1) Richard Cordukes, clerk, St. Mary Bishop Hill, Yorks, rector. C: (1) Thomas Lowes, counsel for p; (2) E. King, counsel for d. Add: (1) William Forth, brewer, York, Yorks, deceased, p's father, C. Forth's husband; (2) Catherine Forth, York, Yorks, deceased, p's mother, W. Forth's widow. P seeks payment of promissory notes totalling £3000 dating from 1750 which d, rector of St. Mary Bishop Hill, allegedly owed p's mother, C. Forth (deceased in 1775). P claims d promised to pay p's commission to join the army, but that d burnt the notes, & never paid the commission. D asserts that in 1750, p's mother attempted suicide when she heard a false rumour that d was to be married. D claims he issued her a £1000 promissory note, payable upon his marriage, to reassure her he would never marry.

1784, Mich	E 112/1699	Bill. LMX 3651.
1785, April 29	E 112/1699	Commission. For d's answer.
1785, June 11	E 112/1699	Answer. Swearing date, filed 16 June.

218. Foster v Jernegan
P: (1) Michael Foster esq., St. Leonard, Shoreditch, Midd, J. Marson's executor; (2) Angela Marson, St. Leonard, Shoreditch, Midd, J. Marson's executrix. D: (1) Elizabeth Jernegan, T. Jernegan's widow & executrix. C: (1) J. A. Stainsby, counsel for ps. Add: (1) James Marson, watch-case maker, St. Leonard, Shoreditch, Midd, deceased, p2's husband; (2) Thomas Jernegan, carpenter, Winchester St., London, d's husband; (3) William Jones, merchant, London. Ps seek foreclosure or repayment of a mortgage from d. In 1769 T. Jernegan mortgaged his leasehold messuage to W. Jones for £1000. In 1772, T. Jernegan defaulted on the repayments, & W. Jones transferred the mortgage to J. Marson. T. Jernegan died in 1777, leaving the mortgage unpaid & d1 his widow & executrix. J. Marson died, leaving ps as executors. Ps claim J. Marson's interest in the mortgaged premises had become absolute.

| 1785, Hil | E 112/1696 | Bill. LMX 3561. |

219. Foxall v Jones
P: (1) Richard Foxall, merchant, London. D: (1) Robert Jones, hatter, London. C: (1) Thomas Lowes, counsel for p. P seeks inj ag d's suit at KB for payment of a £250 promissory note. P claims in 1780 he asked d to account for debts allegedly owed to p. Instead d had p arrested in the Court of Common Pleas claiming p owed d debts. P issued d a £250 promissory note as security for any debts. Now d threatens to proceed to judgement on a verdict he obtained ag p at KB for the note.

| 1785, Hil | E 112/1697 | Bill. LMX 3616; cf. E 112/1724 LMX 4311 Foxall v Jones. |
| 1785, Feb 24 | E 112/1697 | Answer (with attachments). Swearing date; schedule attached of d's account with p. |

220. Foxall v Jones
P: (1) Richard Foxall gent., London. D: (1) Robert Jones, hatter, Birchin Lane, Cornhill, London. C: (1) William Waller, counsel for p; (2) John Lloyd, counsel for d. P seeks discovery of the true account between himself & d. P claims d

owed him debts from business dealings, but that in 1781, d had p arrested in the Court of Common Pleas for £170, but the dispute was resolved. In 1782, p was arrested at KB by another party's suit, & d became p's bail in return for security of a £250 promissory note from p. P also claims in 1784 he lent d 2 promissory notes for £23 & £20. D has sued p at KB for the notes. D asserts p still owes him £248 9s 8d.

1785, Trin	E 112/1724	Bill. LMX 4311; cf. E 112/1697 LMX 3616 Foxall v Jones.
1785, Nov 28	E 112/1724	Answer. Swearing date, filed 1 December; schedule below answer of account between d & p.
1786, Trin	E 112/1724	Exception. P's exceptions concern the promisory notes & accounts.
1786, Nov 14	E 112/1724	Further answer. Swearing & filing date of d's further answer.

221. Fraser v Huxham

P: (1) Thomas Fraser, merchant, underwriter, London; (2) George Ernst De Hahn, merchant, underwriter, Middle Moorfields, Midd; (3) Harry Sedgwick, merchant, underwriter, Newman's Court, Cornhill, London; (4) John Meyer, merchant, underwriter, Angel Court, Throgmorton St., London. D: (1) William Huxham, Charles Town, S. Carolina; (2) Humphrey Courtney, Charles Town, S. Carolina; (3) William Eales, Charles Town, S. Carolina; (4) John Hill, insurance broker, London; (5) James Thomas, clerk, d4's employee. C: (1) J. Pippard, counsel for ps; (2) William Cooke, counsel for ds. Ps seek inj ag the suit of ds1-3 at KB for payment of an insurance policy on the voyage of a ship, the *Providence*, & its cargo of rice from Charles Town, S. Carolina, to London, which ps underwrote for £100 each. Ps claim the policy is void because d4 & his clerk d5 persuaded them to underwrite it knowing the ship had been lost at sea (its crew & letters were rescued by another ship, the *Little Joe*). Ds deny ds4-5 knew the ship had been lost before the policy was underwritten.

1785, Easter	E 112/1700	Bill. LMX 3689.
1785, Nov 12	E 112/1700	Answer. Swearing & filing date of answer of ds4-5; schedule below answer of letters & accounts for ship & cargo.
1786, May 1	E 112/1700	Answer. Filing date of answer of ds1-3, sworn 13 February 1786; schedule below answer of letters & accounts for ship & cargo.

222. Frederick v Alexander

P: (1) Sir Charles Frederick, Hammersmith, Midd, knight of the Bath; (2) Thomas Lenox Frederick esq., Mount St., Berkeley Sq., Midd. D: (1) Thomas Alexander, Tom's Coffee House, Cornhill, London; (2) Peter Mortimer, linen draper, Bond St.; (3) Henry Salomons, notary public, Haymarket; (4) Robert Kennett, upholder, Bond St.; (5) William Facon; (6) Annesley Shee, Great Newport St., Long Acre; (7) George Crossley gent., Adelphi in the Strand. C: (1) Thomas Nedham, counsel for ps; (2) John Lloyd, counsel for d2; (3) W. Ainge, counsel for d1; (4) Thomas Lowes, counsel for d7; (5) James Agar,

counsel for d3. Add: (1) Thomas Freeman. Ps seek inj ag any suit of ds
seeking payment of bills of exchange. In 1784, p2 drew upon p1 3 bills of
exchange amounting to £1612 10s for T. Freeman to get discounted for p2. T.
Freeman never paid p2 the money, but endorsed the bills away. Ds1-2 now
possess the bills & threaten to sue for payment, claiming all the ds have given
value for the bills.

1785, Easter	E 112/1699	Bill. LMX 3648.
1785, June 4	E 112/1699	Answer. Swearing & filing date of d1's answer; 2 schedules included below answer of goods d7 bought from d1 with 2 of the bills of exchange.
1785, June 7	E 112/1699	Answer. Swearing date of d2's answer; schedule below answer of goods d5 bought from d2 with one of the bills.
1785, June 28	E 112/1699	Answer. Swearing date of d3's answer, filed 29 June.
1785, June 28	E 112/1699	Answer. Swearing & filing date of d7's answer.

223. Freeman v Hawkins
P: (1) Robert Freeman, victualler, Brick Lane, Spittalfields, Midd; (2) John
Maker the younger, Princes St., Spittalfields, Midd, p1's trustee. D: (1) Samuel
Hawkins, trustee of the act of Parliament; (2) Sanney Richard Cousemaker,
trustee of the act of Parliament; (3) David Wilmot, trustee of the act of
Parliament; (4) James Hatch, trustee of the act of Parliament; (5) Peter Lefevre,
trustee of the act of Parliament; (6) James Caney, trustee of the act of
Parliament; (7) Daniel Martin, trustee of the act of Parliament; (8) Lawrence
Dermott, trustee of the act of Parliament; (9) Charles Beck, trustee of the act of
Parliament; (10) James Henley, trustee of the act of Parliament; (11) John
Perry, trustee of the act of Parliament; (12) Charles Mills, trustee of the act of
Parliament; (13) John Robinson, trustee of the act of Parliament; (14) Isaac
Colnett, & other commissioners for executing the act. C: (1) John Fonblanque,
counsel for ps. Ps seek payment of £200 purchase money for land from ds.
After an act of Parliament of 19GIII for improving the recovery of small debts
within Tower Hamlets, d14 & the other commissioners for executing the act
agreed in 1779 to purchase land & transfer it to ds1-13 in trust to build a Court
House for Tower Hamlets. Ps claim that in 1780 ds agreed with p2 to buy p1's
land in Whitechapel for £200, the indentures were drawn up, & ds took
possession. Ps claim ds have never paid them the £200.

1785, Trin	E 112/1718	Bill. LMX 4154.

224. French v Mason
P: (1) Andrew French, Batwone, Galway. D: (1) Kender Mason, merchant,
London. C: (1) F. P. Stratford, counsel for p; (2) William Walter, counsel for d.
P, claiming to be heir by distant descent to estates in Montserrat, seeks
discovery from d, current mortgagor, of deeds or other documents which may
support his claim.

1785, Easter	E 112/1701	Bill. LMX 3696.
1785, July 27	E 112/1701	Answer. Filing date.

225. French v Thellufson

P: (1) Andrew French, merchant, London; (2) Daniel Hobson, merchant, London; (3) Benjamin Champion, merchant, London; (4) Thomas Roebuck, merchant, London; (5) John Nutt, merchant, London; (6) Joseph Watkins, merchant, London; (7) William Davis, merchant, London; (8) Jacob Wilkinson, merchant, London; (9) Joseph Nutt, merchant, London; (10) John Whitmore, merchant, London. D: (1) Peter Thellufson, merchant, London, partners with ds2-3, d4's agent; (2) John Cossart, merchant, London, partners with d1 & d3, d4's agent; (3) Edward Simeon, merchant, London, partners with ds1-2, d4's agent; (4) Jean Francois Hubert, merchant, Dunkirk, owner of the ship, *Prudente*; (5) Antoine Francois De Gand, ship's captain. C: (1) E. King, counsel for ps; (2) William Alexander, counsel for ds. Ps seek inj ag ds' suit at cl for payment of an insurance policy. In 1784 ps became the underwriters for a £2000 insurance policy which d4 had caused ds1-3 to prepare for the ship *Prudente* & its cargo on a voyage from Dunkirk to Bordeaux, with d5 as captain. Ps claim the ship was unseaworthy and therefore had to be abandoned with its cargo. Ds are suing for the policy, maintaining ps are still liable.

1784, Mich	E 112/1692	Bill. LMX 3507.
1784, Dec 11	E 112/1692	Answer (with attachments). Swearing & filing date of the answer of ds4-5; schedule attached of the accounts in French of ds4-5 concerning the voyage.
1784, Dec 11	E 112/1692	Answer (with attachments). Swearing & filing date of answer of ds1-3; schedule attached of the accounts in French of ds4-5 concerning the voyage.

226. Garrard v Hunt

P: (1) Jacob Garrard gent., London. D: (1) Thomas Hunt, livery stable keeper, Surrey side, Blackfriars Bridge, London; (2) Thomas Jennings. C: (1) Thomas Lowes, counsel for p; (2) E. King, counsel for d2. P seeks inj ag d2's suit at KB for non-payment of promissory note which p issued d1 allegedly on the understanding that d1 would pay it off before the due date. D1 transferred it to d2 as part-payment of a debt, but failed to pay it off on time. D1 is now in KB prison for (another?) debt. P claims ds are colluding to extort money from him.

| 1785, Easter | E 112/1701 | Bill. LMX 3710. |
| 1785, Nov 11 | E 112/1701 | Answer. Filing date. |

227. Garton v Mosely

P: (1) Jonathan Garton esq., Charlotte St., Bloomsbury, Midd. D: (1) Jacobus Mosely, broker, Coventry St., Westminster, Midd; (2) Michael Jacobs, goldsmith, Prescott St.; (3) Robert Albion Cox, goldsmith, d4's partner; (4) William Merle, goldsmith, d3's partner; (5) Henry Solomon, Coventry St., Westminster, Midd; (6) Thomas Thompson, Coventry St., Westminster, Midd; (7) William Monkhouse; (8) Thomas Beckett, attorney at law; (9) Joseph George Brett, Cockspur St., Charing Cross, Midd. C: (1) Thomas Lowes, counsel for p; (2) J. Crode, counsel for ds8-9. P seeks inj ag ds' suits at KB for payment for bills of exchange. In 1784, p borrowed £200 from d1, upon the security of 3 bills of exchange. P could not pay the bills by the due date, so issued d1 further security of a mortgage on his premises in Erith, Kent, for a further loan of £150. D1 allegedly never paid p the further £150. D1 endorsed a bill to d2, who discounted it with ds3-4. D1 transferred another bill to d5, who issued it to d6, who paid it to d8. D1 transferred the third bill to d9. Ds8-9 allege they were paid the bills for goods, and severally sue p for payment.

1785, Easter	E 112/1708	Bill. LMX 3914.
1785, April 25	E 112/1708	Answer. Swearing & filing date of d8's answer.
1785, April 25	E 112/1708	Answer. Swearing & filing date of d9's answer; schedule below answer of accounts between d1 & d9.

228. Gawler v Shoolbred

P: (1) Samuel Gawler, solicitor, Clements Inn, Midd. D: (1) John Shoolbred, Jane Shoolbred's husband; (2) Elizabeth Rudman, J. Rudman's widow & executrix. C: (1) Josiah Brown, counsel for p; (2) E. King, counsel for d2. Add: (1) Francis Hislop, linen draper, Bradford, Wilts, deceased, Jane Shoolbred's father; (2) John Rudman, yeoman, Metsham, Wilts, deceased, d2's husband; (3) James Spragg gent., Melksham, Wilts, now in KB prison, ds' deponent; (4) Jane Shoolbred, d1's wife, F. Hislop's daughter. P seeks payment of a bond. In 1769, F. Hislop issued a £200 bond to J. Rudman, who transferred the bond to J. Spragg, who assigned the bond to p, his creditor. P, on behalf of J. Rudman, sued among others d1 & his wife Jane, F. Hislop's daughter, for the bond in 1777 in the Court of Common Pleas. D1 got an inj in this Court ag J. Rudman. In 1784 J. Rudman died, leaving d2 his widow & executrix. P claims ds now conspire in refusing to pay the bond. D2 denies F. Hislop owed her husband money.

1785, Trin	E 112/1717	Bill. LMX 4118; amended 28 February 1787 to include more details of earlier litigation between p & ds.
1785, Nov 28	E 112/1717	Commission. For d2's answer.
1785, Dec 24	E 112/1717	Answer. Swearing date of d2's answer, filed 11 January 1786.
1786, Easter	E 112/1717	Replication. P asserts d1's answer (missing) & d2's answer are insufficient.
1786, Easter	E 112/1717	Rejoinder. Ds1-2 maintain their answers are sufficient.

229. Gibson v Ward

P: (1) Thomas Gibson, builder, Portland Place, Midd; (2) James Gibson, builder, Portland Place, Midd. D: (1) William Ward gent.. C: (1) R. Richards, counsel for ps. Ps seeks inj ag d's suit at law for payment of arrears of rent. Ps claim in 1779 they agreed to lease d's premises in Weymouth Mews for 99 years at £8 per annum. Ps claim they have been paying rent for the premises, on which they have built a coach house & stables, but that d refuses to execute the lease.

1785, Hil	E 112/1699	Bill. LMX 3654.

230. Gill v Galloway

P: (1) Thomas Gill, merchant, insurer, Dowgate Hill, London. D: (1) John Galloway, Dublin; (2) Alexander Stillas, merchant, Dublin. C: (1) W. Scafe, counsel for p; (2) John Reade, counsel for d2. Add: (1) John Cadenhead, ship's captain. P, insurance underwriter, seeks inj ag ds' suit at KB for payment of insurance for ds' ship, the *Success*, and cargo which sank in the Delaware river, N. America, on a voyage from Dublin to Philadelphia. P claims the ship was deliberately grounded by the captain J. Cadenhead (whom p alleges was a part owner), and that ds are therefore not entitled to the insurance.

1784, Mich	E 112/1705	Bill. LMX 3815.
1784, Mich	E 112/1705	Commission. For ds' answers.
1784, Dec 7	E 112/1705	Answer. Swearing date of d2's answer.
1785, Jan 26	E 112/1705	Answer. Swearing date of d1's answer in Dublin; filed 4 March 1785. Includes captain's account of voyage.
1785, Trin	E 112/1705	Exception. P's exceptions to d1's answer concern the captain's responsibilities, and whether any cargo was saved.
1785, Trin	E 112/1705	Exception. P's exceptions to d2's answer as those to d1's.

231. Graham v Crooke

P: (1) George Graham, Wapping, Midd. D: (1) Solomon Crooke; (2) George Kirchner. C: (1) Thomas Lowes, counsel for p; (2) F. Walker, counsel for ds. Add: (1) Francis Ewers, carpenter, Princes Square, Midd. P seeks inj ag d2's suit at KB for payment of a promissory note. P claims in 1784 he verbally agreed with d1 to become tenant of a house in Wapping which d1 leased from F. Ewers, & to buy its fixtures from d1. P paid d1 a £30 11s 6d promissory note for the fixtures. When F. Ewers claimed he owned the fixtures, p asked d1 to cancel the note, but d1 had already endorsed it to d2, who got a verdict at KB ag p for payment. D1 asserts the fixtures were his to sell.

1785, Hil	E 112/1718	Bill. LMX 4149.
1785, Feb 1	E 112/1718	Answer. Swearing & filing date of ds' answer; schedule below answer of fixtures.

232. Grant v Aymer

P: (1) James Grant esq., London, previously of Quebec. D: (1) Philip Aymer. C: (1) William Grant, counsel for p. P seeks inj ag d's suit in the Court of Common Pleas. P claims in 1780, while living in Quebec, he hired d as a servant, who mistreated p's family. P claims in 1782 he discharged d from his employ, & struck him with a stick. P claims he paid for the medical treatment of d's injuries & compensation demanded by d, but since p's return to England, d has sued him for assault in the Court of Common Pleas.

1785, Easter	E 112/1724	Bill. LMX 4307.

233. Grant v le Gallais

P: (1) George Grant esq., Bedford Row, Midd. D: (1) Francis le Gallais esq., Kensington Sq., Midd. C: (1) Thomas Evance, counsel for p; (2) Josiah

Brown, counsel for d. Add: (1) Thomas Rowntree, money scrivener, Essex St., Midd, bankrupt; (2) James Sutton, silversmith, Cheapside, London, bankrupt. P seeks relief from d's suit at KB for repayment of loan made jointly to p, T. Rowntree and J. Sutton. D raised the money by selling bank annuities, which the partners agreed to buy back for d with interest. P claims he and Sutton repaid some of the debt, but d claims Sutton was repaying a separate debt. As p's partners have since gone bankrupt, d is suing p for the entire balance.

1785, Easter   E 112/1700   Bill. LMX 3688.
1785, July 13   E 112/1700   Answer. Swearing date.

234. Grant v Lunell

P: (1) George Grant esq., Bedford Row, Midd. D: (1) Peter Lunell, banker, Bristol, assignee for d8 & d10; (2) Richard Aldridge, banker, Bristol, assignee for d8 & d10; (3) John Edye, banker, Bristol, assignee for d8 & d10; (4) Edward Wigan, linen draper, Bristol, assignee for d8 & d10; (5) Nathan Mullens, jeweller, Bristol, assignee of d9 & d11; (6) Joseph Walton, oilman, Little Britain, London, assignee of d9 & d11; (7) Francis Broderip, music seller, Cheapside, London, assignee of d9 & d11; (8) Henry Bicknell, banker, Bristol, partners with ds10-11; (9) James Sutton, goldsmith, banker, Cheapside, London, d11's partner; (10) Thomas Gillam, banker, Bristol, partners with d8 & d11; (11) James Bult, goldsmith, banker, Cheapside, London, partners with ds8-10. C: (1) W. Scafe, counsel for p; (2) John Lloyd, counsel for ds1-4, d8 & d10. P seeks inj ag ds' suits for alleged debts. P claims he had dealings with d9 & d11, partners as bankers. In 1784, d11 also became partners with d8 & d10 as bankers. P claims d10 coerced him into issuing a £2736 1s 6d bill of exchange which d10 alleged p owed d9 & d11. D9 & d11 went bankrupt, with ds5-7 as assignees, who are suing p in the Court of Common Pleas for a £95 debt. D8 & d10 have also gone bankrupt, with ds1-4 as assignees, who are suing p at KB for the bill of exchange. P denies owing either debt.

1784, Mich   E 112/1722   Bill. LMX 4253.
1786, July 5   E 112/1722   Commission. For the answer of ds1-4, d8 & d10.
1786, July 22   E 112/1722   Answer (with attachments). Answer of ds1-4, d8 & d10, sworn by d1, ds3-4, d8 & d10 on this date, sworn by d2 on 26 July; schedule of accounts attached.

235. Grant v Sedley

P: (1) Alexander Grant esq., captain in the 13th Regiment of Foot, p3's son; (2) Richard Brook Webber esq.; (3) Anna Maria Grant, Manchester Square, London, p1's mother. D: (1) Davenport Sedley, moneylender, Swithins Lane, London; (2) John Wilson esq., Mile End, Midd; (3) Massey Stackpoole esq., cornet in the Regiment of Horse Guards; (4) Elizabeth Anthony, Mile End, Midd. C: (1) Thomas Nedham, counsel for ps; (2) William Cooke, counsel for d2 & d4; (3) J. Stanley, counsel for d3; (4) Geo Sloper, counsel for d1. Ps seek inj ag ds' suits at KB for payment of securities. Ps claim in 1781 they issued d1 two £150 bonds & a bond for a £60 annuity, in return for a £300 loan. D1 paid ps £20 cash, a horse & £280 in securities, which ps could not get accepted. D1 transferred the annuity to d2, & persuaded ps to execute a warrant of attorney to enter judgement in KB as security for the annuity. D1 transferred the bonds to ds2-4. Ds now sue ps at KB. D1 claims he only agreed to lend ps £150.

1785, Easter	E 112/1708	Bill. LMX 3898.
1785, May 5	E 112/1708	Answer. Swearing date of answer of d2 & d4, filed 6 May.
1785, Nov 10	E 112/1708	Answer. Swearing & filing date of d3's answer.
1785, Mich	E 112/1708	Exception. Ps' exceptions to d3's answer concerns the acquisition of the securities by ds2-4 from d1.
1785, Dec 13	E 112/1708	Amended bill. Bill amended to address issues raised in exceptions.
1786, Feb 13	E 112/1708	Further answer. Swearing & filing date of d3's further answer.
1787, Jan 23	E 112/1708	Answer. Swearing date of d1's answer, filed 23 January.

236. Grave v Harder

P: (1) John Grave gent., innholder, Furnival's Inn, London. D: (1) Thomas Harder, innholder, London; (2) Robert Gray, innholder, London; (3) William Hanks, innholder, Brentford, Midd; (4) William Cox, innholder, Colnbrook, Midd; (5) William Costar, innholder, Oxon; (6) John Shrubb, innholder, Benson, Oxon; (7) Stephen Wentworth, innholder, Kingston Inn, Oxon; (8) Christopher Bolton, innholder, Farringdon, Berks; (9) George Phillips, innholder, Fairford, Glos; (10) William Brewer, innholder, Cirencester, Glos; (11) Thomas Masters, stage master, Cirencester, Glos; (12) Daniel Masters, stage master, Cirencester, Glos. C: (1) Thomas Nedham, counsel for p. P seeks enforcement of contract allegedly agreed between p and ds. P claims the ds, proprietors of the Light and Heavy Stroud Water Tetbury and Cirencester Stage Coaches, contracted to use his inn, the Bell and Crown, Holborn. P accordingly invested in horses and equipment, but the ds allegedly deny they entered into any such contract.

| 1785, Easter | E 112/1708 | Bill. LMX 3911; cf. E 112/1907 OXFORDSHIRE 54 Costar v Harder, & E 112/1705 LMX 3812 Forbes v Mott. |

237. Gregory v Bateman

P: (1) Barnard Gregory gent., solicitor, Lyons Inn, Midd; (2) Richard Hankins gent., solicitor, Lyons Inn, Midd; (3) Oliver Edwards gent., solicitor, Lyons Inn, Midd; (4) James Best gent., solicitor, Lyons Inn, Midd; (5) John Richardson gent., solicitor, New Inn Buildings, Wych St., Midd. D: (1) Maurice Bateman; (2) Francis Skyrme, W. Skyrme's father. C: (1) Charles Cotton, counsel for ps. Add: (1) William Skyrme gent., deceased, d2's son. Ps seek inj ag ds' suit at KB. Ps1-4, trustees for the Society of Lyons Inn, claim that in 1776 the Society leased chambers to William Skyrme for his lifetime, who in turn let them to p5. W. Skyrme died in 1780, & his father d2 did not inform ps1-4 of his son's death, but asked p5 to pay the rent directly to d1, not via ps1-4. In 1783, p5 quit the chambers, & ps1-4 found out W. Skyrme was dead, & sought reimbursement from ds of rent since his death. Ds are suing p5 at KB for alleged non-payment of rent.

1784, Mich   E 112/1723   Bill. LMX 4263.

238. Gregory v Dennis

P: (1) Henry Gregory, optician, Leadenhall St., London. D: (1) Thomas Dennis, wine merchant, Love Lane, East Cheap, London, p's brother in law. C: (1) Antony Hart, counsel for p; (2) Charles Shuter, counsel for d. P seeks inj ag any future suit by d for payment of an accountable receipt p issued d. P claims he issued the receipt in return for a promissory note which he subsequently paid off to a third party to whom p had transferred it at a discount. D asserts the receipt was given in exchange for a cash loan, and should be repaid.

1784, Mich   E 112/1705   Bill. LMX 3798.
1784, Nov 15   E 112/1705   Answer. Swearing date.
[1785, undated] E 112/1705   Exception. P's exception concerns his dealings with d.

239. Groves v Poole

P: (1) John Groves, bricklayer, Milbank, St., Westminster, Midd, trustee of d1's estate. D: (1) Samuel Gower Poole; (2) Edward Scales; (3) Thomas Wilkinson gent., Friday St., London; (4) James Miller, merchant, Watling St., London. C: (1) E. King, counsel for p; (2) Thomas Nedham, counsel for d2; (3) T. Pippard, counsel for d1 & ds3-4. Add: (1) Josiah Dornford, trustee of d1's estate; (2) John Hawkins, trustee of d1's estate; (3) Edward Webster, trustee of d1's estate; (4) David Grant, trustee of d1's estate; (5) Timothy Brown, trustee of d1's estate; (6) John Young, trustee of d1's estate; (7) Thomas Evans, trustee of d1's estate. P, for himself & the other trustees of d1's estate, seeks payment of profits from ds' brewhouse. In 1781, p filed a bill in this Court ag J. Dornford, J. Hawkins, E. Webster, D. Grant, T. Brown, J. Young & T. Evans (appointed trustees with p in 1778 to receive d1's estate & pay his debts), & ds1-2, against the trustees' sale of d1's estate to d2. P claimed the sale was collusive between ds1-2, to the loss of d1's creditors. As supplement, p adds that in 1784, ds1-2 sold d1's brewhouse to ds3-4. P claims ds1-4, as partners, now receive profits from the brewhouse which should be transferred to the trustees, to pay d1's debts. Ds deny the sale was collusive.

1785, Easter   E 112/1706   Supplementary bill. LMX 3831.
1785, Sept 16   E 112/1706   Answer. Swearing date of answer of ds3-4, filed 4 November.
1785, Sept 16   E 112/1706   Answer. Swearing date of d1's answer, filed 4 November.
1785, Sept 19   E 112/1706   Answer. Swearing & filing date of d2's answer.

240. Halliday v Paulhan

P: (1) John Halliday esq., Parliament St., Midd; (2) Matthias Kitchen gent., Mile End, Midd. D: (1) John Lewis Paulhan, broker, Mark Lane, London, employee of ds3-4; (2) John Francis Blache, broker, Mark Lane, London, employee of ds3-4; (3) William McDowall Colhoun, plantation manager, J.

Mills' employee; (4) George Daniell, plantation manager, J. Mills' employee. C: (1) G. Daniell the younger, counsel for ps. Add: (1) John Mills, Great St. Helens, London, deceased. Ps, for themselves & the other annuity creditors of the estate of J. Mills (deceased), seek payment of annuities & an inj to prevent ds1-2 from paying sums to ds3-4. In 1774, J. Mills & his managers, ds3-4, granted ps annuities payable from a plantation on the island of Nevis in return for £15,000. In 1781, J. Mills went bankrupt, but ds3-4 have continued to manage the plantation, depositing profits from the sale of sugar with their brokers ds1-2, but neglecting to pay ps' annuities.
1784, Mich   E 112/1691   Bill. LMX 3483.

241. Halliwell v Robinson
P: (1) John Halliwell, currier, St. Martin in the Fields, Midd. D: (1) Samuel Robinson, tire smith; (2) Ann Tookey, H. Tookey's widow & executrix; (3) Matthias Stable, coach maker, Hanover Sq., Midd, partners with d4; (4) John Somerville, coach maker, Hanover Sq., Midd, partners with d3. C: (1) Thomas Nedham, counsel for p. Add: (1) Henry Tookey, tire smith, parish of St. Marylbone, Midd, deceased, d2's husband. P seeks payment of a £67 13s debt from ds. In 1778, ds3-4 owed £101 12s to p, £120 to d1, & £55 to H. Tookey. Ds3-4 were unable to pay, so they assigned their estate to p, d1 & H. Tookey in trust to pay their debts, with d1 as principal trustee. In 1783, H. Tookey died leaving d2 his widow & executrix. P claims he is still owed £67 13s from the estate, whereas ds1-2 have been fully repaid. Ds allegedly deny p is still owed money, or assert the estate is insufficient to pay the debt.
1785, Trin   E 112/1702   Bill. LMX 3733.

242. Hardy v Bulmer
P: (1) Elizabeth Hardy, North St., Westminster, Midd. D: (1) Blackett Bulmer; (2) James Milbourne, carver, gilder, the Strand, Midd. C: (1) Charles Shuter, counsel for p; (2) W. Ainge, counsel for ds. Add: (1) John Riley, auctioneer, Long Acre, Westminster, Midd. P, a widow, seeks inj ag any suit of ds for payment of a bond. D1 lent money to p and received as security her household goods and her bond. P asserts she repaid the loan but d1 refused to return her goods, alleging that some had been stolen from his warehouse. Neither will d1 cancel her bond, which d1 had transferred to d2 (who had paid John Riley with it). P wants a true inventory of all the goods, payment for missing ones, and cancellation of the bond.
1785, Trin   E 112/1708   Bill. LMX 3909.
1785, July 2   E 112/1708   Answer. Swearing date of ds' answer.

243. Harrington v Salomons
P: (1) George Harrington gent., Brentford, Midd. D: (1) Henry Salomons, Coventry St., Haymarket, Midd; (2) Abraham Hendriks, Coventry St., Haymarket, Midd; (3) John Martyn, tailor, Rupert St., Westminster, Midd; (4) John Andrews, carpenter, Air St., Piccadilly, London; (5) William Taylor, stone mason, Berwick St., Soho, Midd. P seeks inj ag d2's suit at KB for payment of a bill of exchange. P claims in 1784, d1 agreed to lend him £100, for which p allowed 2 £50 bills of exchange to be drawn upon him in favour of d2. P also executed a warrant of attorney to confess judgement in KB for £200, as

collateral security, at d1's request. P claims d1 never lent him the £100, but d2 paid the bills to d3, who paid one to d4, who paid it to d5. D2 threatens to sue out execution of the judgement in KB ag p, allegedly asserting d1 paid p the £100 in goods.

| 1785, Hil | E 112/1734 | Bill. LMX 4539; truncated; attached to answer from different suit. |

244. Harris v Bruere

P: (1) Mary Simeon Stuart Harris, Kennett, Cambs. D: (1) Goulstone Bruere esq., legatee of Sophia Stuart; (2) Joseph Kaye gent., attorney at law, N. Audley St., Grosvenor Sq., Midd, hired to recover arrears. C: (1) Robert Ledlie, counsel for p; (2) Thomas Lowes, counsel for d1; (3) William Walter, counsel for d2. Add: (1) Sophia Stuart, Warfield, Berks, deceased; (2) Mary Stuart, Lakenham, Suff, deceased. P, a spinster, seeks enforcement of the will of Mary Stuart who made p her sole executrix and legatee. Among the assets p alleged was Mary Stuart's legacy from Sophia Stuart, consisting of arrears of an annuity payable to Sophia. Those arrears were the subject of litigation between d1 and d2, and p also seeks inj to halt that litigation as part of p's claim via Mary to a share of the arrears.

1785, Easter	E 112/1708	Bill. LMX 3912.
[1785, undated]	E 112/1708	Answer. D1's answer.
1785, Nov 18	E 112/1708	Answer. Filing date of d2's answer.

245. Hayward v Hayward

P: (1) William Hayward, merchant, Fenchurch St., London, d1's brother. D: (1) Nathaniel Hayward, merchant, Philpott Lane, London, p's brother, bankrupt; (2) Elizabeth Hayward, Philpott Lane, London, d1's wife; (3) Samuel Prince esq., d1's creditor; (4) James Sutton, d1's assignee; (5) John Francis Rivaz, d1's assignee; (6) Luder Hoffham, d1's assignee. C: (1) R. Richards, counsel for p; (2) Richard Hollist, counsel for d3; (3) John Mitford, counsel for ds4-6. P seeks inj ag ds' suit at KB for payment of p's bond. P took on d1's failing business, and agreed to sell d1 an annuity in return for £1000. P signed d1's bond allowing p to buy the business in exchange for the annuity. P claims he was unhappy with the bond but signed it anyway. D1 did not pay the £1000, so p did not pay the annuity. D1 went bankrupt, and his creditor d3 and assignees d4, d5 and d6 demand payment of arrears of the annuity.

1784, Mich	E 112/1705	Bill. LMX 3827.
1785, Dec 8	E 112/1705	Answer. Filing date of d3's answer.
1786, June 3	E 112/1705	Answer. Filing date of d6's answer.
1787, May 24	E 112/1705	Answer. Filing date of the answer of ds4-5.

246. Hazlehurst v Hole

P: (1) Elizabeth Hazlehurst, Priest Alley, Tower Dock, London, R. Fawcett's cousin & legatee. D: (1) Benjamin Hole esq., Powis Place, Gt. Ormond St., Midd, R. Fawcett's executor & trustee; (2) John Seymour, surgeon, Theobalds Rd., Midd, R. Fawcett's executor & trustee; (3) William Holden, clerk, Chatteris, Ely, Cambs, R. Fawcett's alleged heir at law. C: (1) Arthur Onslow, counsel for p. Add: (1) Robert Fawcett gent., Southampton Row, Bloomsbury, Midd, deceased. P, a widow, seeks payment of £100 left to her by her cousin

R. Fawcett, who died in 1784 appointing ds1-2 as his executors, entrusted to sell his estate & pay his debts & legacies. D3 allegedly claims to be R. Fawcett's heir at law, & disputes the will. Ds also apparently deny the estate is sufficient to pay the debts.

1785, Trin   E 112/1706   Bill. LMX 3857.

247. Heighway v Dawson

P: (1) Richard Heighway, attorney at law, Rathbone Place, Midd. D: (1) Thomas Dawson; (2) Andrew Thompson, tailor, Litchfield St., Midd. C: (1) J. Pippard, counsel for p; (3) Thomas Nedham, counsel for ds. P seeks inj ag d1's suit at cl for payment of promissory notes. P had formerly hired d2 to make clothes, & d2 had hired p as his attorney. P claims d2 became indebted to him, could not pay, but offered to get promissory notes discounted for p. P issued the notes to d2, who did not pay p the discounted money, but endorsed the notes to d1. D1 now sues p for the notes. D2 asserts p owed him far more than he owed p, & that the account is now even.

1784, Mich	E 112/1694	Bill. LMX 3530.
1784, Dec 8	E 112/1694	Answer. Swearing date of d1's answer, filed 11 December.
1784, Dec 11	E 112/1694	Answer. Swearing date of d2's answer, filed 13 December.
1785, Easter	E 112/1694	Replication. P asserts ds' answers are insufficient.
1785, Easter	E 112/1694	Rejoinder. Ds maintain their answers are sufficient.

248. Higgins v Myers

P: (1) Hugh Higgins esq., parish of St. Marylebone, Midd. D: (1) Napthali Hart Myers, merchant, John St., America Sq., London, A. Grant's administrator; (2) Thomas Vardon, merchant, Grace Church St., London, A. Grant's administrator; (3) Peter Robinson, coppersmith, High St., St. Mary White Chapel, Midd, A. Grant's administrator; (4) Robert Tuite esq., Portman Sq., St. Marylebone, Midd, now abroad. C: (1) Robert Comyn, counsel for p. Add: (1) Alexander Grant, merchant, Billitter Lane, London, deceased intestate. P seeks discovery of A. Grant's estate from ds. In 1780, p claims he lent d4 £5000 upon a £10000 bond, with A. Grant as security. D4 went abroad without paying. A. Grant died intestate, and his creditors ds1-3 became his administrators. Ds1-3 allegedly deny d4 borrowed the money, or claim it has been repaid, or that A. Grant's estate is insufficient to pay the debt.

1784, Mich   E 112/1704   Bill. LMX 3778.

249. Hooper v Raben

P: (1) John Hooper gent., solicitor, London. D: (1) John Raben, coal merchant, Holborn, London; (2) John Devey gent., Mile End, Midd; (3) Mathias Fleming; (4) Thomas Hamlen, Southwark, Surrey. C: (1) S. S. Cox, counsel for p. P seeks inj ag d1's suit at KB for payment of a promissory note. P claims in 1784, he (as d2's solicitor) recovered sums due to d2, for which p issued d4 (d2's agent) a £14 promissory note. P claims d2 persuaded him to issue him another £14 note, promising to cancel the first. D4 endorsed the 1st note away. D2 endorsed the 2nd note to d1, who, in cooperation with ds2-3, is now suing p at KB for payment. Ds allegedly claim p issued the 2nd note for a separate debt.

1785, Hil   E 112/1717   Bill. LMX 4120.

250. Horsley v Fuller

P: (1) John Horsley, brass founder, Haberdasher's Walk, Hoxton, Midd. D: (1) Richard Fuller the younger, banker, London, partner of other ds; (2) John Halford, banker, London, partner of other ds; (3) John Vaughan, banker, London, partner of other ds. C: (1) Robert Ledlie, counsel for p; (2) William Alexander, counsel for ds. Add: (1) Richard Oakes, timber merchant, Snowhill, London; (2) Richard Fuller the elder, banker, London, deceased, ds' partner. P seeks inj ag ds' suit at KB for payment of bills of exchange. R. Oakes drew bills on p, promising to pay them off by the due date. Oakes discounted them at the bank of ds & R. Fuller the E. P claims the ds assured him that they held Oakes's premises as security and p would not have to pay the bills. Nonetheless, p filed a bill ag any suit for payment of the bills. Oakes went bankrupt, R. Fuller the elder died, and the surviving ds sued p for payment of the bills.

1784, Mich	E 112/1705	Bill. LMX 3820.
1784, Nov 20	E 112/1705	Answer. Swearing date of ds' answer.
1784, Mich	E 112/1705	Exception. P's exceptions concern compensation ds received for Oakes's bad debts from the sale of his premises, and payment by Oakes's debtors.
1785, Jan 16	E 112/1705	Amended bill. More detailed account of Oakes's dealings with ds.
1785, March 26	E 112/1705	Further answer. Filing date.

251. Horton v Biggar

P: (1) John Shadwell Horton esq., Bedford St., Covent Garden, London. D: (1) Robert Biggar, wholesale draper, London, d2's partner; (2) John Hamilton, wholesale draper, London, d1's partner. C: (1) Thomas Finch, counsel for p; (2) William Alexander, counsel for ds. Add: (1) Richard Hatchett, linen draper, Tavistock St., Covent Garden, London. P seeks inj ag ds' suit at KB for payment of 2 bills of exchange. P claims that in 1784 R. Hatchett owed debts to ds, & drew 2 bills of exchange totalling £246 10s 6d upon p to pay ds, promising to pay them off before the due dates. Hatchett since went insolvent & died, & ds had p arrested at KB for payment of the bills. Ds assert that Hatchett drew the bills upon p as payment for debts p owed Hatchett.

1785, Trin	E 112/1718	Bill. LMX 4165a.
1785, Oct 26	E 112/1718	Answer. Ds' answer, sworn by d2 on this date, sworn by d1 & filed on 27 October.

252. Hughes v Baldwyn

P: (1) John Hughes, sail maker, Red Lyon St., Wapping, Midd; (2) Edward Simon gent., Mile End, Old Town, Midd. D: (1) Richard Baldwyn, linen draper, Smithfield, London; (2) John Knight, yeoman, 9 Boulton Row, Piccadilly, London; (3) Thomas Woolloton, linen draper, Oxford St., Midd. C: (1) Charles

Shuter, counsel for ps; (2) Thomas Evance, counsel for d1; (3) Richard Hollist, counsel for d3. Add: (1) John Henry Aickles, 9 Boulton Row, Piccadilly, London. Ps seek inj ag ds' suits at KB for payment of 2 bills of exchange. In 1783, p1 issued two £250 bills to J. H. Aickles in return for a £500 loan, which Aickles never advanced him. Ds then sued ps for the bills at KB. D3 asserts he received the bills in payment for debts & goods, & paid one of them to d1 in return for goods. D1 denies any acquaintance with d2 or Aickles.

1784, Mich	E 112/1717	Bill. LMX 4119.
1784, Nov 25	E 112/1717	Answer. Swearing date of d1's answer; schedule below answer of goods for which d3 paid d1 one bill.
1785, Hil	E 112/1717	Exception. Ps' exceptions to d1's answer concern the relationship between d2, J. H. Aickles, d1 & d3.
1785, Sept 14	E 112/1717	Answer (with attachments). Swearing date of d3's answer, filed 16 September; schedules attached of d3's accounts with d1, etc.
1786, April 13	E 112/1717	Further answer. Swearing date of d1's further answer, filed 15 April.
1786, Easter	E 112/1717	Replication. Ps assert d3's answer is insufficient.
1786, Easter	E 112/1717	Rejoinder. D3 maintains his answer is sufficient.

253. Hunter v Sharrer

P: (1) Thomas Hunter, warehouseman, Blackfriars, London. D: (1) Thomas Sharrer, silk broker, London, p's brother-in-law; (2) James Collins Walker, silkman, Carey Lane, London. C: (1) Robert Steele, counsel for p; (2) E. King, counsel for ds. Add: (1) Whittaker Wright, Macclesfield, Ches, misnamed William in original bill. P seeks inj ag d2's suit claiming penalties for an allegedly usurious promissory note d2 issued p, but then refused to pay. P sued d2 and secured payment, claiming d2 had issued the note as payment for silk brokered on p's behalf by d1. Ds assert the note was not issued for silk, but as security against a loan for a lesser amount than that stated in the note.

1785, Trin	E 112/1701	Bill. LMX 3695.
1785, June 28	E 112/1701	Answer. Filing date of ds' answer.
1785, Mich	E 112/1701	Exception. P's exceptions concern whether the note was issued for silk.
1785, Nov 16	E 112/1701	Amended bill. Corrects Wright's name; maintains silk was bought by p, then sold to Wright and d2.
1786, Jan 20	E 112/1701	Further answer. Swearing date of ds' further answer, denying d2 issued the note for silk, or that d1 was concerned in any such transaction.
1786, Hil	E 112/1701	Exception. P's exceptions to ds' further answer concern ds' transactions regarding the silk.

254. Ingram v Wiltshire
P: (1) Joseph Ingram, clerk, Oxon. D: (1) Richard Wiltshire, gambling house owner, 52 Berwick St., Soho., Midd. C: (1) John Lloyd, counsel for p; (2) J. Johnson, counsel for d. P seeks inj ag d's suit in KB for non-payment of penal bond supposedly covering both gambling debt and further loan, plus interest. Imprisoned for running illegal E.O. (evens or odds) gambling tables, d claims bond covers only loan not gambling debt. P denies this, but also seeks repayment of all his gambling losses.

1785, Trin	E 112/1701	Bill. LMX 3698.
1785, June 6	E 112/1701	Answer. Filing date.

255. Irwin v Eaton
P: (1) Joseph Irwin gent., Greenwich New Rd., Surrey. D: (1) Daniel Eaton, paper maker, late of Bowers Mill, Surrey; (2) William Priddle, attorney; (3) John Snelling; (4) John Mills; (5) William Mappleback. C: (1) R. Pratt, counsel for p. P seeks inj ag ds' suit at KB for payment of a bond p issued to d1 in return for a loan. P claims he paid d1 bills of exchange which exceeded the debt, and expected to receive in return the bond and the balance. Instead d1 transferred the bond to d2, his attorney. D2 and the other ds sued p at KB, had him imprisoned and his goods seized for non-payment of the bond.

1785, Hil	E 112/1708	Bill. LMX 3905.

256. Jackson v Mackreth
P: (1) Elizabeth Jackson, St. Paul's Churchyard, London, W. Jackson's widow & executrix. D: (1) Robert Mackreth esq., Cork St., Westminster, Midd; (2) Josiah Lucas esq., Hampton, Midd, d3's husband; (3) Mary Lucas, Hampton, Midd, d2's wife, J. Bennett's executrix; (4) John Raincock. C: (1) E. King, counsel for p; (2) Samuel Romilly, counsel for ds2-3; (3) Henry Boulton, counsel for ds' answers to amended bill. Add: (1) William Jackson, St. Mildreds in the Poultry, London, deceased, p's husband; (2) John Dawes, merchant, London; (3) Thomas Dawes, merchant, London; (4) Arthur Evans, deceased; (5) John Bennett, deceased. P (widow & executrix of W. Jackson, deceased in 1782) seeks inj ag the suits at cl of ds1-3 for payment of bonds. In 1768, p's husband issued with J. Dawes & T. Dawes a £10,000 bond to A. Evans (since deceased), a £5000 bond to d1, & with d1 & d4 a £4000 bond to J. Bennett. P claims her husband's estate was insufficient to pay his debts. D1 asserts the estate is sufficient to pay the bonds or part thereof.

1784, Mich	E 112/1693	Bill. LMX 3508.
1784, Nov 22	E 112/1693	Answer. Swearing & filing date of answer of ds2-3.
1784, Nov 23	E 112/1693	Answer. Swearing & filing date of d1's answer; schedules included below answer of d1 & W. Jackson's accounts.
1784, Mich	E 112/1693	Exception. P's exceptions to d1's answer concern the bonds possessed by d1.
1785, Hil	E 112/1693	Exception. P's exceptions to the answer of ds2-3 concern the bonds possessed by d1.
1785, Trin	E 112/1693	Replication. P asserts the answer of ds2-3 is insufficient.

1785, Trin	E 112/1693	Rejoinder. Ds2-3 maintain their answer is sufficient.
1785, Dec 13	E 112/1693	Amended bill. P's amended bill in particular seeks discovery of how d1 acquired all the bonds issued by W. Jackson.
1786, Jan 31	E 112/1693	Answer. Swearing & filing date of answer of ds2-3 to amended bill.
1786, Jan 31	E 112/1693	Answer. Swearing & filing date of d1's answer to amended bill.

257. Jackson v Whittenbury

P: (1) Joseph Jackson, letter founder, Salisbury Court, London, p2's husband; (2) Mary Jackson, Salisbury Court, London, p1's wife, J. W. Pasham's widow & executrix. D: (1) John Whittenbury, warehouseman, Watling St., London; (2) Samuel Swann, warehouseman, Watling St., London; (3) William Brocklehurst, warehouseman, Watling St., London; (4) John Collier, linen draper, Newgate St., London. C: (1) Charles Shuter, counsel for ps & d4; (2) J. Stanley, counsel for ds1-3. Add: (1) John Wheeler Pasham, printer, Shoemaker Row, Blackfriars, London, deceased, p2's former husband. Ps seeks inj ag the suit of ds1-3 at KB for payment of a promissory note. Ps claim in 1783, p2's late husband J. W. Pasham lent a £100 promissory note to d4, who agreed to pay it off by the due date, & issued it to ds1-3 for debts. Pasham died, leaving p2 his widow & executrix, who married p1. D4 could not pay off the note, & issued ds1-3 other notes instead. Ds1-3 refused to accept a composition in lieu of d4's debts, & are suing ps at KB for the note. D4 claims ds1-3 have been repaid & should cancel the note, but ds1-3 assert d4 still owes them for goods.

1785, Hil	E 112/1710	Bill. LMX 3981.
1785, Nov 15	E 112/1710	Commission. For the answer of ds1-3.
1785, Dec 9	E 112/1710	Answer. Answer of ds1-3, sworn by d1 & d3 on this date in Manchester; sworn by d2 on 16 December, filed 17 December.
1786, Jan 27	E 112/1710	Answer. Swearing date of d4's answer.
1786, June 23	E 112/1710	Amended bill. Ps add that ds1-3 have obtained a verdict at KB ag them.
1787, Feb 12	E 112/1710	Commission. For the answer of ds1-3 to ps' amended bill.
1787, April 21	E 112/1710	Answer. Answer of ds1-3, sworn by d1 & d3 on this date in Manchester, sworn by d2 on 12 May, filed 14 May; schedule below answer of goods ds1-3 issued d4.

258. James v Fearon

P: (1) William Ford James esq., barrister, Inner Temple, London. D: (1) Anthony Fearon, tailor, d in original bill, bankrupt; (2) John Robinson, woollen draper, Bedfordbury, London, d1's assignee; (3) James Rosier, button maker, parish of St. Clements Danes, London, d1's assignee. C: (1) Sylvester Douglas, counsel for p; (2) Josiah Brown, counsel for ds. P seeks to add ds2-3 to his bill filed in this Court ag A. Fearon seeking an inj ag Fearon's suits at KB for payment of alleged debts. P claims he had employed Fearon as a tailor from 1777-9, but

Fearon did not issue him a true account of debts owed by p. In 1785, Fearon went bankrupt, and ds2-3 became his assignees, who threaten to revive Fearon's suits ag p.

1784, Mich	E 112/1786	Supplementary bill. LMX 6189.
1785, Feb 25	E 112/1786	Answer. Swearing date of d1's answer to original bill.
1785, June 1	E 112/1786	Answer. Swearing & filing date of the answer of ds2-3 to supplementary bill.

259. Jennings v Poole

P: (1) Thomas Jennings, merchant, London. D: (1) John Poole, stockbroker, London. C: (1) E. King, counsel for p; (2) J. Bicknell, counsel for d. P seeks inj ag d's suit for payment of £100 in promissory notes. In 1780 p issued d £4000 in bank annuities. The stock rose on the day of the contract, so p also issued d 2 promissory notes for £75 & £25. P claims d then persuaded him to wager that if the stock's value rose, p would pay d the difference. The stock rose, so p allegedly issued d £100 in promissory notes. P claims the notes, issued for a gambling debt, are void, but d is suing p for payment. D asserts he only seeks payment of the £75 & £25 notes issued as payment for the stock.

1784, Mich	E 112/1698	Bill. LMX 3638; cf. E 112/1706 LMX 3859 Jennings v Poole.
1785, April 28	E 112/1698	Answer. Swearing date, filed 29 April.
[1785, Easter, undated]	E 112/1698	Exception. P's exceptions to d's answer concern the notes allegedly issued after the wager.

260. Jennings v Poole

P: (1) Thomas Jennings, merchant, London. D: (1) John Poole, stockbroker, London. C: (1) E. King, counsel for p; (2) J. Bicknell, counsel for d. P seeks inj ag d's suit for payment of £100 in promissory notes. P claims in 1780 he bought £4000 in bank annuities from d, who persuaded him to wager ag the stock's value rising. The stock rose, so p allegedly issued d £100 in promissory notes. P claims the notes, issued for a gambling debt, are void. D now denies the notes were issued either as a gambling debt or for annuities, but claims p issued them in return for loans from d.

1784, Mich	E 112/1706	Amended bill. LMX 3859; amended 1 June 1785; cf. E 112/1698 LMX 3638 Jennings v Poole.
1786, July 10	E 112/1706	Further answer. Swearing date of d's further answer, filed 13 July.

261. Johnson v Whicker

P: (1) Elizabeth Johnson, Thames St., London. D: (1) John Whicker, cordwainer, Southwark, Surrey, d2's husband; (2) Mary Ann Whicker, Southwark, Surrey, d1's wife, under 21 years; (3) Thomas Mayow gent., Hackney, Midd, A. Mayow's husband, executor & trustee. C: (1) J. Hawkins, counsel for p; (2) J. Pippard, counsel for d1. Add: (1) Ann Mayow, deceased, d3's wife. P, a spinster, seeks payment of £200 in government securities. P claims that in 1768 d3's wife, A. Mayow, died leaving d3 as her executor &

trustee to invest £200 in securities for the benefit of d2, for when she reached 21 years. In 1785, when d2 was 18 or 19 years old, her husband d1 sold the securities to p for £96. P claims that d3 refuses to transfer the securities, asserting they are entrusted for d2 until she is 21 years.

| 1785, Easter | E 112/1718 | Bill. LMX 4141. |
| 1785, May 4 | E 112/1718 | Answer. Swearing date of d1's answer, filed 9 May. |

262. Johnston v Green

P: (1) William Johnston esq., stationer to the Board of Ordnance, Hampton Court, Midd. D: (1) Richard Green, clergyman, Strand, Westminster, Midd. C: (1) J. Bicknell, counsel for p; (2) J. Simeon, counsel for d. Add: (1) John Bullock, stationer to the Board of Ordnance; (2) Mary Green, pencutter, Strand, Westminster, Midd, d's wife. P, stationer to the Board of Ordinance, seeks inj ag d's suit at cl for payment of £66. In 1784, p claims he & J. Bullock bought pens & quills from d totalling £52 14s, at 12 months credit. P issued d a £25 promissory note in part payment, of which he paid d £15 15s. Before the 12 months were up, d got a verdict at cl ag p for £66. P claims he only owes d £37 19s, the remainder of the £52 14s debt. D asserts his wife Mary runs the pencutting business, & that she sold J. Bullock more pens than are listed in p's schedule.

1785, Hil	E 112/1702	Bill. LMX 3727; 2 schedules below bill of pens & quills p allegedly bought from d.
1785, Feb 18	E 112/1702	Answer. Swearing & filing date; 2 schedules below answer of pens p allegedly bought.
1785, April 13	E 112/1702	Amended bill. P refers to his colleague J. Bullock & d's wife M. Green; 2 schedules below amended bill of pens p & J. Bullock allegedly bought.
1785, April 21	E 112/1702	Answer. Swearing & filing date of d's answer to amended bill.

263. Jonas v Jonas

P: (1) Lazarus Jonas, merchant, parish of St. Andrew, Holborn, Midd, formerly Lazarus Solomon. D: (1) Dorothy Jonas, merchant, Catherine Square, Midd, (The Widow Jonas, Son and Co. are defendants); (2) Nathaniel Barber, tobacconist, East Smithfield, nr Tower Hill, Midd, assignee of bankrupt d1's estates. C: (1) J. Morgan, counsel for p. P seeks inj ag ds' suit for payment of allegedly unpaid accounts, and also seeks proof of actual accounts. P claims d1, now bankrupt, actually owes him money, and together with d2, assignee of d1's estates, collude to extort money from him.

| 1785, Trin | E 112/1701 | Bill. LMX 3714. |

264. Jones v Cartwright

P: (1) Rice Jones gent., officer of Revenue of Excise, East St., St. George the Martyr, Midd. D: (1) George William Cartwright, officer of Revenue of Excise. C: (1) R. Richards, counsel for p. P, an Excise officer, seeks inj to prevent d, another Excise officer, from receiving further monies from the General Excise Office as commn for seizing smuggled goods which were subsequently

condemned and sold off. P alleges that d reneged on their partnership to divide the proceeds of the goods equally.
1785, Hil   E 112/1701   Bill. LMX 3720.

265. Kane v Cullen
P: (1) Michael Kane gent., Great Russell St., Bloomsbury, Midd. D: (1) Thomas Cullen gent., Ostend. C: (1) J. Johnson, counsel for p. P seeks inj ag d's suit for payment of a bond. P claims in 1784 he allowed d to draw several bills of exchange upon him, to be paid off by the due date. D was unable to pay the bills, & asked p for a £600 bond & a warrant of attorney to confess a judgement for £166, with which to raise money to pay off the bills. P issued d the same, but d is now suing p at KB for the bond, allegedly claiming p issued it in return for a valuable consideration.
1785, Hil   E 112/1704   Bill. LMX 3783.

266. Kelly v Meyrick
P: (1) John Kelly esq., Theobalds, Herts. D: (1) John Meyrick esq., Parliament St., Midd, agent to the 33rd Regiment of Foot; (2) James Meyrick esq., Parliament St., Midd, agent to the 33rd Regiment of Foot. C: (1) William Waller, counsel for p; (2) Arthur Onslow, counsel for ds. P seeks discovery of actual price ds received for p's army commissions. P claims that in 1779 he bought an ensign's commission in the 33rd Regiment of Foot for £400, and later a lieutenant's commission for £200. In 1783, p directed ds, agents for the regiment, to sell his commissions. Ds assert they sold the commissions for £400 in total, but p claims they received a far higher price.
1785, Trin   E 112/1718   Bill. LMX 4143.
1786, Feb 1   E 112/1718   Answer. Swearing & filing date of ds' answer.

267. Kent v Isaac
P: (1) Rowley Kent, surgeon, Bethnall Green, Midd, bankrupt. D: (1) Gershon Isaac, Bury St., St. Mary Axe, London, bankrupt, signs his name in Hebrew characters; (2) John Faux, silversmith, Worship St., London, d1's assignee; (3) Alexander Phillips, Bury St., St Mary Axe, London, d1's assignee; (4) Hananel Mendes da Costa, included as d in amended bill; (5) Jacob Mendes da Costa, included as d in amended bill. C: (1) John Bicknell, counsel for p; (2) Charles Abbot, counsel for ds. P seeks inj ag suit in KB of ds2-3, d1's assignees, for payment of p's bond to d1 (bankrupt). P had issued the bond to d1, who stood as security for another bond of p's. P (now also bankrupt) claims he repaid d1 with bills of exchange, and that the bond should have been cancelled. Ds claim that p paid d1 for other debts, not the bond.
1785, Easter   E 112/1701   Bill. LMX 3715.
1785, April 21   E 112/1701   Answer. Filing date of the answer of ds1-3.
1785, April 30   E 112/1701   Amended bill. P claims his payments to d1 covered not only his bond to d1, but also their further joint bond to ds4-5, and p's purchase of jewellery from d1.
1785, May 27   E 112/1701   Further answer. Ds1-3 deny d1 was bound to offset p's bills of exchange ag the bond, the joint bond to ds4-5 or p's purchase of

jewellery, claiming the bills were worth less than p alleges.

1785, May 30   E 112/1701   Answer. Swearing date of the answer of ds4-5 to amended bill.

268. Kenworthy v Allen

P: (1) John Kenworthy, linen draper, Ironmonger Lane, London, p2's partner; (2) Edward Kenworthy, linen draper, Ironmonger Lane, London, p1's partner. D: (1) Thomas Allen, d6's assignee; (2) Robert Macky, d6's assignee; (3) Thomas Greg, d6's assignee; (4) Stratford Canning, d6's assignee; (5) Henry Smith, d6's assignee; (6) John Marlar, bankrupt. C: (1) Richard Hollist, counsel for ps. Add: (1) James Pell, deceased; (2) Richard Down. Ps seeks inj ag the suit of ds1-5 for payment of a promissory note. In 1781, ps sought an inj in this Court ag any suit of d6 (bankrupt), his assignees ds1-5, & J. Pell (since deceased) & R. Down for payment of a £8000 promissory note, which ps claim they only lent d6. Ps add by way of supplement that d6's bankruptcy was collusive with ds1-5.

1784, Mich   E 112/1709   Supplementary bill. LMX 3958.

269. Keys v Horne

P: (1) Michael Keys, St. Martin in the Fields, Midd, p2's husband; (2) Eleanor Keys, St Martin in the Fields, Midd, p1's wife and B. Horne's executrix. D: (1) Thomas Horne, initially designated B. Horne's brother, then uncle; (2) Henry Sterry, Hatton Gardens, London. C: (1) J. Johnson, counsel for ps. Add: (1) Benjamin Horne, St. Georges Fields, Southwark, Surrey, deceased. P1 & his wife p2, executrix of B. Horne (deceased), seek payment of a half share of bank annuities standing in the names of B. Horne & ds, his alleged trustees, left to p2. Ds allegedly deny they are B. Horne's trustees of the annuities, & claim ignorance of the will.

1784, Mich   E 112/1700   Bill. LMX 3669.

270. Kynaston v Millar

P: (1) Thomas Kynaston esq., Grosvenor Place, Hanover Sq., Midd, impropriate rector of St. Botolph without Aldgate. D: (1) William Millar, the Minories, London. C: (1) John Reade, counsel for p. P, impropriate rector of St. Botolph without Aldgate since 1760, seeks payment for arrears of tithes from d, who has occupied a house in the Minories for ten years. D allegedly denies his house lies within the rectory.

1785, Easter   E 112/1696   Bill. LMX 3555.

271. Kynaston v Sermitte

P: (1) Thomas Kynaston esq., Grosvenor Place, Hanover Sq., Midd, impropriate rector of St. Botolph without Aldgate. D: (1) Thomas Sermitte, Houndsditch, High St. Aldgate, London. C: (1) John Reade, counsel for p. P, impropriate rector of St. Botolph without Aldgate since 1760, seeks payment for arrears of tithes from d, who has occupied a house in Houndsditch for two years. D allegedly denies his house lies within the rectory.

1785, Easter   E 112/1696   Bill. LMX 3556.

272. Lee v Butler

P: (1) Robert Lee, mariner, parish of St. Paul, Shadwell, Midd. D: (1) John Butler, seaman, parish of St. Paul, Shadwell, Midd. C: (1) Charles Shuter, counsel for p. Add: (1) Robert Lumley, mariner, Scarborough, Yorks. P seeks inj ag d's suit for non-payment of wages. P hired d as seaman on voyage to W. Indies but paid the promised wages to Robert Lumley, a mariner apparently entitled to the money as d was his indentured apprentice.

1785, Trin   E 112/1701   Bill. LMX 3716.

273. Levy v Lloyd

P: (1) Israel Levy, silversmith, Deptford, Kent. D: (1) Edward Lloyd, innkeeper, Deptford, Kent. C: (1) J. Bicknell, counsel for p. P seeks inj ag d's suit in the Court of Common Pleas seeking a refund for goods p sold d. P claims in 1780, d was appointed boatswain of the East India Company's ship, the *Neptune*, & bought goods from p in return for a £128 respondentia bond. P claims d sold the goods in the East Indies at a profit, but after his return in 1783, d sued p, alleging the goods were not worth £128.

1785, Hil   E 112/1711   Bill. LMX 3989.

274. Lincoln v Oriel

P: (1) Charles Lincoln, optician, Leadenhall St., London. D: (1) Philip Oriel, stationer, Aldersgate, London, J. Fryday's executor; (2) Mary Fryday, under 21 years, J. Fryday's natural daughter; (3) Elizabeth Fryday, under 21 years, J. Fryday's natural daughter. N/f: (1) Samuel Kinsey gent., guardian & next friend of ds2-3. C: (1) Josiah Brown, counsel for p; (2) E. King, counsel for d1; (3) Thomas Evance, counsel for ds2-3; (4) J. Johnson, counsel for d1's answer to amended bill. Add: (1) Mary Fryday, Chelsea Rd., Hanover Square, Midd, deceased, J. Fryday's widow & executor; (2) John Fryday, deceased, M. Fryday the E's husband, father of ds2-3. P seeks payment of a mortgage or foreclosure on ds' 2 houses. P claims in 1777, M. Fryday (J. Fryday's widow) & d1, J. Fryday's executors, mortgaged 2 houses in Chelsea Rd. to p for £200, which they never repaid to p. M. Fryday died in 1783. Ds2-3, J. Fryday's natural daughters, claim J. Fryday left the premises to M. Fryday only for her lifetime, to descend to ds2-3 after her death.

1784, Mich	E 112/1724	Bill. LMX 4330; amended 8 May 1787 to question d1's right to the mortgaged premises.
1785, Sept 21	E 112/1724	Answer. Swearing date of d1's answer, filed 22 September.
1786, June 22	E 112/1724	Answer. Answer of ds2-3, sworn by S. Kinsey & filed on this date.
1787, June 27	E 112/1724	Answer. Swearing date of d1's answer to amended bill.
1788, Hil	E 112/1724	Replication. P asserts ds' answers are insufficient.
1788, Hil	E 112/1724	Rejoinder. Ds2-3 maintain their answer is sufficient.

275. Longman v Rennett

P: (1) James Longman, music seller, shopkeeper, Cheapside, London, p2's partner; (2) Francis Broderip, music seller, shopkeeper, Cheapside, London, p1's partner. D: (1) Charles Rennett, attorney at law, Inner Temple, London; (2) Charles Dibdin gent., composer, St. George in the Fields, Surrey. C: (1) W. Scafe, counsel for ps. Ps seek inj to prevent d1 printing or selling d2's music. Ps claim that in 1769 p1 bought the copyright for d2's musical works, *The Padlock, The Recruiting Serjeant & The Jubilee* for a term of 14 years with a reversionary term of a further 14 years. Ds allegedly deny p1 bought a reversionary term, & assert that the second term of 14 years has been bought by d1, who prints & sells the music, & has sought an inj in this Court to prevent ps from doing the same.

1785, Hil   E 112/1718   Bill. LMX 4165.

276. Lowe v Frord

P: (1) James Lowe, J. Ward's executor. D: (1) John Frord, administrator of his wife Elizabeth; (2) Robert Paterson, J. Phillips's executor. C: (1) J. A. Stainsby, counsel for p. Add: (1) Joseph Ward, parish of St. Marylebone, Midd, deceased; (2) Robert Peele, deceased, J. Ward's assignee; (3) Robert Mort, deceased, J. Ward's assignee; (4) Alexander Purvis, deceased, E. Frord's former husband; (5) John Phillips, deceased; (6) Joshua Hurst; (7) Elizabeth Frord, deceased, d1's wife, A. Purvis's widow & executrix. P, J. Ward's executor, seeks revival & execution of a decree which J. Ward (insolvent) obtained in 1771 in this Court compelling his assignees R. Peele & R. Mort, & A. Purvis, J. Phillips & J. Hurst to return the residue of J. Ward's estate to him after paying his debts. In 1779, J. Ward died, leaving p his executor. Ward's assignees have died, so p is reviving the decree ag ds, their legal heirs.

1785, Hil   E 112/1703   Bill of revivor. LMX 3759; cf. E 112/1706 LMX 3830 Clarkson v Ford.

277. Lowes v Hill

P: (1) Thomas Lowes esq., barrister, Middle Temple, London. D: (1) John Hill, upholsterer, Gough Square, London; (2) Edward Shove, draper, Fleet St., London; (3) William Justice, merchant, Bradford, Lancs. C: (1) J. Johnson, counsel for p; (2) R. Richards, counsel for d2. P seeks inj ag d2's suit for payment of bills of exchange and a promissory note which p issued ds2-3 to release d1 from imprisonment for debt, on the understanding that d1 would pay them off before the due date. D1 has not paid them off.

1785, Easter   E 112/1700   Bill. LMX 3662.
1785, April 25   E 112/1700   Answer. Filing date of d2' answer.

278. Marsh v Brown

P: (1) William Marsh, King St., Bloomsbury, Midd. D: (1) Joshua Brown, carpenter, Winslow St., St. Mary le Bone, Midd. C: (1) R. Richards, counsel for p. P seeks discovery of all documents concerning two loans p made to d, upon the security of d's two houses. P alleges principal and interest on the mortgage have not been paid, and seeks foreclosure.

1785, Hil   E 112/1701   Bill. LMX 3719.

279. McLean v Kinnaird
P: (1) John McLean, Kingston, Jamaica; (2) John Moore, Kingston, Jamaica. D: (1) George, Lord Kinnaird, d2's husband; (2) Elizabeth, Lady Kinnaird, d1's wife. C: (1) Richard Hollist, counsel for ps. Add: (1) Allan McLean, deceased, former plaintiff; (2) Griffin Ransom esq., deceased, former defendant; (3) William Gray; (4) John Macdonald; (5) Thomas Smith; (6) Attorney General. Ps seek revival of a suit filed in this Court in 1782 by p1 & A. McLean seeking an inj ag the suit at law of G. Ransom, W. Gray, John Macdonald, T. Smith & the AG for payment of a bill of exchange. The suit abated when G. Ransom died, leaving d2, his daughter & administratrix. A. McLean also died, & ps seek revival.
1785, Hil   E 112/1713   Bill of revivor. LMX 4033.

280. Miller v Clarke
P: (1) John Miller, merchant, New York, N. America. D: (1) Richard Clarke, merchant, New Broad St., London; (2) Elias Smerdon, merchant, Copthall Buildings, London; (3) Thomas Lempriere, merchant, Winchester St., London, bankrupt; (4) Owen Neill, ship's captain; (5) Benjamin Kidney, merchant, Laurence Poultney Lane, London, d3's assignee; (6) Henry Smerdon, Rotterdam, Holland; (7) John Ellis, Rotterdam, Holland; (8) John Fiot, merchant, College Hill, London, d3's assignee. C: (1) William Alexander, counsel for p; (2) John Mitford, counsel for d1; (3) J. Bicknell, counsel for d2. P seeks inj to prevent d1 paying d2 for a ship, the *London*. P claims in 1783 in New York, at d3's request, he bought the ship (registered in his name) & cargo, with d4 as ship's captain & p's trustee. D4 sailed the ship to Newfoundland, Italy & London, paid the cargo profits to d2, & allowed d3 to sell the ship to ds6–7, who sold it to d2, who has chartered it to d1. D3 allegedly went bankrupt in 1784, with d5 & d8 as his assignees, who claim the ship. P claims d3 never reimbursed him, so he is intitled to the ship & cargo.

1784, Mich	E 112/1694	Bill. LMX 3520; cf. E 112/1709 LMX 3954 Miller v Tate.
1784, Dec 1	E 112/1694	Answer. Swearing & filing date of d1's answer.
1785, Feb 14	E 112/1694	Answer. Swearing date of d2's answer.

281. Miller v Tate
P: (1) John Miller, merchant, London. D: (1) John Tate, merchant, Bucklersbury, London, d6's trustee; (2) John Barton, merchant, Milk St., London, d6's trustee; (3) Arthur Edie, merchant, Tokenhouse Yard, London, d6's trustee; (4) William Grove, merchant, Broad St., London, d6's trustee; (5) James Senols, upholsterer, Fenchurch St., London, d6's trustee; (6) Elias Smerdon, merchant, Copthall Buildings, London. C: (1) William Alexander, counsel for p. Add: (1) Richard Clarke, merchant, New Broad St., London; (2) Thomas Lempriere, merchant, Winchester St., London, bankrupt; (3) Owen Neill, ship's captain; (4) Benjamin Kidney, merchant, Laurence Poultney Lane, London, T. Lempriere's assignee; (5) Henry Smerdon, Rotterdam, Holland; (6) John Ellis, Rotterdam, Holland; (7) John Fiot, merchant, College Hill, London, T. Lempriere's assignee. P, by way of supplement, seeks for ds1–5 to be added as defendants to his bill filed in this Court in 1784 ag d6, T. Lempriere, O. Neill,

R. Clarke, B. Kidney, J. Fiot, H. Smerdon & J. Ellis, seeking possession from d6 of a ship, the *London*. P now adds that d6, being pressed by creditors, has transferred his estate to ds1-5 to pay his debts.

| 1785, Trin | E 112/1709 | Supplementary bill. LMX 3954; cf. E 112/1694 LMX 3520 Miller v Clarke. |

282. Mills v Sharp

P: (1) Thomas Mills, publican of the Marshall and Anchor, the Minories, London. D: (1) Thomas Sharp, carpenter, the Minories, London. C: (1) Thomas Nedham, counsel for p; (2) John Mitford, counsel for d. Add: (1) Bartholomew Edwards, Haydon Sq., Little Minories, London, previously arbitrator between p and d. P seeks inj ag d's suit, and discovery of d's accounts. D sues for payment for carpentry work he performed at p's public house. P claims d borrowed money and bought goods on account from p, amounting to a sum greater than the carpentry bill. D asserts he repaid the borrowed money, and will deduct the price of goods from the carpentry bill. Previous attempts to settle by the arbitration of B. Edwards failed.

| 1785, Trin | E 112/1700 | Bill. LMX 3685; schedule of accounts below bill. |
| 1785, June 6 | E 112/1700 | Answer. Swearing date, filed 7 June. Since filing his bill, p has brought a writ of error in Exchequer upon the judgement at KB in favour of d. |

283. Mullens v Sutton

P: (1) Nathan Mullens, jeweller, Bristol; (2) Francis Broderip, music seller, Cheapside, London; (3) Joseph Walton, oilman, Little Britain, London. D: (1) James Sutton, goldsmith, late of Cheapside, London, d2's partner; (2) James Bult, goldsmith, Cheapside, London, d1's partner; (3) Solomon Henry. C: (1) William Walter, counsel for p; (2) Thomas Nedham, counsel for d3. Ps seek inj ag d3's suit for recovery of leasehold premises assigned by d1 to d3 before ds1-2 went bankrupt. Ps, assignees of the estates of ds1-2, suspect an agreement between d1 & d3 to return the premises to d1 when he is solvent again.

1784, Mich	E 112/1701	Bill. LMX 3717.
1784, Dec 15	E 112/1701	Answer. Filing date of d3's answer.
1785, Easter	E 112/1701	Replication. Ps deny d3's answer is sufficient.
1785, Easter	E 112/1701	Rejoinder. D3 maintains his answer is sufficient.
1785, April 12	E 112/1701	Answer. Swearing & filing date of d1's answer.

284. Nelthropp v Brantingham

P: (1) Henry Nelthropp, attorney of KB, Birmingham, Warw; (2) William Hough esq., Bloomsbury, Midd; (3) Joseph Harris, merchant, London. D: (1) Thomas Brantingham, white lead manufacturer, Devonshire St., London, a Quaker; (2) Henry Noah, Crosby Sq., Bishopgate St., London; (3) Ephraim Hart; (4) Charles Geary Eames. C: (1) J. Johnson, counsel for ps; (2) Thomas Nedham, counsel for d1. Ps seek inj ag d1's suit at KB for payment of bills of exchange. Ps claim in 1781 ds agreed to lend them £500 upon bills of exchange, if they advanced d1 £100. Ps apparently issued the £100 & bills, but ds never paid them. D2 allegedly claimed the bills were picked from his pocket & issued ps indemnification. D1 denies any involvement other than that he sold white lead to d2, who paid him with ps' bills of exchange, for which d1 is now suing ps.

| 1785, Hil | E 112/1692 | Bill. LMX 3499. |
| 1785, Feb 11 | E 112/1692 | Answer. Swearing date of d1's answer; 2 schedules below answer of white lead d1 sold d2, & ps' bills of exchange which d2 paid d1. |

285. Neville v Galbraith

P: (1) Thomas Neville esq., New Norfolk St., Midd, previously resident in Jamaica. D: (1) Archibald Galbraith, merchant, Jamaica. C: (1) J. Stanley, counsel for p; (2) J. Bicknell, counsel for d. Add: (1) George Campbell, merchant, Jamaica, deceased, d's partner. P seeks inj ag d's suit at KB for payment for cargo. In 1783, d got a judgement ag p for £263 15s in the Supreme Court of Judicature for Jamaica. D claims in 1780 a privateer, the *Ballatoe*, owned by d & his partner G. Campbell (since deceased), together with p's ship, the *Lady Parker*, captured an enemy ship, the *Anna Catherina*, laden with sugar. D asserts p received all the profits from the sale of sugar, & sued p for a share. D is now suing p at KB on the judgement. P claims he paid d & Campbell their share already.

1785, Easter	E 112/1748	Bill. LMX 4958.
1786, July 5	E 112/1748	Commission. For d's answer.
1787, May 28	E 112/1748	Answer (with attachments). D's answer sworn at Kingston, Jamaica, on this date, filed 23 October 1687; account attached of sale of the *Anna Catherina*'s cargo.
1787, Nov 28	E 112/1748	Amended bill. P claims he paid d & Campbell their share.

286. Partridge v Emes

P: (1) Charles Partridge, cider merchant, Thames St., London. D: (1) Edward Emes the younger, broker & auctioneer. C: (1) Thomas Lowes, counsel for p; (2) John Crode, counsel for d. Add: (1) John Hanna esq., Westminster, Midd. P seeks compensation from d for his furniture & goods. In 1783, p mortgaged his premises in Thames St. & Kennington, Surrey, to J. Hanna for a £20 annuity. In 1784 p was imprisoned in KB, & requested d to pay off the mortgage. P claims d duped him into issuing as security an absolute bill of sale of his premises, upon which d has now possessed p's furniture & goods, worth more than the mortgage. P claims d has also refused to accept payment of the mortgage. D asserts the sale of the furniture only covers p's debts to him.

| 1784, Mich | E 112/1716 | Bill. LMX 4091. |
| 1785, Jan 12 | E 112/1716 | Answer. Swearing date; schedule below answer of d's accounts with p. |

287. Passman v Haffey

P: (1) John Passman, slopseller, Leadenhall St., London, p2's husband; (2) Mary Passman, Leadenhall St., London, p1's wife, T. Rogers's daughter & administratrix. D: (1) John Haffey gent., slopseller; (2) Christopher Corrall. C: (1)

Richard Hollist, counsel for ps. Add: (1) Thomas Rogers gent., deceased intestate, p2's father. Ps seeks revival of the suit filed in this Court in 1782 by p1 & T. Rogers (p2's father), seeking inj from any suit of ds for payment of a £1000 bond, which p1 & T. Rogers paid for d1's trade as slopseller. Ps claim the trade was misrepresented to them & seek cancellation of the bond. The suit abated when T. Rogers died intestate in 1784, leaving p2 his administratrix.

1784, Mich   E 112/1707   Bill of revivor. LMX 3880; cf. E 112/1707 LMX
                                       3879 Passman v Woodmason.

288. Passman v Woodmason

P: (1) John Passman, slopseller, Leadenhall St., London, p2's husband; (2) Mary Passman, Leadenhall St., London, p1's wife, T. Rogers's daughter & administratrix. D: (1) James Woodmason, stationer, Leadenhall St., London, J. Haffey's assignee; (2) Robert Wigram, merchant, Crossby Square, London, J. Haffey's assignee; (3) Christopher Corrall. C: (1) Richard Hollist, counsel for ps; (2) T. Pippard, counsel for ds1-2; (3) W. Scafe, counsel for d3. Add: (1) Thomas Rogers gent., deceased intestate, p2's father; (2) John Haffey gent., slopseller, bankrupt. Ps seek inj ag any suit of ds1-2 for payment of a £1000 bond. In 1782, p1 & T. Rogers (p2's father) got an inj in this Court ag J. Haffey & d3, claiming d1 had misrepresented Haffey's trade as slopseller to persuade p1 & Rogers to buy the trade for £1000 bond. In 1784, ps revived the suit when it abated after Rogers died intestate, leaving p2 his administratrix. Ps add as supplement that J. Haffey has gone bankrupt, & they now seek cancellation of the bond by his assignees, ds1-2. D1 denies misrepresenting the trade to p1 & Rogers.

1785, Trin   E 112/1707   Supplementary bill. LMX 3879; cf. E 112/1707
                                       LMX 3880 Passman v Haffey.
1786, May 27   E 112/1707   Answer. Answer of ds1-2, sworn by d2 on
                                       this date, sworn by d1 & filed on 29 May.
1786, July 5   E 112/1707   Answer. Swearing date of d3's answer, filed
                                       10 July.

289. Pattman v Percivall

P: (1) John Pattman gent., Lyon St., Bloomsbury, Midd. D: (1) Samuel Percivall, victualler, Long Acre, Midd; (2) John Bell, attorney at law, New Compton St., Soho, Midd, employed by p & d1. C: (1) John Lloyd, counsel for p. Add: (1) Thomas Baker, tallow chandler, St. Martin's Lane, Midd. P seeks payment of a debt from the sale of T. Baker's stock. P claims in 1784 T. Baker executed a warrant of attorney for confessing a judgement at KB to p & d1, to whom T. Baker owed debts. P & d1 later employed d2 to sue out execution on the judgement ag T. Baker's stock in trade. P claims ds sold the stock for £115 10s. Ds allegedly deny receiving profits from the sale of stock, or deny T. Baker executed the warrant to p for any debt.

1784, Mich   E 112/1707   Bill. LMX 3870.

290. Poelnitz v Corbett

P: (1) Hon. Frederick, Baron de Poelnitz, Charlotte St., Rathbone Place, Midd, p2's husband; (2) Hon. Anna, Baroness de Poelnitz, Charlotte St., Rathbone Place, Midd, p1's wife, previously wife of Hugh, Earl of Percy. D: (1) Andrew

Corbett esq., married to p2's sister; (2) Herman Berens, merchant, London, p1's agent; (3) Joseph Berens, merchant, London, p1's agent. C: (1) Richard Reynolds, counsel for ps. Add: (1) Hon. Hugh, Earl of Percy, son & heir of Hugh, Duke of Northumberland, p2's previous husband; (2) Abraham Chambers esq., Hanover Sq., Midd. Ps seek inj ag d1's suit in the Mayoralty Court of London for payment of £562 10s. D1 claims in 1776, p2 received £900 from A. Chambers, in return for a £150 annuity, for which d1 was security. In 1779, p2 was divorced by her previous husband, Hugh, Earl of Percy, & received a £1600 annuity. P2 since married p1. D1 claims he had to pay Chambers £562 10s arrears of the £150 annuity, which p2 now owes him. P2 asserts she has not been liable for the debt since her divorce. D1 has obtained a verdict ag ps, & has attached £562 10s and an account of the annuity in the hands of ds2-3, p1's agents.

1784, Mich	E 112/1698	Bill. LMX 3632.
1785, Jan 22	E 112/1698	Answer. Swearing & filing date of d1's answer; schedule included below answer of p2's debt to d1.

291. Pooley v Smith

P: (1) Thomas Pooley gent., Isleworth, Midd, M. Jones's executor. D: (1) Thomas Smith, customs officer, Tower St., Midd, M. Jones's trustee of £100 annuities; (2) Governor & Co., Bank of England. C: (1) James Agar, counsel for p; (2) Richard Jackson, counsel for d2. Add: (1) Margaret Jones, Hanover Square, Midd, deceased. P seeks an inj ag d1 & a writ of distringas ag d2, the Bank of England, preventing them from selling bank annuities or d1 receiving dividends therefrom. P claims in 1784, M. Jones bought £100 Bank of England annuities in her name & that of d, her trustee. M. Jones then died, leaving p her executor. D now refuses to transfer the annuities to p, allegedly claiming he alone paid for the annuities.

1785, Trin	E 112/1706	Bill. LMX 3863, filed 20 July 1785.
1785, Nov 24	E 112/1706	Answer. Swearing date of d2's answer, filed 25 November.

292. Prichard v Rogers

P: (1) Joshua Jones Prichard gent., Doctors Commons, London. D: (1) Vitorino Rogers, victualler, Wapping, Midd; (2) Joseph Mayo, mariner. C: (1) J. Jones, counsel for p. P seeks inj ag d2's suit in the Court of Common Pleas for payment of £31. P claims in 1781, d1 (as d2's attorney) hired p to commence an action at KB to recover £31 owed to d2 from a voyage on a ship, the *Lively Privateer*. P claims he spent £14 17s 5d in prosecuting the suit, & recovered the full £31. P claims he is willing to pay the £31 to d1, as d2's attorney, in addition to £10 10s costs p owes d1, but that d2 now denies d1 is his attorney, & is suing p for the £31. P also claims d1 has not paid his £14 17s 5d costs.

1785, Hil	E 112/1717	Bill. LMX 3136 (misnumbered; should be 4136).

293. Priestman v Ayley

P: (1) William Priestman, Princes St., Soho, Midd. D: (1) Mary Ayley. C: (1) J. Pippard, counsel for p; (2) Joseph Stacpoole, counsel for d. P seeks inj ag d's suits in the Palace Court for £5 maintenance of p's alleged child. In 1775 p claims he had several encounters with d in a tavern. In 1776, d sought an allowance from p, claiming she had given birth to p's daughter, but apparently refused to make an affidavit to that effect. D brought several suits ag p for £5 maintenance for the child. P denies the child is his, asserting d is a prostitute. D claims she is an honest woman, & denies p asked her to make any affidavit.

1785, Trin   E 112/1698   Bill. LMX 3636.
1785, June 21   E 112/1698   Answer. Swearing date, filed 23 June.
1785, Trin   E 112/1698   Exception. P's exceptions concern d's suits ag
                                           him for maintenance.

294. Pringle v De Berdt
P: (1) William Pringle, merchant, Glanville St., Rathbone Pl., Midd; (2) James Mather, merchant, Birchin Lane, London; (3) John Sims, merchant, London St., London, added when bill was amended; (4) Ebba Stevenson, Canon St., London, P. Stevenson's widow & administratrix. D: (1) Dennis De Berdt, merchant, London. C: (1) William Hood, counsel for ps; (2) James Frower, counsel for d. Add: (1) Peter Stevenson, deceased, p4's husband. Ps seek inj ag d's suit for payment of an insurance policy. In 1784, d drew up a £500 policy on a ship, the *Ann*, bound from Maryland to London, with ps1-3 & P. Stevenson as underwriters. The *Ann* sank, & ps allege the captain had been incompetent & the ship in poor condition, though d had assured them otherwise. P. Stevenson died, leaving p4 his widow & administratrix. Ps deny they are liable to pay the policy. D denies misleading ps.

1785, Easter   E 112/1713   Bill. LMX 4092; amended 7 February 1786 to
                                           include p3.
1786, May 13   E 112/1716   Answer. Swearing date, resworn 17 May, filed
                                           18 May.

295. Randolph v Tombs
P: (1) William Randolph, merchant, Bristol, Bristol; (2) William Jones, merchant, Bristol, Bristol; (3) Levi Ames, merchant, Bristol, Bristol; (4) Thomas William Jolly, merchant, London; (5) Thomas Walker, ship's captain, Bristol, Bristol, commander of the *Prince Alfred*. D: (1) Richard Tombs, ship builder, Bristol, Bristol; (2) Anthonio Jose de Souza, ship's captain, d3's son, commander of the brig, *Santa Anna*; (3) Luis de Souza, imprisoned in KB, d2's father, part owner of the *Santa Anna*; (4) Anselmus Anthony Hartsen, Amsterdam, part owner of the *Santa Anna*'s cargo; (5) Jacob de Fflines, Amsterdam, part owner of the *Santa Anna*'s cargo; (6) Theophilus Christian Blauchenhagen, merchant, London, issued power of attorney by ds4-5; (7) Henry Cutler, merchant, London, issued power of attorney by ds4-5; (8) Caetano Dias Santos, merchant, London; (9) George Barclay; (10) William Boulton. C: (1) R. Richards, counsel for ps; (2) J. Stanley, counsel for d1; (3) Richard Hollis, counsel for d3; (4) John Mitford, counsel for ds6-7; (5) Cha. Shuter, counsel for d8; (6) J. Jones, counsel for ds9-10. Add: (1) William Drake, admiral, commander in chief in the Downs. Ps1-4, owners of a private ship of war, the *Prince Alfred*, & p5, the ship's captain, seek inj ag d1's suit at KB for £1002 19s 7d repair costs for a Portuguese brig, the *Santa Anna*, captained by d2 which p5 captured. The Court of Admiralty, Bristol, restored the brig to its

owners & awarded repair costs & £7000 damages ag the ps. Ps claim d1 issued an estimate of £396 11s 11d, but then claimed this was only part of the cost. D3 (d2's father, part-owner of the brig) claims p5 had ignored Admiral W. Drake's certificate proving the brig's neutrality. D3 assigned the brig to ds9-10 as security for loans, and d8 has had d3 imprisoned for debts. Ds6-7 received power of attorney from owners of the brig's cargo including ds4-5.

1785, Trin	E 112/1700	Bill. LMX 3690.
1785, June 27	E 112/1700	Answer. Swearing date of answer of ds6-7.
1785, Nov 16	E 112/1700	Answer. Swearing date of d8's answer, filed 18 November; schedule below answer of d3's debts to d8.
1785, Nov 28	E 112/1700	Answer (with attachments). Swearing & filing date of d1's answer; schedule below answer of repairs estimate; copy attached of affadavit of the estimate sworn 17 May 1783.
1785, Mich	E 112/1700	Exception. Ps' exception to d1's answer concerns whether £396 11s 11d is sufficient to repair the brig.
1785, Dec 22	E 112/1700	Answer. Swearing date of d3's answer.
1786, Jan 24	E 112/1700	Answer. Filing & swearing date of answer of ds9-10.

296. Rawlinson v Wyatt

P: (1) Jane Wise Rawlinson, Bampton, Midd, C. Rawlinson's widow & executrix. D: (1) James Wyatt, architect, Queen Ann St. East, Midd; (2) Samuel Wyatt, architect, Berwick St., Soho, Midd. C: (1) W. Scafe, counsel for p; (2) J. Johnson, counsel for d2. Add: (1) Charles Rawlinson gent., Lestwithiel, Corn, deceased, p's husband. P claims in 1772 her husband C. Rawlinson obtained a 14-year patent for his invention of a method for slating roofs. In 1785 C. Rawlinson died leaving p his executrix. P claims ds have employed the slating method without paying 2s 6d per square yard to her, as holder of the patent. D2 asserts he paid C. Rawlinson, & subsequently p, for his use of the method.

1785, Trin	E 112/1716	Bill. LMX 4093; schedule below bill of slating performed by d1 following Rawlinson's method.
1786, May 12	E 112/1716	Answer (with attachments). Swearing date of d2's answer; 2 schedules attached of buildings slated by d2 using the method, & payments made to C. Rawlinson & p.

297. Raymond v Farquharson

P: (1) Sir Charles Raymond, London, bart.. D: (1) James Farquharson esq., Gough Square, London. C: (1) R. Richards, counsel for p; (2) Richard Hollist, counsel for d. P seeks inj ag d's suit at KB for payment of an insurance policy. P claims in 1781, he & d were part-owners of a ship in the service of the East India Company, the *Blandford*, bound for Bengal, underwritten by p. They agreed with other ship-owners for the EIC to insure each other mutually for return voyages only. The *Blandford* was captured on the apparent outward journey between Madras & Bengal. D now sues p for the insurance, alleging the ship was returning from Madras, its ultimate destination.

1784, Mich	E 112/1734	Bill. LMX 4531.
1784, Nov 18	E 112/1734	Answer. Swearing & filing date.

298. Rennett v Haxby

P: (1) Charles Rennett gent., solicitor, Inner Temple, London. D: (1) Thomas Haxby, music seller, York, Yorks. C: (1) Robert Ledlie, counsel for p. P adds a supplement to his bill ag d seeking compensation for breach of copyright. In 1783 p sued d in this Court, claiming he had sole copyright to Bach's operas 16 & 18, Bach's 3rd set of concertos & other music books, of which d had been selling pirate copies. By way of supplement, p claims that in 1784 he bought the 14-year copyrights for John Garth's 6 sonatas & Charles Dibdin's operas, of which d has also been selling pirate copies.

1785, Hil	E 112/1718	Supplementary bill. LMX 4152.

299. Rennett v Longman

P: (1) Charles Rennett gent., Inner Temple, London. D: (1) James Longman, music seller, Cheapside, London; (2) Francis Fane Broderip, music seller, Cheapside, London. C: (1) Robert Ledlie, counsel for p; (2) William Waller, counsel for ds. Add: (1) John Garth, composer, Durh. P seeks to supplement his bill filed in 1780 in this Court ag ds seeking compensation & an inj to prevent ds breaching copyright. P claimed he owns the copyright for works by Bach, Fischer & other music books, of which ds had printed, imported & sold pirate copies. P adds as supplement that since his bill was filed ds have continued to sell pirate copies, including J. Garth's works, whose copyright p owns. Ds claim they stopped selling Garth's works when p bought the copyright.

1784, Mich	E 112/1758	Supplementary bill. LMX 5276; amended 24 January 1785 to include ds' alleged sale of Garth's works.
1785, Jan 12	E 112/1758	Answer. Swearing date of ds' answer to supplementary bill, filed 13 January; schedule below answer of music sold by ds.
1785, April 6	E 112/1758	Answer. Swearing & filing date of ds' answer to p's amended supplementary bill.

300. Rennett v Thompson

P: (1) Charles Rennett gent., solicitor, Inner Temple, London. D: (1) Samuel Thompson, music seller, St. Paul's Church Yard, London, partner of ds2-3; (2) Ann Thompson, music seller, St. Paul's Church Yard, London, partner of d1 & d3; (3) Peter Thompson, music seller, St. Paul's Church Yard, London, partner of ds1-2. C: (1) Robert Ledlie, counsel for p; (2) Charles Shuter, counsel for ds. Add: (1) John Garth, composer, Durh; (2) Charles Dibdin, composer, London; (3) James Longman, music seller, Cheapside, London, prior owner of some of the music with previous partner Charles Lukey (deceased); (4) Francis Fane Broderip, music seller, Cheapside, London, J. Longman's partner. P seeks inj ag any suit of ds, Messrs Thompson & Co., challenging p's sole right to print and sell the music of certain operas; p also seeks inj ag ds printing or selling copies of the operas. P claims he bought sole copyright after the rights of ds (previous holders) reverted to the composers at the end of a 14-year term. Ds claim they own the music outright because the composers never reclaimed their copyright.

1784, Mich	E 112/1705	Bill. LMX 3808.
1785, Jan 15	E 112/1705	Answer. Swearing and filing date of ds' answer.
1785, Jan 24	E 112/1705	Amended bill. P details the 14-year term of copyright, & ds' sale of music after their rights had allegedly expired.
1785, Feb 11	E 112/1705	Further answer. Swearing date of ds' further answer; includes schedule of music books bought and sold by ds.

301. Righton v Wilks

P: (1) Basil Righton, cooper, London. D: (1) Joseph Wilks, merchant, London; (2) George Walker, wine merchant, Exchange Alley, London. C: (1) J. S. Harvey, counsel for p; (2) R. Richards, counsel for d1. Add: (1) William Sealy, wine merchant, London. P seeks inj ag d1's suit at KB for payment of a bill of exchange. P claims in 1784 he & W. Sealy drew bills of exchange for £231 12s & £128 12s respectively, & endorsed them to d2 for d1's use, to be paid off before the due date. P asserts d1 never used his £231 12s bill, but refused to give it back to be cancelled. D1 is now suing p at KB for the bill, alleging p issued the bill for goods received from d2, who endorsed it to d1.

1784, Mich	E 112/1703	Bill. LMX 3763; cf. E 112/1703 LMX 3760 Sealy v Wilks.
1784, Nov 23	E 112/1703	Answer. Swearing & filing date of d1's answer.
1784, Mich	E 112/1703	Exception. P's exceptions to d1's answer concern d1's acquisition of the bill of exchange.

302. Riley v Caesar

P: (1) John Riley, upholder, auctioneer, Long Acre, Westminster, Midd. D: (1) Carlos Caesar, grocer, Holborn Bridge, London; (2) Robert Jaques. C: (1) W. Ainge, counsel for p; (2) William Scafe, counsel for d1. Add: (1) John Glidden. P seeks inj ag d1's suit for payment of promissory note allegedly endorsed by p. P accuses ds of forging his signature on the note. D1 claims the note was tendered to him by J. Glidden, and that d1 recognised the endorser on the note as p (his and d2's previous landlord). D1 denies d2 has anything to do with the dispute.

| 1784, Mich | E 112/1705 | Bill. LMX 3816; cf. E 112/1708 LMX 3908 Caesar v Hankey. |
| 1784, Nov 29 | E 112/1705 | Answer. Swearing date of d1's answer. |

303. Riley v Williams

P: (1) John Riley, victualler, Kensington, Midd. D: (1) David Williams gent., solicitor, Inner Temple, London. C: (1) E. King, counsel for p. Add: (1) William Williams, broker, Lambeth, Surrey, insolvent. P seeks inj ag d's suit for

payment of a note of hand. To clear part of a debt d's friend W. Williams owed p, d paid p cash for his friend's note of hand. P signed the note supposedly to enable d to claim repayment from his friend later. Williams then became insolvent, so d claims p's endorsement of the note renders him liable to pay it.
1785, Easter   E 112/1700   Bill. LMX 3687.

304. Roberts v Townsend

P: (1) Thomas Roberts esq., Castle St., Midd, d4's brother, D. Roberts's son; (2) Henry Leicester gent., clerk, Castle St., Midd, employed by D. Roberts. D: (1) Theyer Townsend, linen draper, Cheapside, London; (2) John Haslam, linen draper, Cheapside, London; (3) William Railton, linen draper, Cheapside, London; (4) John Roberts, army agent, p1's brother, D. Roberts's son; (5) William Randall the younger, Marsham St., Westminster, London; (6) Thomas Hume Bowles, the War Office; (7) James Hay, tailor, Charles St., Covent Garden, Midd; (8) Mr Birch, mercer, May's Buildings, Bedfordbury, Midd; (9) Mr Simpson, mercer, May's Buildings, Bedfordbury, Midd. C: (1) E. King, counsel for ps; (2) John Loyd, counsel for d7; (3) J. Pippard, counsel for ds1-3; (4) J. Bicknell, counsel for d5. Add: (1) David Roberts esq., Castle St., Midd, father of p1 & d4. Ps seek inj ag the suit of ds1-3 for payment of a bill of exchange. Ps claim in 1784, d4 persuaded his brother p1 to draw a £250 bill of exchange in favour of p2, who endorsed it to d4, who promised to indemnify ps. D4 endorsed the bill to d5, who delivered it to d6, who paid it to d7, who transferred it to ds8-9, who delivered it to ds1-3. Ds1-3 are suing ps & D. Roberts at KB for payment of the bill, to which D. Roberts has filed a bill in Chancery ag ds1-3. Ds1-3, d5 & d7 claim they were issued the bill as payment for goods or debts.

1785, Hil   E 112/1711   Bill. LMX 3986.
1785, March 13   E 112/1711   Answer. Swearing date of d7's answer, filed 12 April; schedule below answer of clothes d6 bought from d7 with the bill.
1785, April 15   E 112/1711   Answer. Swearing date of the answer of ds1-3, filed 16 April.
1785, April 30   E 112/1711   Answer. Swearing date of d5's answer.

305. Robinson v Franter

P: (1) Thomas Robinson, ironmonger, Benjamin St., West Smithfield, Midd. D: (1) James Franter, ironmonger, Dudley, Worcs; (2) Myles Bourn gent., Dudley, Worcs. C: (1) John Lloyd, counsel for p. P seeks inj ag ds' suit at KB for payment of bills of exchange. D1 drew 2 bills on p in favour of d2, which p accepted. P claims he later paid sufficient to cover the bills, but failed to secure the instruments which remained in d2's possession. Ds deny the bills were paid off and assert p still owes the money.
1784, Mich   E 112/1705   Bill. LMX 3813.

306. Rogers v Dudman

P: (1) Victori Rogers, victualler, Hermitage St., Wapping, Midd. D: (1) John Dudman, slopseller, Wapping, Midd. C: (1) Thomas Lowes, counsel for p; (2) John Crode, counsel for d. P seeks inj ag d's suit at KB for a £100 note. In 1779, p, then an innkeeper, agreed to give credit to sailors at his inn to buy clothes in d's shop, for a commission from d. P claims he paid sums to d, but d never paid him the commission, & had him arrested for a £150 debt in 1781. P issued 2 notes for £50 & £100 to d, who allegedly agreed not to cash the £100 note in lieu of the commission. D has since had p arrested for the £100 note. D claims p forfeited the commission by not paying for the clothes on time.

1785, Trin	E 112/3562	Bill. LMX 3562.
1785, June 27	E 112/1696	Answer. Swearing date; schedule below answer of accounts between d & p.

307. Ross v Austin

P: (1) Isaac Ross, shipbreaker, Rotherhithe, Surrey. D: (1) William Austin, mariner, Wapping, Midd. C: (1) Thomas Lowes, counsel for p. P seeks inj ag d's suit in the Court of Common Pleas for £20. P claims he paid £70 bail for d who absconded after being arrested for assault. Upon d's return, p made him captain of p's ship bound for Africa. D neglected to procure certificates when the ship was impressed into government service, & avoided giving an account of the cargo to p. D allegedly employed p to purchase a share in a ship for him, but called off the negotiation & paid p £20 as a gratuity. D is now suing p for the £20, allegedly claiming he only lent p the money.

1785, Easter	E 112/1702	Bill. LMX 3722.

308. Ross v Bray

P: (1) Isaac Ross, shipbreaker, Rotherhithe, Surrey. D: (1) John Bray, lighterman to the Office of Ordnance, Prescott St., Goodmans Fields. C: (1) Geo. Wood, counsel for p; (2) F. Walker, counsel for d. P seeks discovery of sums received by d for the hire of p's sloop by the Office of Ordnance. P claims in 1780 he employed d to hire p's sloop, the *Prince of Wales*, to the Office of Ordnance. P claims the office employed the sloop for over 2 years, & paid d the earnings, who never paid p. D asserts the sloop needed repairs, for which d paid, & was not used for many voyages.

1784, Mich	E 112/1702	Bill. LMX 3723; amended 7 June 1785 to request that d account with p for the earnings.
1785, April 8	E 112/1702	Answer. Swearing date; schedule below answer of d's accounts with p.
1785, Mich	E 112/1702	Replication. P asserts d's answer is insufficient.
1785, Mich	E 112/1702	Rejoinder. D maintains his answer is sufficient.

309. Rowe v Maxwell

P: (1) Milward Rowe esq., Palace of Kensington, Midd. D: (1) Charles Maxwell, chemist, apothecary, Fleet St., London; (2) Edward Ashwell esq., Leighton Buzzard, Beds, d1's trustee; (3) John Forbes, merchant, Aldermanbury, London, d1's trustee; (4) Margaret Maxwell, d1's daughter & beneficiary; (5) Charlotte Maxwell, d1's daughter & beneficiary; (6) Governor & Co., Bank of England. C: (1) John Spranger, counsel for p. Add: (1) Isabella Maxwell, St. Clements Danes, Westminster, Midd, deceased, d1's wife; (2) Henry Gardiner, deceased, I. Maxwell's nephew; (3) Thomas Hudson esq., Twickenham, Midd, deceased,

d1's trustee. P seeks inj ag ds transferring bank annuities. P claims d1 issued him bonds for loans, with annuities as security. D1 then entrusted the annuities for his daughters and his wife's nephew (since deceased). D1 subsequently added houses as further security for the loan, and disclosed to p that the annuities were in trust. P claims he should at least be paid the dividends on the annuities.
1785, Hil   E 112/1705   Bill. LMX 3828.

310. Rutter v Gibbons

P: (1) Samuel Rutter the younger, carcass butcher, Newgate Market, London. D: (1) Benjamin Gibbons gent., Hatton St., London. C: (1) William Scafe, counsel for p. P seeks inj ag d's suit at KB for payment of 2 promissory notes for £15 each. P claims before 1779 he owed d £30. In 1779 p went bankrupt, & his assignees possessed his estate, & issued p a certificate of assignment of his estate in 1781. D refused to sign p's certificate until p issued him the promissory notes for the £30. D then sued p for the notes. P claims the notes are void because the £30 debt was incurred before his bankruptcy.
1785, Easter   E 112/1697   Bill. LMX 3583.

311. Scudamore v Smith

P: (1) John Scudamore esq., Stafford St., Hanover Sq., London. D: (1) Walter Smith, linen draper, Oxford St., London, bankrupt, partners with d2; (2) William Turner, linen draper, Oxford St., London, bankrupt, partners with d1; (3) Thomas Woolloton, assignee of ds1-2; (4) Charles Miller, assignee of ds1-2; (5) William Salte, assignee of ds1-2; (6) John Knight; (7) John Wilding, clerk, d8's servant; (8) John Henry Aickles. C: (1) Henry Boulton, counsel for p; (2) J. Stanley, counsel for ds1-5. P seeks inj ag the suit of ds1-2 in the Exchequer of Pleas for payment of a £250 bill of exchange which p issued with 3 other £250 bills to d7 (d8's clerk) in 1783. P claims d8 was supposed to get the bills discounted for him, but instead d8 endorsed one bill to d6, who endorsed it to ds1-2, who went bankrupt in 1784 with assignees ds3-5. P had an indictment preferred ag d8 at the Sessions of the Peace, Guildhall, but ds1-2 got a judgement for the bill in the Exchequer of Pleas. Ds1-2 claim they sold d6 goods for the bill.

1785, Hil	E 112/1700	Bill. LMX 3665.
1786, Jan 24	E 112/1700	Answer. Swearing & filing date of answer of ds1-2; schedule below answer of d6's accounts with ds1-2.
1786, Feb 9	E 112/1700	Answer. Sworn by d3 & filed on this date; sworn by ds4-5 on 23 January 1786.
1786, Hil	E 112/1700	Exception. P's exceptions to the answer of ds1-2 concern the indictment, & payment for the bills.
1786, May 10	E 112/1700	Amended bill. P seeks discovery of the 3 other bills.
1787, Nov 26	E 112/1700	Further answer. Swearing & filing date of further answer of ds1-2 to amended bill.
1787, Dec 14	E 112/1700	Exception. P's exceptions to the 1st further answer of ds1-2 concern d6's payment for goods bought with the bill from ds1-2.

1788, Feb 6	E 112/1700	Amended bill. 2nd amended bill concerns the due date for payment of the bills.
1788, Nov 18	E 112/1700	Further answer. Swearing date of further answer of ds3-5 to 2nd amended bill; filed 26 November.
1788, Nov 27	E 112/1700	Further answer. Filing date of further answer of ds1-2 to 2nd amended bill; sworn by d2 on 18 November; sworn by d1 on 25 November.

312. Sealy v Wilks

P: (1) William Sealy, wine merchant, London. D: (1) Joseph Wilks, merchant, London; (2) George Walker, wine merchant, Exchange Alley, London. C: (1) J. S. Harvey, counsel for p; (2) R. Richards, counsel for d1. Add: (1) Basil Righton, cooper, London. P seeks inj ag d1's suit at KB for payment of a bill of exchange. P claims in 1784 he & B. Righton drew bills of exchange for £128 12s & £231 12s respectively, & endorsed them to d2 for d1's use, to be paid off before the due date. P asserts d1 never used his £128 12s bill, but refused to give it back to be cancelled. D1 is now suing p at KB for the bill, alleging p issued the bill for goods received from d2, who endorsed it to d1.

1784, Mich	E 112/1703	Bill. LMX 3760; cf E 112/1703 LMX 3763 Righton v Wilks.
1784, Nov 23	E 112/1703	Answer. Swearing & filing date of d1's answer.
1784, Mich	E 112/1703	Exception. P's exceptions to d1's answer concern d1's acquisition of the bill of exchange.

313. Shoolbred v Fowle

P: (1) John Shoolbred, merchant, London. D: (1) Thomas Fowle, haberdasher, Newgate St., London; (2) William Stark, merchant, London; (3) William McLeod, merchant, Charles Town, S. Carolina., d4's partner; (4) John Bethune, merchant, Charles Town, S. Carolina, d3's partner; (5) Henry Shoolbred, p's agent. C: (1) William Walter, counsel for p; (2) J. Pippard, counsel for ds. P seeks relief from ds' suit at KB for debts which p claims are overstated by mistake. P incurred the debts with his partners when their ship & cargo sailing from Charles Town, S. Carolina to East Florida and West Indies was captured by Americans, and the partners were evacuated from Charles Town.

1784, Mich	E 112/1701	Bill. LMX 3700.
1786, Feb 28	E 112/1701	Answer. Filing date.
1786, Feb 28	E 112/1701	Answer. Filing date.

314. Singleton v Mitchell

P: (1) Lawrence Singleton gent., London. D: (1) Thomas Mitchell the elder, tailor, Bucklers Bury, London, previously W. Singleton's colleague; (2) Thomas Mitchell the younger, tailor, Bucklers Bury, London; (3) Thomas Tooley, tailor. C: (1) Thomas Lowes, counsel for p; (2) R. Richards, counsel for ds. Add: (1) William Singleton, trader, deceased, p's father. P seeks inj ag ds' suit at KB for payment of a debt that p alleges is unjustly inflated. P claims ds compelled him to sign a note under threat of imprisonment, but ds claim the debt is accurate, arising from tailor's bills, loans made by ds to p, & debts p's father W. Singleton owed ds.

| 1785, Easter | E 112/1700 | Bill. LMX 3664. |
| 1786, May 10 | E 112/1700 | Answer. Filing date of ds' answer; schedule of accounts included. |

315. Skynner v Durrant

P: (1) Richard Skynner. D: (1) John Durrant. C: (1) W. Scafe, counsel for p; (2) Thomas Evance, counsel for d. P seeks inj ag d's suit at KB for payment for a bag of tea. P claims d had hired him to transport goods by horse, at a cost of £20. P bought 4 bags of tea from d, whose price would be set off ag d's £20 debt to p. P asserts that only 3 bags were delivered, but d is suing him at KB for the price of the fourth bag. D claims he is suing p, not for a fourth bag, but for £5 7s 3d still owing for the 3 bags after the £20 was set off.

| 1785, Trin | E 112/1703 | Bill. LMX 3761. |
| 1785, Nov 15 | E 112/1703 | Answer. Swearing date, filed 16 November. |

316. Smart v Morris

P: (1) Richard Smart gent., Eastham, Essex. D: (1) Thomas Morris, upholder, St. Paul's Church Yard, London. C: (1) John Henniker, counsel for p. Add: (1) William Worth gent., Plaistow, Essex. P seeks discovery of any other incumbrances upon d's mortgaged premises. In 1782, d allegedly mortgaged his 2 messuages in St. Paul's Church Yard to W. Worth for £350. In 1784 W. Worth transferred the mortgage to p for £350. D apparently paid p some of the mortgage, but then denied ever mortgaging the premises to Worth, or claimed the premises are subject to incumbrances prior to p's mortgage.

| 1785, Trin | E 112/1704 | Bill. LMX 3781. |

317. Smith v Douglas

P: (1) William Smith esq., Clapham, Surrey, assignee of ds1-2; (2) John Randall esq., Southampton St., Bloomsbury, Midd, assignee of ds1-2; (3) James Jackson, ropemaker, New Rd., St. George in the East, Midd, assignee of ds1-2. D: (1) Thomas Douglas, mariner, dealer, chapman, Holborn, London, bankrupt; (2) James Adams, merchant, dealer, chapman, Mincing Lane, London, bankrupt; (3) Samuel Hartley, merchant, London. C: (1) John Mitford, counsel for ps; (2) J. Stanley, counsel for d3. Add: (1) John Shoolbred, merchant, nominated by ps to ascertain true accounts. Ps, assignees of the estates of ds1-2, bankrupts, seek discovery of the disposal of elephant ivory acquired in Africa by d2 for d1, owner of ship of which d2 was master. Ps allege d1 and d3, a merchant, defrauded d2 of his part of the ivory.

1785, Trin	E 112/1701	Bill. LMX 3694; 2 schedules of accounts between d1 & d3 included below bill.
1785, Nov 7	E 112/1701	Answer. Filing date of d3's answer.
1786, Hil	E 112/1701	Exception. Ps' exceptions to d3's answer concern d3's shipping of the ivory & the insurance thereon.
1786, Trin	E 112/1701	Amended bill. Ps allege more explicitly d3's collusion to defraud.

1787, Feb 12	E 112/1701	Further answer. Filing date of d3's further answer, including copy of his correspondence with Messrs Buchanan & Co., insurers of the ivory.

318. Smith v Robertson

P: (1) Elizabeth Smith, Gt. Russell St., Bloomsbury, Midd, J. Smith's sister; (2) Eleanor Smith, Gt. Russell St., Bloomsbury, Midd, J. Smith's sister. D: (1) William Robertson esq., Clapham, Surrey, J. Smith's agent. C: (1) John Mitford, counsel for ps; (2) F. Walker, counsel for d. Add: (1) James Smith, naval lieutenant, deceased, ps' brother. Ps, spinsters, seek discovery of a true account of the finances of their brother J. Smith (deceased) from d, his agent. Ps, sole heirs and beneficiaries in their brother's will, claim d witholds some of the deceased's assets. D disputes their accounting.

1785, Hil	E 112/1701	Bill. LMX 3718.
1785, May 14	E 112/1701	Answer. Filing date.
1785, Trin	E 112/1701	Replication. Ps deny d's answer is sufficient.
1785, Trin	E 112/1701	Rejoinder. D maintains his answer is sufficient.

319. Smith v Thompson

P: (1) John Smith, clerk, Taunton, Som, J. Andrews's employee. D: (1) William Thompson, innholder, the Saracen's Head, Friday St., London. C: (1) E. King, counsel for p; (2) Josiah Brown, counsel for d. Add: (1) John Andrews, currier, Taunton, Som; (2) William Osborne, bookkeeper, Gerrards Hall, Basing Lane, London, J. Andrews's employee. P seeks inj ag d's suit at KB for payment of 3 drafts for money. In 1784, p (J. Andrews's clerk) issued d 3 drafts for £154 18s in his own name upon W. Osborne (J. Andrews's bookkeeper), as alleged security for payment for the housing of J. Andrews's wagon at d's inn. D now sues p for the drafts. D claims p issued the drafts as payment, not security, on behalf of J. Andrews, who is under 21 years.

1785, Trin	E 112/1703	Bill. LMX 3766.
1785, Nov 7	E 112/1703	Answer. Swearing & filing date.
1785, Mich	E 112/1703	Exception. P's exception asks whether d had not promised to consider the drafts as security rather than payment.

320. Sowerby v Myers

P: (1) Robert Sowerby, slopseller, Fenchurch St., London. D: (1) Jonas Myers, silversmith & slopseller, Chatham, Kent, d2's brother; (2) Lazarus Myers, silversmith, Chatham, Kent, d1's brother. C: (1) Thomas Evance, counsel for p; (2) J. Pippard, counsel for ds. Add: (1) Thomas Lowten gent., solicitor, Inner Temple, London, arbitrator of the dispute in KB. P seeks payment of 2 promissory notes from ds. P claims in 1783 he accepted cash & the 2 notes for a composition of 15 shillings in the pound from d1, who could not pay a £204 14s debt he owed p. When ds did not pay the notes, p had them arrested at KB, where the dispute was referred to the arbitration of T. Lowten, who awarded damages to p. Ds then obtained an inj ag p in this Court, alleging p had agreed to accept only 5 shillings in the pound composition, with the notes as security only.

| 1785, Trin | E 112/1696 | Bill. LMX 3564. |
| 1785, June 13 | E 112/1696 | Answer. Swearing & filing date of ds' answer. |

321. Stacpoole v Barnhouse

P: (1) Joseph Stacpoole esq., barrister, Middle Temple, London; (2) Philip Bromfield esq., captain in the service of the East India Company, Soho, Midd. D: (1) John Barnhouse, sailor, 3rd mate on a ship, the *St. Anne*. C: (1) James Sheridan, counsel for ps; (2) John Lloyd, counsel for d. Add: (1) Sir William James, Eltham Park Farm, Kent, bart., deceased; (2) Thomas Wetherhead, yeoman, London, agent for J. Anthony & the crew of the *St. Anne*; (3) Joseph Anthony, ship's captain, the *St. Anne*. Ps seek inj ag d's suit at KB. Ps claim that in 1782 Sir W. James's privateer, the *St. Anne* (commanded by J. Anthony), captured 2 French ships, later condemned as droits & perquisites of Admiralty. James petitioned for recovery of profits from the ships' sale, but died. In 1784 the Court of Admiralty awarded the profits, including a £6000 share to the crew, most of whom were born on the estate of p1's family in Ireland. The crew appointed p1 & p2 (James's friend) as their trustees of the £6000. D, 3rd mate on the *St. Anne*, claims ps refused to pay his share to J. Anthony & his agent T. Wetherhead, & now sues ps at KB.

1785, Hil	E 112/1785	Bill. LMX 6169.
1785, Nov 21	E 112/1785	Answer. Swearing & filing date.
1785, Nov 28	E 112/1785	Exception. Ps' exceptions concern whether d issued his power of attorney to J. Anthony.

322. Stephenson v Pearson

P: (1) Christopher Stephenson, merchant, Shadwell, Midd. D: (1) Margaret Pearson, North Shields, Northumb. C: (1) W. Waller, counsel for p. Add: (1) John Stephenson, ship's captain. P seeks payment from d of £38 15s for beef & pork. P claims in 1783 he delivered the meat to J. Stephenson, captain of d's ship, the *Two Friends*, bound for Madeira & America. J. Stephenson failed to pay p before setting sail. Last Trinity term, p sued d at KB for payment, but could not prove d's ownership of the ship. D asserts she owned only a 32nd share of the ship, & that J. Stephenson was the principal owner, & that the ship sank on the voyage.

1784, Mich	E 112/1695	Bill. LMX 3550.
1785, Feb 12	E 112/1695	Commission. For d's answer.
1785, April 19	E 112/1695	Answer. Swearing date, filed 2 May.

323. Stevens v Wills

P: (1) John Stevens, victualler, Saffron Hill, Midd. D: (1) Thomas Wills, pressmaker, Giltspur St., London, d2's husband; (2) Sarah Wills, Giltspur Lane, London, d1's wife. C: (1) John Lloyd, counsel for p; (2) William Waller, counsel for ds. P seeks payment of a £140 mortgage on premises copyhold of the manor of Highbury in Islington which ds made to p in 1784. Ds have not paid the mortgage. Ds offer p possession of the premises until they can redeem them.

| 1785, Easter | E 112/1698 | Bill. LMX 3635. |
| 1786, Feb 24 | E 112/1698 | Answer. Swearing date of ds' answer. |

| 1786, Easter | E 112/1698 | Replication. P asserts ds' answer is insufficient. |
| 1786, Easter | E 112/1698 | Rejoinder. Ds maintain their answer is sufficient. |

324. Stevenson v Axe

P: (1) John Stevenson, mariner, Islington, Midd. D: (1) William Axe, tailor, Birchin Lane, London; (2) Isaac Pratt, hardwareman, Carey St., Midd. C: (1) Richard Hollist, counsel for p; (2) Thomas Nedham, counsel for d1. P seeks inj ag d1's suit at KB for payment of a £560 respondentia bond. In 1774, p was hired by the EIC as chief mate of a ship, the *Rochford*, bound for China. P had ironmongery and cloth delivered to the ship by ds, for which p paid with blank respondentia bonds. Ds filled in the bonds to the amount of £560. On the voyage, p discovered the cloth to be damaged, & could only sell it at a discounted price. Ds now sue p at KB for the full bond. D1 denies the cloth was damaged.

| 1785, Easter | E 112/1698 | Bill. LMX 3631. |
| 1785, May 2 | E 112/1698 | Answer. Swearing & filing date of d1's answer; schedule included below answer of accounts between d1 & p. |

325. Stokoe v Byrne

P: (1) Mary Stokoe, Paternoster Row, Spitalfields, Midd, over 70 years old. D: (1) Patrick Byrne, Hog Lane, Oxford Rd., Midd, d2's husband; (2) Catherine Byrne, d1's wife. C: (1) R. Richards, counsel for p. P, a spinster, seeks inj ag ds' suit at KB for payment of an alleged bond. P claims in 1781 d2 lived in her house as her servant. P, over 70 years old, claims she entrusted the management of her affairs to d2, who abused p, ran up debts in p's name, stole p's money, & brought her husband d1 & child from Ireland to live in p's house. Ds eventually left the house, but are suing p for an alleged bond which they claim p owes them.

| 1785, Hil | E 112/1702 | Bill. LMX 3745. |

326. Stuart v Careless

P: (1) James Stuart gent., Finchley, Midd. D: (1) William Careless, hairdresser, parish of St. James, Westminster. C: (1) William Alexander, counsel for p; (2) John Holt, counsel for d. P seeks execution of a lease by d. P claims in 1774, he leased a messuage in Warwick St., parish of St. James, to d, for 21 years at £42 per annum. D allegedly demolished & altered parts of the messuage, reducing the value of the property, and then quit the premises, all contrary to the lease. D pleads that he may not be sued because the lease was never executed (though he often requested p to do so), & that he agreed only to rent the premises on a yearly basis, not for 21 years.

1784, Mich	E 112/1699	Bill. LMX 3646.
1785, April 11	E 112/1699	Answer. Swearing date of d's plea & answer, filed 12 April.
1785, Trin	E 112/1699	Exception. P's exceptions to d's answer concern the particulars of their agreement to let the premises.

1785, Nov 8	E 112/1699	Further answer. Swearing date of d's further answer, filed 9 November.
1786, Hil	E 112/1699	Replication. P asserts d's answers are insufficient.
1786, Hil	E 112/1699	Rejoinder. D maintains his answers are sufficient.
1786, Jan 23	E 112/1699	Amended bill. P claims d promised to execute the lease.

327. Swaine v Cope

P: (1) William Swaine, hop merchant, Southwark, Surrey, p2's partner & d4's trustee; (2) John Swaine, hop merchant, Southwark, Surrey, p1's partner. D: (1) John Cope the younger, yeoman, Ayton, Yorks, d4's brother & trustee, J. Cope the E's son & executor; (2) Ann Cope, J. Cope the E's widow & executrix; (3) George Wadbrook, malster, Kingston upon Thames, Surrey, d4's trustee; (4) Thomas Cope, brewer, parish of St. Luke, Midd, d1's brother, J. Cope the E's son. C: (1) W. Ainge, counsel for ps. Add: (1) John Cope the elder, father of d1 & d4. Ps, for themselves & the other creditors of d4 in 1780, seek repayment of debts owed them by d4. In 1780, d4 assigned his estate to p1, d1 & d3 in trust to pay off his creditors. D1, d4 & their father J. Cope the E persuaded ps to pay off d3 & allow them to continue running d4's brewing business, in return for a dividend of 8 shillings in the pound. In 1781, J. Cope the E died, leaving d2 (his widow) & d1 his executors. Ps claim the business was mismanaged & will not now yield the value of the dividend.

1785, Easter   E 112/1716   Bill. LMX 4089.

328. Thackray v Garford

P: (1) Robert Thackray, broker, merchant, London; (2) William Hanson, broker, merchant, London. D: (1) John Garford, broker, London; (2) Mr Samuel Baker, merchant, Lynn, Norf. C: (1) E. King, counsel for ps; (2) John Lloyd, counsel for ds. Ps seek inj ag d2's suit in KB for breach of supposed contract negotiated by d1. D2 is suing for lost profits in a deal for whale oil which ps deny ever concluding.

1784, Mich	E 112/1701	Bill. LMX 3702.
1785, April 27	E 112/1701	Answer. Filing date of d1's answer.
1785, April 27	E 112/1701	Answer. Filing date of d2's answer.

329. Thorne v Shafto

P: (1) Thomas Thorne, C. Barrow's assignee; (2) George Addis, C. Barrow's assignee; (3) Thomas Winsloe esq., College Priest, Devon, C. Barrow's assignee. D: (1) Robert Shafto, A. Shafto's husband; (2) John Shafto; (3) Frances Duncombe, T. Duncombe's daughter; (4) George Marchant; (5) Rt. Hon. Jacob, Earl of Radnor, d6's husband; (6) Ann, Countess of Radnor, d5's wife, heiress of Lord Feversham; (7) James Bowater esq., d8's husband; (8) Frances Bowater, d7's wife, heiress of Lord Feversham; (9) Jonathan Collett, administrator de bonis non of T. Betts. C: (1) J. A. Stainsby, counsel for ps. Add: (1) Charles Barrow, bankrupt; (2) Thomas Duncombe esq., deceased, d3's father, d1's father in law; (3) Rt. Hon. Anthony, Lord Feversham, deceased, Baron of Downton, Wilts; (4) Thomas Betts, glass manufacturer,

St. Martin in the Fields, Midd; (5) Ann Shafto, d1's wife, T. Duncombe's daughter. Ps, as assignees of C. Barrow (bankrupt), are assuming the prosecution of Barrow's suit in this Court. In 1779, Barrow sued T. Duncombe & ds4-9 in this Court to compel them to execute a lease. In 1755, Lord Feversham had leased a messuage to T. Betts for 47 years, who in 1758 leased it to d4, who sold his interest in it to Barrow in 1770. Lord Feversham died leaving the premises to T. Duncombe, who sued to eject Barrow at KB in 1778. In 1780 T. Duncombe died, so Barrow revived his suit ag T. Duncombe's daughters d3 & Ann Shafto, d1's wife. In 1782, Barrow went bankrupt with ps as his assignees, who now seek execution of the lease & inj ag ds' suit at KB.

1785, Hil   E 112/1702   Supplementary bill. LMX 3724.

330. Tweedie v Wilson

P: (1) Walter Tweedie, silversmith, Holiwell St., St. Clements Danes, Midd. D: (1) Elizabeth Wilson, warehousewoman, parish of St. Mary le Strand, Midd. C: (1) Robert Ledlie, counsel for p. P seeks for the lease of 2 properties to be assigned to him. P claims d agreed to sell him the premises which he already rents. P paid a deposit, but did not pay the balance because d did not assign the lease. D allegedly asserts she never agreed to sell the property.

1785, Easter   E 112/1708   Bill. LMX 3907.

331. Twigg v Moorhouse

P: (1) Joseph Twigg, gauze weaver, Gutter Lane, London, partner & brother of ps2-3; (2) William Twigg, gauze weaver, Gutter Lane, London, partner & brother of p1 & p3; (3) Samuel Twigg, gauze weaver, Gutter Lane, London, partner & brother of ps1-2. D: (1) Joseph Moorhouse the elder, banker, Lombard St., London; (2) William Willis, banker, Lombard St., London; (3) John Tysoe Reade, banker, Lombard St., London; (4) Joseph Moorhouse the younger, banker, Lombard St., London; (5) James Wood, banker, Lombard St., London; (6) Thomas Ludlam, personal representative of W. Copeland; (7) Benjamin Dixon, personal representative of W. Copeland. C: (1) John Mitford, counsel for ps; (2) J. S. Harvey, counsel for ds1-5; (3) J. A. Stainsby, counsel for d7. Add: (1) William Copeland, merchant, Cannon St., London, deceased; (2) Samuel Glover, merchant, Coleman St., London, bankrupt; (3) Samuel Huxley, merchant, Coleman St., London, bankrupt. Ps seek inj ag ds' suit at cl for payment of a £250 promissory note. In 1783, ps issued the note to S. Glover & S. Huxley, who agreed to pay it off by the due date. Glover & Huxley endorsed it to W. Copeland (since deceased), who deposited it with his bankers, ds1-5. Glover & Huxley went bankrupt, & ps allegedly paid Copeland 1/2 the value of the note. Copeland died owing ds1-5, who, with Copeland's representatives, ds6-7, are suing ps for the note.

1784, Mich	E 112/1698	Bill. LMX 3641.
1784, Dec 11	E 112/1698	Answer (with attachments). Swearing date of answer of ds1-5, filed 13 December; schedule attached of W. Copeland's accounts with the bank of ds1-5.
1785, Jan 27	E 112/1698	Answer. Swearing & filing date of d7's answer.

1785, Hil   E 112/1698   Exception. Ps' exceptions to answer of ds1-5
                                   concern the promisory note in the accounts
                                   of ds1-5.

332. Vezian v Jacobs

P: (1) Andrew Vezian, merchant, London. D: (1) Michael Jacobs; (2) George
Frederick Stras. C: (1) J. S. Harvey, counsel for p. P seeks inj ag d1's suit at KB
for payment of a promissory note. P claims in 1783, d2 borrowed a £130
promissory note from him, promising to pay it off by the due date. D2
endorsed the note to d1, possibly as a result of a wager on the stock market.
D1 sought payment for it from p, & has now obtained a judgement ag p at KB.
1785, Hil   E 112/1711   Bill. LMX 3991.

333. Von Holm v Sheperd

P: (1) John Von Holm, tobacconist, Little Hermitage St., Midd, parish of St.
George in the East.. D: (1) William Sheperd, mariner, Old Bethlem, London. C:
(1) William Walter, counsel for p. P and d jointly owned a ship trading to
Holland, which d sold or exchanged at Rotterdam. P seeks half share of
proceeds from last voyage and from sale of ship, but d claims p has already
received his share.
1785, Hil   E 112/1701   Bill. LMX 3705.

334. Wallace v Swaddle

P: (1) Michael Wallace, merchant, Halifax, Nova Scotia. D: (1) Hannah
Swaddle, Newington Butts, Surrey; (2) James Mac Taggart, merchant, Bristol,
W. Foster's administrator; (3) John Thomas, Newcastle upon Tyne,
Northumb, d4's husband; (4) Isabella Thomas, Newcastle upon Tyne,
Northumb, d3's wife; (5) Philip Protheroe, merchant, Bristol, d6's partner; (6)
Mark Davis, merchant, Bristol, d5's partner; (7) Barbara Foster, Jamaica, W.
Foster's widow. C: (1) William Alexander, counsel for p & d2; (2) Robert
Dallas, counsel for ds5-6; (3) William Cooke, counsel for ds3-4. Add: (1)
William Foster, ship's captain, deceased intestate, B. Foster's husband. P
seeks inj ag any suit of d1 ag d2, & payment for his ship, the *Britannia*. In
1781 p hired W. Foster to captain the *Britannia* from Nova Scotia to the West
Indies. At Jamaica W. Foster sold the ship & cargo, omitted to pay p the
proceeds, but bought another ship, the *Commerce*. In 1782 W. Foster insured
the *Commerce's* voyage from Jamaica to Bristol with ds5-6, but the ship sank
with all hands, & d2 bought W. Foster's administration from ds3-4. D1, W.
Foster's creditor, threatens to sue d2 for payment of W. Foster's debts. P
claims ds5-6 refuse to pay him from the insurance, but have instead paid d2 &
d7. Ds5-6 claim to be willing to pay the remaining insurance as the Court
directs.
1785, Hil   E 112/1713   Bill. LMX 4023.
1785, June 15   E 112/1713   Commission. For d2's answer.
1785, Nov 21   E 112/1713   Answer. Swearing date of d2's answer;
                                     schedule below answer of accounts of W.
                                     Foster's estate.
1786, April 21   E 112/1713   Answer. Swearing date of the answer of ds3-4.
1787, Feb 12   E 112/1713   Commission. For the answer of ds5-6.

138

1787, April 17	E 112/1713	Answer. Swearing date of the answer of ds5-6; schedule below answer of W. Foster's accounts with ds5-6.
1788, Trin	E 112/1713	Replication. P asserts the answers of ds2-6 are insufficient.
1788, Trin	E 112/1713	Rejoinder. D2 & ds5-6 maintain their answers are sufficient.

335. Waters v Hooper

P: (1) William Waters, Richmond Buildings, Soho, Midd; (2) James Soundy, Long Acre, Covent Garden, Midd. D: (1) Mathew Hooper, grocer, Fleet Market, London, d2's husband; (2) Hannah Hooper, Fleet Market, London, d1's wife. C: (1) Michael Schooll, counsel for ps; (2) Richard Hollist, counsel for ds. Add: (1) William Crawford, upholsterer, High Holborn, Midd, ps' creditor; (2) Samuel Payne, linen draper, Southampton St., Covent Garden, Midd, bankrupt, ps' creditor; (3) Jacob Fletcher, wine merchant, St. Martin in the Fields, London, ps' creditor. Ps seek inj ag ds' suit at KB for payment of a draft. In 1779, ps bought furniture on credit to stock a hotel, which they then failed to open. Ps agreed to assign the stock to their creditors, W. Crawford, S. Payne & J. Fletcher in trust to pay their debts. Ps also issued a £50 9s draft to Payne, who endorsed it to d1, & then went bankrupt. D1 refused to become ps' creditor under the trust, &, with his wife d2, sues ps at KB.

| 1785, Trin | E 112/1722 | Bill. LMX 4256. |
| 1786, July 3 | E 112/1722 | Answer. Swearing date of ds' answer, filed 5 July. |

336. Watkins v Towers

P: (1) George Watkins, silk weaver, Wood St., Cheapside, London. D: (1) John Towers, trustee of the Union Fire Office; (2) Henry Rutt, trustee of the Union Fire Office; (3) Francis Hamilton, trustee of the Union Fire Office. C: (1) Thomas Lowes, counsel for p; (2) J. Stanley, counsel for ds. Add: (1) Samuel Clarke, weaver, Printing House Lane, Blackfriars, London. P seeks payment of an insurance policy. In 1781, p bought the workshop, stock in trade & furniture of S. Clarke for £700. P insured the premises ag fire with ds, trustees of the Union Fire Office, at a cost of £10 10s. P's premises were then destroyed by fire & p sought compensation from ds. Ds refuse to pay fully for the policy, claiming that p could not produce an adequate account of his property, much of which, ds suspect, was not on the premises during the fire.

1785, Trin	E 112/1707	Bill. LMX 3875.
1786, May 4	E 112/1707	Answer. Swearing date of ds' answer, filed 3 May.
1786, Mich	E 112/1707	Replication. P asserts ds' answer is insufficient.
1786, Mich	E 112/1707	Rejoinder. Ds maintain their answer is sufficient.

337. Webb v Bridge

P: (1) Daniel Webb gent., Fleet St., London. D: (1) Thomas Bridge, broker, Bread St., London. C: (1) Thomas Lowes, counsel for p. Add: (1) Olginpea

Bridge, p's wife, d's sister; (2) Joseph Williams, planter, New Black River, Jamaica, d's attorney. P seeks inj to prevent d from selling an estate in Jamaica, & seeks the equity of redemption of the estate. P claims in 1759 he married Olginpea, the sister of d, his broker. In 1761, p mortgaged his estate in Jamaica to d for £1500. In 1771, p made absolute conveyance of the estate to d as security for the mortgage, after p's cattle & slaves were stolen. In 1778, p went insolvent with d as his assignee. In 1781, d's attorney J. Williams seized the estate. P claims the profits from the estate will have paid off his debts to d by now.

| 1785, Trin | E 112/1703 | Bill. LMX 3751. |

338. Wewitzer v Middleton

P: (1) Ralph Wewitzer gent., Covent Garden, Midd. D: (1) Jane Middleton, W. Middleton's widow, re-named Britton, d2's wife, in amended bill; (2) Richard Britton, Chelsea, Midd, d1's husband. C: (1) J. Johnson, counsel for p; (2) J. Pippard, counsel for ds. Add: (1) William Middleton, Chelsea, Midd, deceased intestate, d1's previous husband. P seeks inj ag d2's suit for payment of a promissory note. In 1780, W. Middleton had p arrested for an alleged £14 debt. P had his effects sold to pay his creditors, & issued W. Middleton a £20 promissory note. P's creditors lodged a detainer causing p to be imprisoned in KB. W. Middleton died intestate in 1782, leaving d1 his widow. In 1783, d2 had p arrested at KB for non-payment of the note. Ds claim they are now married, & allege p issued W. Middleton the note as payment for goods.

1785, Easter	E 112/1720	Bill. LMX 4211.
1785, May 6	E 112/1720	Answer. Swearing & filing date of ds' answer.
1785, Trin	E 112/1720	Exception. P's exceptions to ds' answer ask whether d1 is W. Middleton's administratrix, & how d2 acquired the note.
1785, July 2	E 112/1720	Amended bill. P re-names d1 as d2's wife.
1786, Jan 20	E 112/1720	Further answer. Swearing date of ds' further answer, filed 24 January; 2 schedules below of p's imprisonment & debts.
1786, Hil	E 112/1720	Exception. P's exceptions to ds' further answer concern the amount of the promisory note.
1786, Trin	E 112/1720	Replication. P asserts ds' answers are insufficient.
1786, Trin	E 112/1720	Rejoinder. Ds maintain their answers are sufficient.

339. Wilkinson v Kaye

P: (1) Thomas Wilkinson, tallow chandler, Conduit St., Midd. D: (1) Joseph Kaye gent., Hanover Square, Midd. C: (1) W. Ainge, counsel for p. Add: (1) John Allanby gent., Fleet St., London, deceased. P seeks relief from d's suit in the Court of Common Pleas for payment of rent. P claims in 1768, d & J. Allanby (since deceased) leased a messuage in Bond St. to him at £50 per annum for 21 years. In 1777 the messuage burnt down, & p has lived elsewhere ever since. D asserts p continues in possession of the premises & is liable for the rent since 1777, for which d sued p in 1784 in the Court of Common Pleas.

1784, Mich	E 112/1732	Bill. LMX 4494; amended 27 January 1785 to include details of p's lease & payment of rent.
1784, Nov 27	E 112/1732	Answer. Swearing date.
[1785, undated]	E 112/1732	Exception. P's exceptions concern p's lease & payment of rent.

340. Williams v Dixon

P: (1) David Williams, glazier & builder, Great Marylebone St., Midd. D: (1) James Dixon, glass merchant. C: (1) R. Richards, counsel for p. Add: (1) Edward Wilmot, p's attorney. P seeks inj ag d's suit at law for foreclosure or repayment of mortgages. In 1778, p mortgaged his house in Marylebone St. to d for £1071 15s 10d, which d claimed p owed him for glass. In 1779, p mortgaged another house to d for a £600 debt d claimed p owed him. P also issued d bonds as security for both mortgages. In 1783, d sought to foreclose, so p transferred another mortgage held by p's attorney, E. Wilmot, to d. D now sues p for repayment of the mortgages.

| 1785, Hil | E 112/1699 | Bill. LMX 3657; amended 30 April 1785. |

341. Williams v Jordan

P: (1) William Williams gent., Kington, Heref. D: (1) Thomas Jordan gent., brewer, Goodmans Fields, Midd; (2) John Searle; (3) Thomas Simpson; (4) John Huggan. C: (1) R. Richards, counsel for p. Add: (1) John Rogers Morgan, brewer, Vine Court, Goodmans Fields, Midd, bankrupt. P seeks inj ag d1's suit for payment of a £500 bond. In 1780 d1 employed as a managing clerk J. R. Morgan, who executed d1 a £500 bond to ensure Morgan's satisfactory performance of the post, with p as security. In 1783 Morgan quit the post, but d1 did not surrender the bond, nor pay Morgan's wages. Morgan went bankrupt, with ds2-4 as assignees. D1 now sues p for the bond, claiming Morgan owes him money.

| 1785, Easter | E 112/1747 | Bill. LMX 4953. |
| 1785, April 29 | E 112/1747 | Answer (with attachments). Swearing & filing date of d1's answer; schedule attached of d1's accounts with Morgan. |

342. Wilson v Carr

P: (1) Sir Thomas Spencer Wilson, Charlton House, Kent, bart., p2's husband; (2) Dame Jane Spencer Wilson, Charlton House, Kent, p1's wife, J. Maryon's grand-neice, M. M. Weller's daughter. D: (1) Samuel Carr. C: (1) W. Ainge, counsel for ps. Add: (1) John Maryon, clerk, White Roothing, Essex, deceased, p2's grand-uncle, impropriate rector of Hampstead; (2) Margaretta Maria Weller, deceased, p's mother. Ps seek payment to p2 (impropriate rector of Hampstead) for great tithes from d, who farms parish land. In 1760, p2's grand-uncle J. Maryon willed the rectory to p2's mother M. M. Weller for her life time (deceased in 1777), then to p2. D allegedly claims his land is exempt from payment or subject only to a modus, but ps assert they got a decree in this Court earlier in the year compelling another parishioner to pay for the full tithes.

| 1785, Trin | E 112/1702 | Bill. LMX 3748; cf. E 112/1710 LMX 3964 Wilson v Errington. |

343. Wilson v Errington
P: (1) Sir Thomas Spencer Wilson, Charlton House, Kent, bart., p2's husband; (2) Dame Jane Spencer Wilson, Charlton House, Kent, p1's wife, impropriate rector of Hampstead. D: (1) Joseph Errington; (2) John Webb; (3) Joseph Berks; (4) Thomas Alsop; (5) Richard Marsh. C: (1) W. Ainge, counsel for ps; (2) Richard Hollist, counsel for d1 & ds3-4; (3) F. Walker, counsel for d5. Ps seek payment to p2 (impropriate rector of Hampstead) for great tithes from ds, who farm titheable parish land. Ps assert they got a decree in this Court earlier in the year compelling another parishioner to pay for the full tithes. D1 & ds3-5 claim their land is within St. John's Wood, part of the monastery of Kilburne, & therefore exempt from tithes.
Alternative titles: Wilson v Marsh.

1785, Trin	E 112/1710	Bill. LMX 3964; cf. E 112/1702 LMX 3748 Wilson v Carr.
1785, Dec 3	E 112/1710	Answer. Swearing date of d5's answer, filed 5 December.
1786, Jan 23	E 112/1710	Answer. Swearing date of d1's answer, filed 31 January.
1786, Jan 23	E 112/1710	Answer. Swearing & filing date of the answer of ds3-4.

344. Windale v Houstoun
P: (1) William Windale gent., Jermyn St., Westminster, Midd. D: (1) George Hawles Houstoun gent., attorney, London, attorney of the Court of the Mayor of London. C: (1) J. Johnson, counsel for p. P seeks inj ag d's suit for payment of a £600 bond. P claims in 1784, d, one of the 4 attornies of the Court of the Mayor of London, sold his office to p for £1110, part of which p paid with a £600 bond. P claims since his purchase, d has refused to allow him the profits accruing to the office, or an associated collection of books. D allegedly asserts that when he was drunk, p compelled him to agree to sell the office.

1785, Hil	E 112/1696	Bill (with attachments). LMX 3570 (mistakenly attached to a replication from E 112/1688 3370).

345. Woodhouse v Adderley
P: (1) Charles Woodhouse gent., Kensington, Midd, p2's son; (2) Harcourt Woodhouse esq., Welwyn, Herts, p1's father. D: (1) Thomas Adderley gent., Lee near Lewisham, Kent; (2) William Hemmings, bricklayer, Lambeth Marsh, Surrey; (3) Edward House, distiller, Old Bailey, London, d4's partner; (4) William Bateman, distiller, Old Bailey, London, d3's partner. C: (1) Thomas Lowes, counsel for ps. Ps seek inj ag any suit of ds for payment of 2 bills of exchange. In 1783, p1 drew 2 bills of exchange for £100 each upon p2 & endorsed them for ds1-2 to discount for p1. Ds1-2 never paid p1 the money, but d2 endorsed one bill to ds3-4. Ds1-2 allegedly claim p1 issued the bills as security for a debt, & threaten to sue ps.

1785, Trin	E 112/1702	Bill. LMX 3738.

INDEX TO PLEADINGS, 1784–5
NAMES

Beeford, George, attorney's clerk, 169
Beldon
  Thomas the elder, 170
  Thomas the younger, 170
Bell
  John, attorney at law, 289
  Thomas, merchant, 159
Bennett, John, 256
Berens
  Herman, merchant, 290
  Joseph, merchant, 290
Berks, Joseph, 343
Bernard, Maurice, 190, 206
Best, James, solicitor, 237
Bethune, John, merchant, 313
Betts, Thomas, glass manufacturer, 329
Bickhaffer
  Henry, tailor, 167
  Mary, 167
Bicknall, Bicknell
  Henry, banker, 234
  J., John, 153, 154, 161, 166, 171, 182, 183,
    184, 185, 189, 205, 259, 260, 262, 267,
    273, 280, 285, 304
Biggar, Robert, wholesale draper, 251
Billingham
  Jane, 168
  Thomas, corn chandler, 168
Birch, –, mercer, 304
Blache, John Francis, broker, 240
Blackaby, John, porter, 169
Blackburn, William, watchmaker, 206
Blauchenhagen, Theophilus Christian,
  merchant, 295
Bliss, James, solicitor, 170
Boddam, Thomas, 171
Bolton, Christopher, innholder, 236
Bontein, James, 235
Botfield, Thomas, iron manufacturer, 191
Boucher, Jonathan, clerk, 172
Boulton
  Henry, 179, 256, 311
  William, 295
Bourke
  John, 161
  Michael, 171
Bourn, Myles, 305
Bouvilla, Elias, 173
Bowater
  Frances, 329
  James, 329
Bowden, Joseph, currier, 174
Bowles, Thomas Hume, 304
Boxall, John, innholder, 216
Bradley, James, carpenter, 202
Branscomb, James, stock broker, 152
Brantingham, Thomas, white lead
  manufacturer, 284
Brassett
  Charles, 175

John, yeoman, 175
Bray, John, lighterman to the Office of
  Ordnance, 308
Brest, William George, 165
Brett, Joseph George, 227
Brewer, William, innholder, 236
Bride, Richard, clerk, 299
Bridge
  Olginpea, 337
  Thomas, broker, 337
Bristow, John, engine maker, 176
Britton, Richard, 338
Brockbank, John, merchant, 198
Brocklehurst, William, warehouseman, 257
Broderip, Francis Fane, music seller, 234, 275,
    283, 299, 300
Brome
  George, wharfinger, 169
  John, 169
Bromfield, Philip, captain in the service of the
  EIC, 321
Brown
  Ann, 169
  George, attorney at law, 177, 178
  Jane, servant, 177
  Joshua, carpenter, 278
  Josiah, 228, 233, 258, 274, 319
  Peter, merchant, 153
  Sarah, 177
  Timothy, 239
  William, cabinet maker, 179
Brownell
  John, 180
  Phillis, 180
  Robert Christian the elder,
    shipwright, 180
  Robert Christian the younger, 180
Bruce, Richard, merchant, 159
Bruere, Goulstone, 244
Brunet, Jean Jacques Antonio, moneylender,
  173
Bullock, John, stationer to the Board of
  Ordnance, 262
Bulmer, Blackett, 242
Bult, James, goldsmith, 283, goldsmith and
  banker, 234
Bunn, John, solicitor, 299
Burdett
  Elizabeth, 181
  Thomas Francis, 181
Burkitt, Alexander Sheafe, 182
Burnbee, William, porter, 169
Burnsall
  David, 183
  George, 183
Butcher, Robert Holt, clerk, 184
Butler
  Jane, 185
  John, seaman, 272
Byde, Thomas Plumer, 202

144

Byrne
Catherine, 325
Patrick, 325
Byron, Rt. Hon. William, Lord, 186

Cadenhead, John, ship's captain, 230
Caesar, Carlos, grocer, 187, 302, grocer and
tea dealer, 188
Calmel, Peter, 202
Campbell
George, merchant, 285
J., 189
Caney, James, 223
Canning, Stratford, 268
Capper, James, 189
Careless, William, hairdresser, 326
Carr, Samuel, 342
Carroll, Thomas, coachman, 235
Carter, Thomas, merchant, 159
Cartwright, George William, officer of
Revenue of Excise, 264
Carver, Edward, 190, 191
Carvick, John, stock broker, 152
Casamajor, Justinian, 161
Cawthorn, George, merchant, 159
Cecil
Ann, 192
John, apothecary, 192
Chambers, Abraham, 290
Champion
Alexander, merchant, 159
Benjamin, merchant, 225
Charnock, Robert, merchant, 187
Christian, Robert, 161
Christie
James, auctioneer, 193
Robert, merchant &
underwriter, 153
Clark
Henry, cheesemonger, 194
Sibella, 194
William, 179
Clarke
John, coal factor, 195, 196
Ralph, coal factor, 195
Richard, merchant, 280, 281
Samuel, weaver, 336
Clarkson, Thomas, 197
Colhoun, William McDowall, plantation
manager, 240
Collet(t)
Jonathan, glassman, 198
Jonathan, 329
Collier, John, linen draper, 257
Colnett, Isaac, 223
Comyn, Robert, 248
Condell, Henry, music master, 299
Cooke
William, 221, 235, 334
William, fireman, 336

Cooper
James, bookseller, 208
Thomas, 178
Cope
Ann, 327
John the elder, 327
John the younger, yeoman, 327
Thomas, brewer, 327
Copeland, William, merchant, 331
Corbett, Andrew, 290
Cordukes, Richard, clerk, 217
Cornwall, Thomas, 178
Corrall
Christopher, 287, 288
Christopher, laceman, 207
Corry, James, yeoman, 174
Cossart, John, merchant, 225
Costar, William, innholder, 236
Cotton, Charles, 237
Courtney, Humphrey, 221
Cousemaker, Sanney Richard, 223
Cox
Henry, innkeeper, 178
Robert Albion, goldsmith, 227
S.C., 154
S.S., 249
William, innholder, 236
Crabb, James, merchant, 159
Cracraft, Richard, money scrivener, 171
Crawford, William, upholsterer, 335
Crease, William, innholder, 216
Crode, J., John, 227, 286, 306
Crooke, Solomon, 231
Crossley, George, 222
Cruger, Henry, merchant, 199
Crump, Joseph, merchant & underwriter, 205
Cullen, Thomas, 265
Curling, George, merchant & underwriter, 153
Cutler, Henry, merchant, 295

D'Avenant, Thomas, Colonel, 177
D'Hancarville, Victor, 173
Dallas, Robert, 334
Daniell
G. the younger, 240
George, plantation manager, 240
Darwin, John Thorold, hatter, 152
Davi(e)s
David, jeweller, artificial flower maker, 201
John, 200
Mark, merchant, 334
William, merchant, 153, 225
Dawes
John, merchant, 256
Thomas, merchant, 256
Dawson, Thomas, 247
De Berdt, Dennis, merchant, 294
de Fflines, Jacob, 295
De Gand, Antoine Francois, ship's captain, 225

Reynolds
George, 192
Richard, 290
Rich
Harris, porter, 169
Peter, 193
Richards, R., 168, 174, 177, 181, 190, 191,
229, 245, 264, 277, 278, 295, 297, 301,
312, 314, 325, 340, 341
Richardson
James, stock broker, 152
John, grocer, 185
John, solicitor, 237
Righton, Basil, cooper, 301, 312
Riley
John, auctioneer, 242, auctioneer and
upholder 302
John, victualler, 303
William, servant, 169
Rivaz, John Francis, 245
Rive, Peter De La, merchant, 159
Robarts, John Chapman, hosier, 182
Roberts
David, 304
John, army agent, 304
Thomas, 304
Robertson, William, 178, 318
Robinson
–, 173
John, 223
John, woollen draper, 258
Peter, coppersmith, 248
Samuel, tire smith, 241
Thomas, ironmonger, 305
Roebuck, Thomas, merchant, 225
Rogers
George, officer & commissioner of the
navy, 155
Thomas, 287, 288
Rogers
Victori, victualler, 306
Vitorino, victualler, 292
Romilly, Samuel, 256
Roper
Francis, 166
William, pattern maker, 194
Rosier, James, button maker, 258
Ross
Gilbert, merchant, 207
Isaac, shipbreaker, 307, 308
Round, Rev. Benjamin, clerk, 202
Rowe, Milward, 309
Rowley, Thomas, merchant, 159
Rowntree, Thomas, money scrivener, 233
Rudman
Elizabeth, 228
John, yeoman, 228
Rumney, Mary, 169
Russell, James, cornet, 205
Rutt, Henry, trustee of the Union Fire Office, 336

Rutter, Samuel the younger, carcass butcher,
310
Ryan, Edward, 204

Salomons, Solomon, Henry, 227, 243, notary
public 222
Salte, William, linen draper, 215, 311
Sands
David, 189
David, upholder, 152
Santos, Caetano Dias, merchant, 295
Scafe
H., 188
W., William, 157, 180, 202, 207, 230, 234,
275, 288, 296, 302, 310, 315
Scales, Edward, 239
Schooll, Michael, 335
Scudamore, John, 311
Scurrah, William, broker, 326
Seacombe, John, 180
Sealy, William, wine merchant, 301, 312
Searle
John, 341
Joseph, servant, 299
Sedgwick, Harry, merchant, underwriter, 221
Sedley, Davenport, moneylender, 235
Senols, James, upholsterer, 281
Sermitte, Thomas, 271
Seymour, John, surgeon, 246
Shafto
Ann, 329
John, 329
Robert, 329
Sharp, Thomas, carpenter, 282
Sharrer, Thomas, silk broker, 253
Shee, Annesley, 222
Sheperd, William, mariner, 333
Sheridan, James, 321
Shoolbred
Henry, 313
Jane, 228
John, 228
John, merchant, 313, 317
Shove, Edward, draper, 277
Shrubb, John, innholder, 236
Shuter, Cha., Charles, 165, 187, 238, 242, 252,
257, 272, 295, 300
Silver, William, 197
Simeon
Edward, merchant, 225
J., 262
Simmons
Ann, 196
Edward, mariner, 196
Simon, Edward, 252
Simpson
–, mercer, 304
Thomas, 341
Sims, John, merchant, 294
Sinclair, Robert, merchant & underwriter, 153

Tombs, Richard, ship builder, 295
Tomlins
    F. E., 177
    T. E., 178
Tookey
    Ann, 241
    Henry, tire smith, 241
Tooley, Thomas, tailor, 314
Toulmin, Oliver, merchant, 171
Towers, John, trustee of the Union Fire Office,
    336
Townsend, Theyer, linen draper, 304
Tuite, Robert, 248
Tumbrook, Frederick, 219
Turner
    John, 235
    William, linen draper, 215, 311
Tweedie, Walter, silversmith, 330
Twigg
    Joseph, gauze weaver, 331
    Samuel, gauze weaver, 331
    William, gauze weaver, 331

Vardon, Thomas, merchant, 248
Vaughan
    Benjamin, merchant, 153
    John, banker, 250
Venden, Shadrack, 193
Vezian, Andrew, merchant, 332
Vidgen, John, 308
Vigne, Robert, merchant & underwriter, 153
Von Holm, John, tobacconist, 333

Wadbrook, George, malster, 327
Wadham, James, linen draper, 213, 214
Walker
    F., 231, 308, 318, 343
    George, wine merchant, 301, 312
    James Collins, silkman, 253
    John, merchant, 159, 159
    Thomas, ship's captain, 295
Wallace, Michael, merchant, 334
Waller, William, W., 159, 164, 167, 179, 180,
    213, 214, 220, 266, 299, 322, 323
Wallis
    Alexander, 192
    Samuel, 155
    Samuel, officer & commissioner of
    the navy, 155
Walrond, Mainswete, planter, 161
Walter, William, 224, 244, 283, 313, 333
Walton, Joseph, oilman, 234, 283
Ward
    Joseph, 197, 276
    William, 229
Warren
    Alport Peter, 193
    John, 193
Waters, William, 335

Watkins
    George, silk weaver, 336
    Joseph, merchant, 225
Watkiss, George Turner, iron manufacturer,
    191
Watts
    John, upholsterer, 189
    Joseph, 189
Webb
    Daniel, 337
    John, 343
Webber, Richard Brook, 235
Webster, Edward, 239
Weddell, Samuel, woollen draper, 194
Welcker, John, music seller, 299
Welford, Mary, 160
Weller, Margaretta Maria, 342
Wentworth, Stephen, innholder, 236
West, Edward, victualler, 169
Wetherhead, Thomas, yeoman, 321
Wewitzer, Ralph, 338
Wheeler, John, 214
Whicker
    John, cordwainer, 261
    Mary Ann, 261
White, Joseph, innholder, 216
Whitlock, George, clerk, 163
Whitmore, John, merchant, 153, merchant &
    underwriter, 225
Whittenbury, John, warehouseman, 257
Wigan, Edward, linen draper, 234
Wigram, Robert, merchant, 288
Wilding, John, clerk, 311
Wilkinson
    Jacob, merchant, 153, merchant &
    underwriter), 225
    Martin, 299
    Thomas, 239
    Thomas, tallow chandler, 339
Wilks, Joseph, merchant, 301, 312
Williams
    Catherine, 167
    David, 167
    David, glazier & builder, 340
    David, solicitor, 303
    Sir John, officer and commissioner of the
    navy, 155
    Joseph, planter, 337
    Robert, 183
    Stephen, linen draper, 213
    William, 341
    William, broker, 303
Willis
    David, woollen draper, 326
    James, 191
    William, banker, 331
Willock, John, surveyor, 326
Wills
    Sarah, 323
    Thomas, pressmaker, 323

Wilmot
  David, 223
  Edward, 340
Wilson
  Elizabeth, warehousewoman, 330
  Dame Jane Spencer, 342, 343
  John, 235
  John, merchant, 159
  Sir Thomas Spencer, 342, 343
  Thomas, merchant, 159
Wiltshire
  Richard, gambling house owner, 254
  Richard, victualler, 179
Windale, William, 344
Wingfield, James, hatter, 326
Winsloe, Thomas, 329
Withers, John, linen draper, 213
Wood
  Geo., 308
  James, banker, 331
Woodgate, Robert, 202

Woodhouse
  Charles, 345
  Harcourt, 345
Woodmason, James, stationer, 288
Woodroffe, Richard, victualler, 343
Woolloton, Wooloton,
  Thomas, 311
  Thomas, linen draper, 215, 252
Worth, William, 316
Wright, Whittaker, 253
Wyatt
  James, 152
  James, architect, 296
  John, merchant, 152
  Samuel, architect, 296
  Thomas, 152
Wylie, Robert, merchant, 213, 214

Young
  John, 239
  Samuel, porter, 169

INDEX TO PLEADINGS, 1784–5
SUBJECTS

LONDON RECORD SOCIETY

Chairman: H.S.Cobb, MA, FSA, FRHS

Hon. Secretary: H.J.Creaton, BA, MPhil, ALA
Hon. Treasurer: G.G.Harris, MA
Hon. General Editors: V.A.Harding, MA, PhD, FRHS
                    S.O'Connor, BA, PhD

The London Record Society was founded in December 1964 to publish transcripts, abstracts and lists of the primary sources for the history of London, and generally to stimulate interest in archives relating to London. Membership is open to any individual or institution; the annual subscription is £12 (US $22) for individuals and £18 (US $35) for institutions. Prospective members should apply to the Hon. Secretary, Miss H.J.Creaton, c/o Institute of Historical Research, Senate House, London WC1E 7HU.

The following volumes have already been published:

1. *London Possessory Assizes: a calendar*, edited by Helena M. Chew (1965)
2. *London Inhabitants within the Walls, 1695*, with an introduction by D.V.Glass (1966)
3. *London Consistory Court Wills, 1492–1547*, edited by Ida Darlington (1967)
4. *Scriveners' Company Common Paper, 1357–1628, with a continuation to 1678*, edited by Francis W. Steer (1968)
5. *London Radicalism, 1830–1843: a selection from the papers of Francis Place*, edited by D. J. Rowe (1970)
6. *The London Eyre of 1244*, edited by Helena M. Chew and Martin Weinbaum (1970)
7. *The Cartulary of Holy Trinity Aldgate*, edited by Gerald A. J. Hodgett (1971)
8. *The Port and Trade of early Elizabethan London: Documents*, edited by Brian Dietz (1972)
9. *The Spanish Company*, edited by Pauline Croft (1973)
10. *London Assize of Nuisance, 1301–1431: a calendar*, edited by Helena M. Chew and William Kellaway (1973)
11. *Two Calvinistic Methodist Chapels, 1748–1811: the London Tabernacle and Spa Fields Chapel*, edited by Edwin Welch (1975)
12. *The London Eyre of 1276*, edited by Martin Weinbaum (1976)
13. *The Church in London, 1375–1392*, edited by A. K. McHardy (1977)
14. *Committees for the Repeal of the Test and Corporation Acts: Minutes, 1786–90 and 1827–8*, edited by Thomas W. Davis (1978)

15. *Joshua Johnson's Letterbook, 1771–4: letters from a merchant in London to his partners in Maryland*, edited by Jacob M. Price (1979)

16. *London and Middlesex Chantry Certificate, 1548*, edited by C. J. Kitching (1980)

17. *London Politics, 1713–1717: Minutes of a Whig Club, 1714–17*, edited by H.Horwitz; *London Pollbooks, 1713*, edited by W.A. Speck and W.A. Gray (1981)

18. *Parish Fraternity Register: Fraternity of the Holy Trinity and SS.Fabian and Sebastian in the parish of St. Botolph without Aldersgate*, edited by Patricia Basing (1982)

19. *Trinity House of Deptford: Transactions, 1609–35*, edited by G.G.Harris (1983)

20. *Chamber Accounts of the sixteenth century*, edited by Betty R. Masters (1984)

21. *The Letters of John Paige, London Merchant, 1648–58*, edited by George F. Steckley (1984)

22. *A Survey of Documentary Sources for Property Holding in London before the Great Fire*, by Derek Keene and Vanessa Harding (1985)

23. *The Commissions for Building Fifty New Churches*, edited by M.H.Port (1986)

24. *Richard Hutton's Complaints Book*, edited by Timothy V. Hitchcock (1987)

25. *Westminster Abbey Charters, 1066–c. 1214*, edited by Emma Mason (1988)

26. *London Viewers and their Certificates, 1508–1558*, edited by Janet S. Loengard (1989)

27. *The Overseas Trade of London: Exchequer Customs Accounts, 1480–1*, edited by H.S.Cobb (1990)

28. *Justice in Eighteenth-century Hackney: the Justicing Notebook of Henry Norris and the Hackney Petty Sessions Book*, edited by Ruth Paley (1991)

29. *Two Tudor Subsidy Assessment Rolls for the City of London: 1541 and 1582*, edited by R.G.Lang (1993 for 1992)

30. *London Debating Societies, 1776–1799*, compiled and introduced by Donna T. Andrew (1994 for 1993)

31. *London Bridge: selected accounts and rentals, 1381–1538*, edited by Vanessa Harding and Laura Wright (1995 for 1994)

32. *London Consistory Court Depositions, 1586–1611: list and indexes*, by Loreen L.Giese (1997 for 1995)

33. *Chelsea settlement and bastardy examinations, 1733–66*, edited by Tim Hitchcock and John Black (1999 for 1996)

34. *The church records of St Andrew Hubbard Eastcheap, c. 1450–c. 1570*, edited by Clive Burgess (1999 for 1997)

35. *Calendar of Exchequer Equity pleadings, 1685–6 and 1784–5*, edited by Henry Horwitz and Jessica Cooke (2000 for 1998)

Most volumes are still in print; apply to the Hon. Secretary, who will forward requests to the distributor. Price to individual members £12 ($22) each, to non-members £20 ($38) each.